LIFE FOR HEALTH

How to solve chronic disease
and increase healthspan
using life insurance

Jeremy Shane

First published in 2025 by Intellectual Perspective Press
© Copyright Jeremy Shane

All rights reserved. No part of this publication may be reproduced, stored in or introduced into a retrieval system, or transmitted, in any form, or by any means (electronic, mechanical, photocopying, recording or otherwise) without the prior written permission of the Publisher.

The right of Jeremy Shane to be identified as the author of this work has been asserted in accordance with the Copyright, Designs and Patents Act 1988.

This book is sold subject to the condition that it shall not, by way of trade or otherwise, be lent, resold, hired out, or otherwise circulated without the publisher's prior consent in any form of binding or cover other than that in which it is published and without a similar condition including this condition being imposed on the subsequent Purchaser.

The purpose of this book is to educate and entertain. The author and Intellectual Perspective Press shall have neither liability nor responsibility to any person or entity with respect to any loss or damage caused, or alleged to have been caused, directly or indirectly, by the information contained in this book.

Book Interior and E-book Design by Amit Dey (amitdey2528@gmail.com)

To find out more about our authors and books visit:
www.intellectualperspective.com

For Ollie and Eliza

TABLE OF CONTENTS

Free for You x

Introduction: Increasing Healthspan xi

Part I Ending Chronic Disease 1

   1. Life for Health's Moment 3

   2. First Principles of Solving Chronic Disease. 11

   3. Visualizing Multimorbidity's Cost. 21

   4. Solving Multimorbidity Adds a Decade of Health and Trillions of Wealth. 44

Part II Beyond Health Insurance 51

   5. The Misconception at the Heart of the System's Failure 53

   6. The Four Types of Medicine 57

   7. Rockefeller, Roosevelt, and The End of Epidemic Disease. 64

   8. Ending Heart Disease: The Good, The Bad, and The Ugly 73

   9. 1973: The Schism of Science and Finance 84

   10. The Rock, Paper, Scissors Vortex. 102

   11. Hastening a Reckoning. 120

Part III Life for Health 125

   12. Life for Health—A Roadmap 127

   13. Life for Health Structure and Entities. 131

   14. The Participant's Experience 141

15. Envisioning Success. 150

16. Two Systems Are Better Than One 156

17. The Economics of Life for Health 162

18. What's "In It" for Life Insurers?. 179

19. Life for Health in Medicaid. 188

PART IV Realizing Predictive/Preventive Medicine 195

20. Prevention, Prediction, Trust, and Transparency 197

21. How Participation and Trust Accelerates Cures. 208

22. Getting Longitudinal. 218

23. From Health Data to Health Narratives 227

24. Data Privacy, Ownership, Control, and Compensation 231

25. Realizing Predictive/Preventive Medicine 239

PART V Looking Forward. 247

26. The Big Unlocks. 249

27. Ending Cancer As We Know It. 251

28. Understanding And Preventing ADRD 260

29. Pricing Drugs For Access And Outcomes 266

30. Ensuring Medicare's Solvency. 286

31. Engineering Food for Health 289

32. Conclusion: Look Long, and Begin 293

Acknowledgments 297

About Jeremy Shane. 298

Index 300

TABLE OF FIGURES

Figure 3.1. Visualizing Multimorbidity's Cost 22

Figure 3.2: Visualizing the Median Age of Multimorbidity Onset 23

Figure 3.3. Multimorbidity Distribution by Age Range, 2019 Hospital Admissions 27

Figure 3.7. Chronic Disease Cascade as a % of Population and Health Spend 36

Figure 3.8. Chronic Disease Cascade in Medicare. 38

Figure 3.9: Population Breakdown by Multimorbidity Status 40

Figure 3.10: Medical Spending by Multimorbidity Status 41

Figure 4.1: Potential Gain in Lifespan / Healthspan 44

Figure 6.1: Visualizing the Four Types of Medicine. 62

Figure 8.1: Decline in Heart Death Rates by Age Group, 1968 - 2012 . . 75

Figure 8.2: UK Cardiac Procedure Volume and Heart-Related Death Rate 77

Figure 8.3: Key Framingham Heart Study Dates and Heart-Related Death Rate 78

Figure 9.1: US Grain Production by Crop Type, 1926 – 2020 95

Figure 9.2: US Obesity and Overweight Rates Over Time 97

Figure 10.1: The Financial and Scientific Realms of Health Care 104

Figure 13.1: Key entities in Life for Health System 131

Figure 16.1: Envisioning Two Systems for Health Care 157

Figure 16.2: Two Systems Spending Over Time. 158

Figure 16.3: Total Health Care Spending With and Without
 Life for Health as 161

Figure 17.1: Annual Medical Expenses, status quo versus Life
 for Health 163

Figure 17.2: Reallocation of Health Insurance Premiums to
 Life for Health 166

Figure 17.3: Financing of Upfront Intervention to Reverse Disease. . 167

Figure 17.4: Realizing the Value of Efforts to Maintain
 Metabolic Health 168

Figure 17.5: Summary of Payment Flows in Life for Health 169

Figure 17.6: Summary of Payment Flows in Direct-to-
 Consumer Arrangement 174

Figure 18.1: Life Insurance Rates With and Without Life for Health. . 184

Figure 19.1: Entities and Payment Flows in Medicaid. 191

Figure 25.1: Relationship Between Age and Payment 242

FREE FOR YOU

This book is enhanced with additional content and a bibliography, along with additional detail about calculations included in the text. You can access all of this extra content at: www.lifeforhealth.com.

You may also sign-up there for ongoing commentary about efforts to solve chronic disease and updates about Life for Health.

INTRODUCTION: INCREASING HEALTHSPAN

> "There are these two young fish swimming along, and they happen to meet an older fish swimming the other way, who nods at them and says, 'Morning, boys, how's the water?' And the two young fish swim on for a bit, and then eventually one of them looks over at the other and goes, 'What the hell is water?'"
>
> —David Foster Wallace, "This is Water"

On the crisp January day in 1961 when John F. Kennedy declared that a torch had been passed to a new generation, Americans lived for about seventy years. Those who reached their sixties spent about six years in ill health, a tenth of their lives. Today, Americans live a decade longer but spend a decade and a half in ill health, almost a fifth of their lives. It's hardly a bargain—more years alive but fewer years in good health.

What happened? Chronic disease happened. The gradual, inexorable buildup of metabolic, respiratory, autoimmune, and behavioral conditions culminating in years of debilitating, costly, and painful illness in the latter half of life. Especially troubling is the growing prevalence of multimorbidity, when a person has three or more chronic conditions.[1]

Life for Health is about how to end that, to reverse multimorbidity, prevent chronic disease, and increase Americans' healthspans. Achieving this will have immense economic and societal value increasing Americans' lifelong savings, reducing unnecessary health spending, ensuring

Medicare's solvency, and paving the way to solve or prevent other lethal disease threats including cancer and Alzheimer's.

In President Kennedy's day, chronic disease tended to kill quickly, often the result of smoking, alcoholism, malnutrition, decades of hard physical labor, or exposure to pollutants. To the extent multimorbidity existed, it happened late in life. Today multimorbidity starts earlier and progresses faster, driven in large part by metabolic dysfunctions manifesting as obesity, diabetes, or cardiovascular disease.[2] Most of the current multimorbidity burden is shouldered by the approximately one third of Americans who have three or more chronic conditions (of which at least one is frequently metabolic in nature). Another quarter of Americans have one or two serious chronic conditions and, absent an intensive reversal and prevention strategy, will progress to advanced disease. The multimorbidity pipeline terminates in Medicare. In 2000, one in four Americans entering Medicare had multimorbidity. Two decades later, more than 40% of new Medicare beneficiaries have multimorbidity, a two-thirds increase.[3] Soon, the rate among new entrants will be one in two. The word "multimorbidity" never appears on death certificates, but it might as well. Beneath most final illnesses multimorbidity lurks, orchestrating the end.

Today's health systems encourage us to think about illnesses as distinct entities, a construct that is deeply at odds with the science of chronic disease. Multimorbidity results from a chain of interconnected conditions, with pathology in one area building up and spreading to other organs and bodily systems. Excess medical spending is the most obvious result, but the socioeconomic costs are even greater. People with multimorbidity have fewer productive working years, earning and saving less and spending more throughout life on medical issues. Metabolic conditions increase the risk of cancer and dementia. Multimorbidity distorts everything else in health care, siphoning critical resources to wage heroic and ultimately futile efforts to halt late-stage illness. If our national aspiration is to life, liberty, and the pursuit of happiness, multimorbidity has us batting zero for three.

What will it take to restore Americans' healthspans? First, we have to stop the bleeding, so to speak. That means **reversing** disease and helping individuals **maintain** their health for decades thereafter. At the same time, we have to preempt future illness, which means efforts to **predict** disease risk and **prevent** onset or progression. Reverse, maintain, predict, and prevent; these are the action verbs of ending chronic disease.

Nothing in that *sounds* controversial, so why has it not been done?

Health care systems and health insurance were not intended to solve a decades-long challenge like chronic disease. They were designed to solve short-term issues, applying low-intensity routine treatment or high-intensity hospitalization for emergencies. After World War II, treatment of heart attacks and cancer was bolted onto the system in place. It made sense at the time since these issues manifested as emergencies and warranted surgery and hospitalization. Our understanding of chronic disease improved in the ensuing quarter century, and it became clear that long lived diseases pose unique scientific and societal challenges. Yet, we never went back to question the system's design. Had we done so, we would have seen that a system built around short-term issues could not solve long-term ones. Chronic disease needs a system of its own, incorporating a continuum of efforts to reverse or forestall pathology rather than treatments for distinct, acute episodes.

This conceptual flaw carried over to health insurance which was designed to blend the risks of frequent but low-cost routine care with infrequent but high-cost emergencies. For all that is wrong with the way health insurers behave—and there is a whole chapter about that!—it is the mismatch between the science of chronic disease and the short-term nature of health insurance that makes all forms, whether fully privatized or socialized, inadequate to solving chronic disease. Long-term, progressive, highly variable disease challenges require a financial framework that links individuals, clinicians, and insurers to work together over long time frames to delay disease onset and increase healthspan. That's why the right financial structure to solve chronic disease is life insurance, not health insurance.

Realizing two systems instead of one requires us to call out another unstated but pervasive idea, that it is desirable and possible for a single health care system to address every kind of medical issue from common colds to car crashes, from high cholesterol to cancer. Science teaches otherwise. Chronic disease is the product of many risk factors, some innate, others environmental. There is tremendous variability in disease risk, speed of progression, and treatment response. Continuing to force fit health insurance to solve chronic disease is as ludicrous as trying to reshape the Washington Monument into the St. Louis Arch.

So we need two systems instead of one. The first solves acute issues including routine, emergency, and elective surgeries using *health* insurance. The second solves chronic, life-threatening, and age-related diseases using *life* insurance.

An additional conceptual barrier to solving chronic disease is that health care has been overtaken by a belief that financial levers are the best way to achieve scientific ends. The amount that is spent becomes divorced from the disease risk that drives spending in the first place. Consider a widely cited statistic from the Centers for Disease Control that about 90% of health dollars are spent on Americans with chronic disease, a fact that—along with others that track health spending as a percent of GDP—frames the debate in terms of what can be done to reduce costs. The right way to frame chronic disease spending is to say something like: "Multimorbidity among 30% of Americans consumes two-thirds of total health spending." Rephrased like that, the arrow of causation flows correctly, from disease to affected population to financial impact. Science drives finance, not the other way around.

It is little wonder that a belief in financialism, expressed through a system and insurance approach designed around short-term issues, leads to short-term thinking. Financialism rewards incrementalism in clinical care, forcing physicians to ratchet treatment intensity (and spending) as symptoms worsen, trapping us in a losing war of attrition as underlying pathology increasingly dictates the terms of battle. The right way to reverse disease is to intervene earlier and decisively even if these measures cost more, at least at first. Absent that, when pathology is widespread and irreversible, the costs just to keep someone with advanced disease alive are astronomical.

Financialism became the dominant ideology of health care in the early 1970s, fed by a growing skepticism of technology and a view that Americans will inevitably seek as much medical treatment as they can, regardless of cost. Absent controls to suppress demand and micromanage how health care is provided, spending would skyrocket. Everything about health care, including return on investment horizons, got shoehorned into annual insurance enrollments and budget cycles. Everything gets paid as it is delivered, which is fine in the emergency room but fatal in chronic disease, where it takes years even decades to realize value. Preventive measures touted by politicians and health system leaders were dead on arrival, disconnected from any long-term framework that quantified and shared the value of avoiding illness.

The financialists succeeded beyond their dreams, and yet in their disregard for the essential nature of chronic disease, we find ourselves with the worst of both worlds—vastly more illness and vastly greater costs. Their folly demonstrates an essential truth: the only way to reduce health *spending* is to solve *disease*, reverse it where it exists and prevent it from happening where it might. It defies everything that health system leaders are taught and believe but the only way to bend the cost curve down is to push the healthspan curve out.

This is not to say that financial arrangements are irrelevant. Far from it, but they must serve scientific ends, rather than the other way around. The time dimensionality and variability of chronic disease requires structures built around assessing outcomes over time, sharing risk and value among individuals, clinicians, drugmakers, and insurers.

The final reason that we have been unable to solve chronic disease is the divide between health care and industries that profit from unhealthy products. This gap is especially true for metabolic issues including obesity, diabetes, and cardiovascular disease, the primary drivers of multimorbidity. As writer and food activist Wendell Berry has said: "People are fed by the food industry, which pays no attention to health, and are treated by the health industry, which pays no attention to food."

The emergence of the Make America Healthy Again (or MAHA) movement, now conjoined with Donald Trump's MAGA movement, reflects the breadth and depth of public unease with unhealthy food. Originally the province of left-leaning eco-warriors, the focus on eliminating unhealthy food, pesticides, and other pollutants is gaining purchase across the political spectrum. This is a good trend insofar as it multiplies the energy available to upend the status quo. Majoritarian coalitions inevitably attract unexpected alliances.

Life for Health, in Brief

Life for Health is a new system to solve chronic disease and increase healthspan using life insurance. It is a comprehensive approach to realize the four-part strategy outlined above, to reverse disease and help individuals maintain healthier trajectories as long as possible. Life for Health reinvests knowledge from reducing prevalence to predict disease risk and prevent onset. In contrast to health insurance, life insurance creates a long-term financial framework that rewards larger investments to reverse disease with years of future returns realized as a portion of lower, future medical costs. Life insurance also enables individuals to share in that value through the policy's built-in savings mechanism.

Life for Health focuses initially on metabolic syndrome, the constellation of issues characterized by high blood pressure, bad cholesterol and blood sugar levels, and excess abdominal weight. Reversing metabolic syndrome is a non-negotiable first step to increasing Americans' healthspan overall since it is at the root of most multimorbidity.

Life for Health as a term describes both a new system to solve chronic disease, and from Parts III onwards, describes a new kind of health company to realize its ideas in practice. Going forward in this book, *Life for Health* when italicized, refers to the overall concept; whereas Life for Health in regular font describes commercial entities and arrangements that are part of a *Life for Health* system.

With that in mind, how does Life for Health work? It combines access to clinicians who help individuals reverse existing disease and maintain better health trajectories, in addition to a universal life insurance policy through which individuals are compensated for success in improving their health prospects. People who join Life for Health are called "participants" rather than patients, policyholders, or consumers. This nomenclature is intentional, reflecting the critical role that individuals play in picking treatments and setting health goals and contributing data to accelerate chronic disease research.

The life insurance policy creates a long-term alignment among participants, clinicians, and insurers. Participants earn payments tied to achieving health outcome goals. Amounts earned are added to the insurance policy's cash balance where they can grow on a tax-deferred basis. The policy also provides access to measures to prevent and treat life-threatening diseases including genetic diseases and cancer.

Participants' primary relationship is with a Life for Health entity. Through this entity, they have access to clinicians with expertise in treating and preventing chronic disease. Clinicians develop intervention plans and health outcomes goals (along with participants), assess participant progress, and ensure access to data, services, or counseling needed to achieve desired outcomes. The clinician-participant relationship can be thought of like a supercharged version of concierge medicine, centered around chronic disease reversal and prevention. Life for Health entities build the network of affiliated clinicians who provide services and partner with top-rated life insurers, who underwrite and issue associated life insurance policies.

The first two to three years of a participant's time in Life for Health focuses on reversing disease and regaining metabolic health. Once accomplished, the relationship shifts to a "maintain" phase, to achieve a continuously better health trajectory over time. In this way, Life for Health brings together the two types of medicine that are necessary to solve chronic and age-related disease. The first, Serious Medicine, encompasses diagnostics and treatments to reverse or halt disease and help people maintain health improvements thereafter. It aims to attack pathology at its source rather than just ameliorating symptoms. The second, Predictive/Preventive Medicine, includes efforts to understand the sources of disease and interactions among organs and bodily systems that hasten pathology's spread.

Life for Health's ultimate goal is to shift the weight of medical investment from reversing disease (as is now required given rising multimorbidity prevalence) to preventing onset in the first place. Thus, everything that participants undergo and experience in the course of their time in Life for Health is reinvested to accelerate understanding of chronic disease in all its manifestations. Life for Health aggregates longitudinal data from participants, using it internally to improve predictive assessments, treatment targeting, and recommendations about preventive measures. Participants may also allow their de-identified data and biosamples (like blood draws) to be included in a data compendium that Life for Health licenses to vetted researchers and product makers. Participants who opt in to have their data included would be compensated through a share in licensing or future product royalties.

Although Life for Health focuses initially on metabolic conditions, it also covers diagnostics and treatment for high stakes medical issues across the lifespan, in keeping with the idea of life insurance. Participants undergo whole genome sequencing upon joining and have access to early detection and diagnostic tests for a range of conditions including prenatal and fetal abnormalities, genetic disease, early cancer detection, immune dysfunction, and neurodegenerative issues. Participants who have a genetic predisposition to cancer or develop a malignancy are guaranteed access to advanced diagnostics and treatment at a top-ranked cancer center.

From a distance, *Life for Health* may not look that different from health insurance. As happens now, participants purchase coverage directly or through their employer and receive treatment from affiliated clinicians. However, Life for Health could not be more different from the status quo in practice. The current system is built around treating symptoms as they arise, valuing and compensating distinct episodes of care. Life for Health is built around long-term health outcomes, to increase healthspan, while advancing scientific understanding of disease. It is the difference between point geometry and calculus.

What's it Worth?

How much would America and Americans gain by solving chronic disease? Economically, Americans stand to gain about $15 trillion in additional wealth from increased healthspan, about half of our current annual GDP. This wealth would be shared among individuals, who will be able to enjoy more years of good health, allowing them to earn and save more; clinicians and product makers who develop technologies to reverse, predict, and prevent disease; insurers and investors who underwrite Life for Health; employers who offer Life for Health plans; and the US and state governments who will realize significant declines in public health insurance programs, especially Medicare and Medicaid.

Life for Health will yield significant societal value as well. Multimorbidity is, in many ways, the most regressive tax there is, disproportionately affecting working class and poorer Americans, reducing their income and wealth. Reversing and preventing disease may be the most progressive policy, synergizing commercial and redistributive interests in a way that benefits everyone.

Life for Health will also ensure the solvency and sustainability of the overall health industry. Our approximately $5 trillion in annual health care spending could drop by 25% to 40% by cutting multimorbidity prevalence by half or more. Reducing prevalence and incidence will take a couple of decades given how much multimorbidity is built up but annual health care savings could realistically total one to two trillion dollars within a decade. Once we turn the corner on multimorbidity, the gains will accelerate, since lower multimorbidity will translate into lower cancer and dementia rates. There is no way to avoid people getting sick towards the end of their lives. With Life for Health, however, the amount of time spent in severe illness, and the costs associated with it, will shrink dramatically regardless of how much lifespans increase.

Some argue that less health spending is not necessarily good economically since clinicians tend to be higher compensated, and many workers rely on health insurers, hospitals, and pharmaceutical companies for employment. As we will see, the converse is true. As in every other industry, employment and earnings grow with productivity and health care has long suffered from low labor productivity. Chronic disease care is for the most part, a financial loser for hospitals and clinicians, requires as many low-wage jobs and high-wage ones, and creates a massive tax on all workers' wage growth. Multimorbidity siphons capital and labor into lower margin activities. Shifting resources from chronic disease "sick care" will be a boon for clinicians, researchers, and technologists, laying the groundwork for new approaches to preventing disease—and financing it—that will be in very high demand globally.

An Outline of What Follows

The first two parts of this book frame the challenge of multimorbidity and the benefits of reversing it, and trace the events that led to the system we now have.

- Part I describes the growth of multimorbidity, what it costs individuals and the system in terms of healthspan and dollars, and how much we stand to gain by slashing prevalence.
- Part II explores how we got to now, to co-opt historian Steven Johnson's phrase.[4] How did the current health care system come to be like this, and why is it impossible to reform from within? It explains why we need to reconceptualize medicine into four, interrelated categories—Routine and Emergency/Elective (covered by health insurance) and Serious and Predictive/Preventive (covered by life insurance).

The last three parts describe the *Life for Health* system in practice.

- Part III describes Life for Health's structure, the key entities, and the role of each, along with the participant experience. It explains how Life for Health approaches can be established alongside health insurance, essentially how the two systems will coexist, and how this can also be achieved in Medicaid. Finally, it details how the economics work, quantifying the benefits to participants, employers, insurers, and clinicians.

- Part IV describes what it will take to establish Predictive/Preventive Medicine as a coequal branch with Routine, Emergency/Elective, and Serious Medicine. It explains the link between predicting disease risk and prevention, and the role of longitudinal data in building understanding about chronic disease, and ways to stop it.

- Part V describes how *Life for Health's* creation enables new approaches to long-standing, seemingly intractable issues. Life for Health longitudinal data will advance our understanding of cancer and Alzheimer's Disease and Related Disorders (ADRD), accelerating work to predict and prevent both. The creation of financial structures to share risk and value over time enables new ways to price breakthrough drugs (like GLP-1s) to lower upfront costs, increase access, and ensure drugmakers have strong incentives to innovate and share in the value of their inventions over time. Finally, it opens the door to solve two political issues closely related to chronic disease, Medicare's long-term solvency and improving the healthiness of Americans' food.

A few themes recur throughout the text. First, chronic disease poses unique scientific and practical challenges that any new system must address. Second, that the forces of science and finance, which were mutually reinforcing for much of the 1900s, underwent a decisive schism in the early 1970s. Since then, efforts to translate medical discoveries into frontline care have—absent political and consumer pressure or emergencies—been severely delayed despite skyrocketing disease prevalence and costs. Third, the nature of the system that has emerged is impervious to disruption or reform from within, hamstrung by financial practices and industrial behaviors suited for short-term issues that are impossible to reconcile with chronic and complex disease. As we stand up and expand Life for Health approaches, repurposing funds now wasted in sick care, health insurance and status quo entities will naturally shrink. Ultimately, we will have two systems, each appropriate to the scientific challenges that each must solve.

David Foster Wallace's quote at the start of this Introduction points out that we all live within default modes of existence—assumptions, ways of thinking, and surroundings that we take for granted without question. Then, suddenly, we have an awakening and a realization that what is does not necessarily have to be, and from this comes constructive scrutiny and creativity. We start to ask: why does it have to be like this? What *could* it be? *Life for Health* represents the application of this thinking to health care. What we have, what everybody hates, is not just a function of greed or mendacity, but whatever the reasons, it need not continue as it has. In fact, it cannot be allowed to do so if we are to live healthier for longer and prosper.

ENDNOTES

1. The co-occurrence of three or more conditions as the criteria for multimorbidity is the most frequently used definition in the US. Note, however, that many health European and Asian academic publications define multimorbidity as two or more chronic conditions.
2. Unless otherwise indicated, "diabetes" in this book refers to Type 2 Diabetes. The clinical definition of metabolic syndrome is the presence of any three of the following: high blood pressure, high levels of triglycerides or low density lipoprotein, elevated blood sugar, or excess abdominal fat.
3. 1999 data is from Wolff, Jennifer L., Barbara Starfield, and Gerard Anderson. "Prevalence, Expenditures, and Complications of Multiple Chronic Conditions in the Elderly." Archives of Internal Medicine 162, no. 20 (November 11, 2002): 2269. https://doi.org/10.1001/archinte.162.20.2269. 2008 and 2018 data are from the Center of Medicare and Medicaid Services Chartbooks on Chronic Conditions among Medicare Beneficiaries.
4. See Johnson, Steven, How We Got to Now: Six Innovations That Made the Modern World, 2015.

PART I

ENDING CHRONIC DISEASE

1. LIFE FOR HEALTH'S MOMENT

> "I could already see that real-world problems didn't neatly lie within territorial boundaries. They jumped right across. And I was dubious of any approach that, when two things were inextricably intertwined and interconnected, would try and think about one thing but not the other."
>
> —Charlie Munger, Vice Chairman,
> Berkshire Hathaway

Health and life are inextricably linked, and yet insurance to manage the risks of illness and death exist in separate worlds. This is baffling, even more so over the last two decades as health insurers have shifted from curing disease to treating symptoms while life insurers have shifted from protecting against early death to managing the risk of outliving income.

The connection between life insurance and chronic disease first occurred to me in the Fall of 2009 when I was running an online health publisher called HealthCentral. We owned over thirty condition-specific communities helping people manage chronic and life-threatening disease, everything from heart disease and diabetes to breast and lung cancer, HIV/AIDS, migraines, mental health, and autoimmune conditions. HealthCentral's communities went beyond clinical information like symptom checkers and drug guides offered by sites like WebMD or MayoClinic.com. Our network of expert patients—people who had lived with and had first-hand experience with a disease—provided practical advice about "living with" issues like managing treatments and symptoms in the context of relationships, diets, travel, job issues, and all the barriers and hacks necessary to navigate health care.

That Fall, I was brainstorming new products with a number of our expert patients, when our diabetes community leader, David Mendosa, observed, "Well, you know, it's next to impossible for someone with Type 2 Diabetes to get life insurance." Wait, what, I asked? Yes, David explained, it was next to impossible to get life insurance at an affordable rate even if a person's diabetes is well-controlled. David spoke with authority. A bear of a man with a Mosaic countenance, he had been among the very first online bloggers on any topic, starting to post about diabetes in the days of Netscape Navigator and listservs. "Why is it so hard?" I asked. Life insurers, David explained, viewed all diabetics as bad risks since they were more likely to have a heart attack, stroke or a lethal low blood sugar event. Their actuarial models were hard-wired to expect early death even if an individual had a history of keeping their diabetes in check.

This struck me as a tremendous opportunity since I love contrarian bets. Back then, about 5% of Americans had been diagnosed with diabetes, but prevalence was increasing quickly. The only medical intervention that seemed to deliver long-term weight loss or diabetes remission was metabolic surgery, more commonly called bariatric or weight loss surgery. (I prefer the term "metabolic surgery" because it counteracts a number of metabolic issues in addition to causing weight loss). Everything else in use around 2010, from diets to drugs, were stopgaps at best. However, metabolic surgery was controversial, dismissed by many in the medical establishment as either a last resort for people with severe obesity or almost a cosmetic procedure, one that was far too risky to be done on a larger scale. As a result, just 150,000 surgeries a year were being performed, less than 1% of the potential market.

This seemed short-sighted. Long-term outcomes data for surgery were very encouraging. Most people who underwent one of the two most effective types of surgeries could lose a quarter of body weight, effectively rebooting their energy intake and inducing diabetes remission.

But metabolic surgeons lacked the media image or acceptability of heart surgery. No doubt this had something to do with deep-seated stigmas about people with obesity, and it forced metabolic surgery into a liminal space closer to plastic surgery than the life-saving kinds featured on Grey's Anatomy.[5] Missing was any kind of system to connect qualified individuals, experienced surgeons, and pricing to increase access. Also absent was an ongoing support structure to ensure surgery recipients achieved long-term health goals, including financial incentives for doing so.

Health insurers were a non-starter. They hated metabolic surgery and did what they could to dissuade its use. Why? Because of health insurer math. Surgery at the time cost more than $20,000 at top centers. Health insurers preferred to pay a few thousand dollars a year to manage the symptoms of diabetes, high blood pressure, or cardiovascular disease. Why spend seven or eight times that amount on a surgery, they figured, if surgery recipients might change coverage in a couple of years before the insurer could earn back their investment in the form of lower health spend? So health insurers routinely denied coverage arguing that the surgery was experimental. When that failed, they added indirect barriers to access requiring potential recipients to complete months of medically-supervised diet plans before qualifying for surgery. The catch was that a person might be disqualified for surgery if they were able to show even small amounts of weight loss, notwithstanding that compliance with a dietary plan is actually a valuable predictor of long-term outcomes for people undergoing surgery. This put people seeking surgery in the bizarre position of trying to *gain weight* to be assured of coverage.

I wondered, why not seek a solution outside health insurance? Since metabolic surgery reduced the risk of death, life insurance seemed a natural possibility. What if life insurers helped to underwrite surgery costs in exchange for recipients buying a ten-year policy? Premiums would be set higher than those for someone without obesity or diabetes but still well below that for someone with both conditions. A portion of the premium would help repay the life insurer for the portion of surgery costs they pay, and the policy could build in premium rebates based on recipients' ability to achieve and maintain weight loss and other metabolic health goals. If the person did not respond as well to surgery, the life insurer was unlikely to be out much revenue, and if they did achieve good outcomes, the insurer would do very well. Importantly, too, potential surgery recipients worried about dying as a result of the surgery or complications—a very small risk but still one that weighed on potential recipients' minds—would secure some financial protection for their loved ones.

Life insurers would gain customers they would not otherwise have had, recipients would gain access, and some financial security if they were nervous about surgery-related death. Clinicians would gain a steadier stream of patients and researchers would get valuable longitudinal data to understand why surgery worked so well. This was years before GLP-1s had even started to be tested for weight loss. While I did not think metabolic surgery was right or necessary for most people, it seemed like there were millions of potential recipients who were being shut out by health insurers from regaining metabolic health.

The idea's economics held up, but life insurers were not interested. Their business had shifted from protecting middle aged workers against premature death to selling annuities, helping aging Baby Boomers manage the risk of outliving their savings. Life insurers were also in a risk averse mood, having just emerged from a decade-long nightmare of winding down unprofitable long-term care policies. There, many companies grossly underpriced long-term health costs (due in large part to rising multimorbidity) but they were loath to tackle another novel idea around metabolic surgery. Venture capital investors had doubts as well. Why finance surgeries with life insurance instead of offering loans like those used with plastic surgery or other elective procedures? Because, I argued, metabolic surgery is not *that kind* of elective surgery, and the people who needed surgery the most were working class, and unable—especially just after the Great Recession—to qualify for or afford a loan.

Chastened but undaunted, I switched the focus to cancer where efforts to target treatments based on tumor genetic anomalies were starting to bear fruit. Here, too, access was a problem. Most Americans did not go to one of the top cancer centers unless their tumor was unusual, their treatment failed, or a malignancy recurred.[6] Here too, it seemed, was an opportunity for insurers. They could sell policy riders covering treatment at a top center, including any travel expenses for the patient or their family.

At the time insurers offered products that allowed whole life policyholders to get a loan or advance against death benefits if they were diagnosed with a terminal illness. Workplace insurer Aflac sold a lump-sum cancer policy in Japan that was especially lucrative. However, the existing policies came with two critical limitations. The illnesses needed to be deemed to be terminal which limited the applicability in first-line care. Also, none of the policies ensured that policyholders could get treated at specific facilities or access to cutting-edge therapies, which was the critical factor to improve life insurers' risk.

In 2020, two economics professors applied a similar line of thinking to cancer immunotherapies, which were proving to induce long-term remission for a sizable minority of recipients.[7] Health insurers were (once again) reluctant to cover these treatments especially when used "off-label" in initial treatment rounds. So, they argued, life insurers should step in and fill the gap. They showed convincingly that life insurers' incremental cost to underwrite immunotherapy would be more than offset by additional time to collect premiums and/or increased policy sales. However, here too, life insurers were unconvinced.

My point in recounting this is not to criticize life insurers as short-sighted but to highlight how much of a conceptual reset is required to fight chronic disease and cancer in new ways.

Also, timing is everything, as illustrated by the old saying on Wall Street: being too early with a great idea is indistinguishable from being wrong. Clearly, using life insurance for metabolic surgery or cancer was premature. So, if the timing a decade ago was wrong, why should now be different?

Because, the times, and minds, *have* changed. No one is happy with health insurers or the way the health care system now works. Not employers, who pay more and more each year only to see workers' health continue to decline. Not clinicians, who are fed up with insurer micromanagement, pressure to deliver higher treatment volumes, and fragmentation in care. Certainly not working Americans or even retirees, who see premiums and out-of-pocket payments consuming more and more of their income, as insurers ramp up prior authorization reviews and claims denials. Officials running health programs for the poor and the elderly see the demographic handwriting on the wall, with earlier multimorbidity and rising late-in-life costs. Even health insurers evince little confidence in their ability to manage chronic disease risk. Drug companies too—as much as they profit from the status quo—see the risk/reward of developing new therapies becoming harder and riskier. No one in the system likes current trends. That disaffection, alone, is insufficient to upend the status quo, but it's a critical shift.

Happily, three other forces are building to make this the right moment. The biggest is scientific. Technologies to reverse metabolic dysfunction are remarkably better, as evidenced by outcomes from using GLP-1 drugs against a range of metabolic issues. Even if the drugs have longer-term issues, scientists have found a rich vein of biochemical gold to mine and refine. GLP-1 drugs are not cure-alls, any more than metabolic surgery is, but their broad efficacy means we have very effective surgical and medicinal approaches to stop obesity, diabetes, and key aspects of cardiovascular disease.

The second change is the emergence of massive computational power, including AI. Given sufficient longitudinal real-world data, it is possible to understand chronic disease heterogeneity, identify the innate and environmental factors that are the greatest drivers of vulnerability and resilience, and trace how pathology develops and spreads. There is much hype about AI and much work to do to ensure the data used to train models is broad, deep, and unbiased. Yet capabilities that even a decade ago would have been dismissed as science fiction are today scientific fact. That's big, especially for life insurers in terms of underwriting risk and predicting long-term outcomes.

Finally, the cultural and political zeitgeist about nutrition and healthspan is changing. Books like *Outlive* by Dr. Peter Attia, *The Longevity Imperative* by economist Andrew Scott, *Ultraprocessed People* by Dr. Chris Van Tulleken, and the work of functional medicine advocates like Dr. Mark Hyman have increased awareness about chronic disease, the importance of increasing healthspan, and the failures of sick care and industrialized food. Their advocacy has started to change minds, and venture-backed healthspan improvement programs (including those launched by Attia and Hyman) provide a glimpse of what could be done on a much larger scale.

Among everyday working Americans, there is a growing awareness and anger about the ubiquity of unhealthy food products engineered to be overconsumed. Take any US interstate highway cross-country and it is quickly evident how hard it is to buy healthy food outside of coastal and well-off cities. Budget supermarkets and convenience stores are stuffed floor to ceiling with death on the installment plan. Searching online for food-stamp eligible items from Walmart or Amazon yields a "Murderer's Row" of ultra-processed, shrink-wrapped products.

So we need to seize this moment, and the momentum that is building, to bring together the threads of dissatisfaction with the status quo, technological breakthroughs, and broader societal awareness of forces that (literally) feed chronic disease. *Life for Health* answers this call and this moment, showing that it is possible to build a profitable and sustainable system to solve chronic disease rewarding long-term outcomes, aligning the interests of Americans with those of clinicians, scientists, and entrepreneurs. Lifespan without healthspan, years without vitality, is an empty promise. We can do better.

ENDNOTES

5. In fact, just two episodes in the show's two decades run have featured metabolic surgery in key plotlines, the first about repairing a botched procedure conducted in Mexico and the second about performing surgery on a character weighing 700 pounds.
6. Julie A. Wolfson et al., "Impact of Care at Comprehensive Cancer Centers on Outcome: Results From a Population-based Study," Cancer 121, no. 21 (July 28, 2015): 3885–93, https://doi.org/10.1002/cncr.29576.. Michael R. Desjardins et al., "Disparities in Cancer Stage Outcomes by Catchment Areas for a Comprehensive Cancer Center," JAMA Network Open 7, no. 5 (May 2, 2024): e249474, https://doi.org/10.1001/jamanetworkopen.2024.9474, and Daniel J. Boffa et al., "Survival After Cancer Treatment at Top-Ranked US Cancer Hospitals Vs Affiliates of Top-Ranked Cancer Hospitals," JAMA Network Open 3, no. 5 (May 26, 2020): e203942, https://doi.org/10.1001/jamanetworkopen.2020.3942.
7. Ralph S J Koijen and Stijn Van Nieuwerburgh, "Combining Life and Health Insurance*," The Quarterly Journal of Economics 135, no. 2 (October 29, 2019): 913–58, https://doi.org/10.1093/qje/qjz037.

2. FIRST PRINCIPLES OF SOLVING CHRONIC DISEASE

Why is chronic disease such a difficult adversary? It's all about time and variability. Pathology can begin in a variety of systems, driven by a confounding array of genetic, environmental, and behavioral factors. Absent decisive intervention, it will progress—here again at varying rates—and as a person ages, the feedback loops between deterioration and disease strengthen. Disease spreads, eventually becoming irreversible. All of this takes decades to unfold, featuring an ongoing battle between the forces of pathology and injury, on one side, and those of resilience and repair on the other.

There is an inconsistency to how chronic disease progresses, with periods of stasis interrupted by tipping-point drops in normal function. Over the years, the shift changes accelerate. In this sense, chronic disease is more like an unwieldy cascade than a linear process. Trickles of seemingly isolated issues coalesce into a waterfall of breakdowns, and eventually, an irreversible flood of multisystem collapse.

Metabolic syndrome often begins with an imbalance in energy intake versus consumption, worsened by certain food ingredients. Surplus fat accumulates along with inflammation, insulin resistance, clogged blood vessels, eventually leading to diminished heart, liver, and respiratory function. The order of manifestations varies. Sometimes high blood pressure appears first. Other times it is obesity or diabetes. However the cascade begins, other dysfunctions follow, undermining the liver and kidneys, increasing stroke risk, hastening arthritis and mobility problems, sleep apnea and depression, vision and peripheral nerve issues, cognition, and greatly increasing cancer risk.

The pace and severity of the cascade is hard to predict during the initial stages. One person may not develop issues until their forties only to progress rapidly to multimorbidity. Another person may develop pathology in their twenties but not enter multimorbidity until decades later. Treatment responses also vary widely. One drug will work very well in some, less so in others, and will be a complete bust in the rest.

The Battle Between Science and Finance

Before there was a concept of "health care," there was medicine. It was rough going for most of human history, as much mysticism and witchcraft as science, but gradually medicine imbibed rationalism, experimentation and evidence. During the first half of the 20th century, science drove medical progress. Antibiotics, blood transfusions, and surgical advances saved millions of wounded soldiers and then, eventually, everyone else. One by one smallpox, polio, tuberculosis, and childhood illnesses were erased by vaccines. World War II fused the forces of science and industry, accelerating a unitary approach to health care delivery. After World War II, researchers zeroed in on heart disease and cancer. Public and private resources ensured that surgical and medical breakthroughs, once standardized, were reproduced and distributed globally.

Then, suddenly in the early 1970s, a loud record scratch. Fueled by rising anti-consumerism, growing awareness of industrial pollution, and inflation, a deep skepticism about abundance and technology set in. Former White House policy aide Jim Pinkerton called it "scarcitarianism," a kind of neo-Malthusian belief that in the face of plenty, less is more. Scarcity is good. Suddenly, at the apogee of American technological prestige, with astronauts on the moon, the realms of medical science and finance split, undergoing a profound schism that remains to this day. The provision of health services, what today we call "health care" became the dominant branch of medicine. Blending financialism and scarcitarianism, it relies on financial levers to constrain access, setting up an all against all competition among physicians, hospitals, and insurers to apportion treatment and compensation. Meanwhile the portion of medicine devoted to research and technology development was liberated, in many ways, freeing scientists to deliver a stream of breakthroughs in molecular biology, medicinal chemistry, imaging, genetics, cell biology, virology, and immunology.

Health care decision-making shifted from inventors to insurers, led by Medicare and Medicaid administrators, hospital executives, and policy experts. They feasted on a steady diet of skepticism about medical technology, establishing layers of oversight to prevent gullible consumers from being duped into excessive care. Their case was buttressed by the misbehavior of exploitive clinicians, hospitals, and drugmakers who thrived amidst increasingly opaque payment rules. As multimorbidity grew, the fraudsters found opportunity in the proliferation of diagnostic codes and fragmented controls. The health care system settled into a cyclical predictability but instead of improving with repetition, it regressed. Each coverage or payment tweak added complexity, widening the gulf between health care delivery and health outcomes. Leaders extolled managerial abstractions like access, affordability, and quality, but interestingly, not long-term outcomes. Failure after failure only intensified efforts to find the elusive magical elixir of incentives and penalties that would—finally!—arrest Americans' shrinking healthspans and rising costs. Eventually, the labyrinth of administrative rules was more than a feature of the system, it was the system.

Health care leaders paid tribute to science in moments of existential peril as with HIV/AIDS, and COVID; when technologies like heart stents or statins proved they could delay costlier surgeries; or in the face of political pressure to cover costly therapies for cancers and rare disease. While scientific knowledge and capabilities accelerated, the speed to graft new insights into clinical practice slowed. Until financial overlords blessed a new approach by shoehorning it into the four corners of reimbursement rules, advances were constrained even if they might have improved Predictive/Preventive Medicine. Even luminaries like Dr. Francis Collins, a long-tenured NIH director, expressed surprise after overcoming prostate cancer at the chasm between clinical knowledge and practice: "I learned from that experience that we've come a long way in how to detect and respond to this cancer in the last ten years. But our health care system hasn't necessarily figured that out."[8]

Health Insurers Lose Their Nerve

In the late 1990s, Wall Street traders spoke gleefully of the "Greenspan put," named after the then-Fed chairman. Financial institutions believed that in the event of a major financial crisis or threats of a big economic downtown, the Fed would lower rates and ensure liquidity, minimizing downside risk. For decades, health insurers profited from a different safety net, the Medicare put. Knowing that the biggest costs of advanced disease correlated with age, they aimed to spend as little as possible on working-age Americans, treating disease symptoms as they arose while underlying pathology continued to fester. Medicare would be left holding the bag for expensive treatments after a person with multimorbidity turned 65.

It worked for decades, and in fact insurers figured out after the ACA's passage in 2010, how to attract healthier seniors into Medicare Advantage (MA) plans that paid them a fixed price for each person covered. Just before COVID, more than half of America's seniors were covered under MA, a doubling from the proportion enrolled in MA plans just a decade earlier. Then, after COVID, one insurer after another began to abandon MA, claiming the coverage was no longer possible.

Insurers blamed Medicare officials' decision to hold the prices paid to insurers below inflation. No doubt that hurt, but many other industries such as energy and transportation overcame much greater price volatility or adverse regulatory decisions. The real story is that multimorbidity costs came home to roost. Recall that the proportion of seniors entering Medicare with multimorbidity increased by two thirds from 2000 to 2020. Meanwhile, seniors who had entered MA plans with one or two chronic conditions progressed into multimorbidity. What had once been immensely profitable became—without warning in the retelling of insurance CEOs—an irreversible revenue drain.

Insurers' stampede out of MA coverage speaks volumes about their inability to solve chronic disease. It's an acknowledgement of their failure over the previous quarter century to halt chronic disease as they benefitted from sick care payment rules. Live by financialism, die by financialism.

The good news is that health insurers' quiet admission suggests that diverting misspent premiums to underwrite *Life for Health,* a real system to solve chronic disease, is much more feasible than insurers admit publicly. As Life for Health approaches pick up chronic disease risk, health insurers can shrink to focus on routine, emergency, and elective situations, the exact challenges for which their industry was designed.

Will health insurers fight efforts to carve out chronic disease? Of course, they would love to keep having their cake (i.e. premium hikes) and eating it too! The beauty of Life for Health is that the shift does not have to happen all at once. It can start with issues relating to metabolic syndrome, including obesity, diabetes, and cardiovascular issues, and expand over time to encompass autoimmune, respiratory, and behavioral conditions. Health insurers will fight publicly, but privately their financial arms will smile. Chronic disease accounts for much of their revenue but even more of their costs. Increasingly, their profitability comes from vertical integration of health delivery, including ownership of physician groups, hospital systems, pharmacy benefit managers, and health analytics consultancies. Inasmuch as the big health conglomerates have failed to stop multimorbidity, it is an open question if they want to keep trying.

Questions About Life for Health

Often, when I discuss *Life for Health*, people zero in immediately on questions of implementation. How could it coexist with health insurance? Would the existence of two systems worsen duplication and fragmentation? Would clinicians work within Life for Health the same way they do now with hospitals or health insurers? Who pays clinicians and hospitals in Life for Health? What would Life for Health mean for employer-based coverage? What assurance would employers or participants have that they would pay less under Life for Health than they do now?

There are legal and practical questions, too, especially around the role of life insurers. Would life insurers have to become health insurers? (No.) Can Life for Health be realized within existing life insurance laws and regulations? (Yes.)

Others ask about the relationship with participants. What ensures that they will stay involved for the long term? What happens if participants do not have a favorable outcome or cease treatment? How does Life for Health encourage people to make better health choices? How much control would participants have over how their data is used?

Finally, there are issues of access and equity, as in the current system. Life insurance is often seen as a luxury good, so how would poorer Americans participate? Can Life for Health be integrated into programs like Medicaid? (Yes.) What about environmental drivers of chronic disease, especially unhealthy food and exposure to pollutants? How realistic is it to think that Life for Health could end metabolic syndrome and other chronic diseases unless these other socioeconomic problems are solved as well?

First Principles and Success Metrics

The answers to these and other questions (addressed in Parts III and IV) reflect the following first principles, foundational ideas that shape how *Life for Health* is designed.

Science drives finance, not the other way around. Efforts to solve chronic disease must be driven by scientific inquiry and data. Finance must work in service of science to increase access and affordability, quantify value, and enable benefits and risks to be shared among participating entities over time.

Intervene earlier and decisively. The earlier we intervene to prevent, halt, or reverse chronic disease the better. Treating symptoms without reversing or preventing pathology is a recipe for disaster, allowing disease burden to accumulate, driving up costs and shortening healthspans.

The participant's interest is the system's interest. The status quo is centered around the needs of health insurers, hospitals, and clinicians. Ending chronic disease requires a system designed around participants and their outcomes. As a general principle, whatever helps participants reverse or prevent disease and maintain health will always be the best outcome, medically *and* financially, for the system overall.

Trust and transparency in all things. Americans trust their clinicians but rightfully distrust the system. *Life for Health* must build participants' confidence that everyone in the system is aligned around improving their health outcomes. The system must be transparent in all things, especially financial arrangements.

Longitudinal data is necessary to solve chronic disease. Chronic disease is a problem of long time horizons and high variability. Solving for these requires a broad commitment to gather data and biosamples (such as blood draws) as continuously as possible over many years. Data density and diversity will help disentangle complex interactions among biology, the environment, and life situations. Waiting until a person is symptomatic or diagnosed with a condition to start gathering data is too late. Longitudinal data allows researchers to rewind history, going back to uncover disease contributors that were not discoverable with earlier technologies. Unlike history, biology not only rhymes, it repeats.

Long-term outcomes matter most. Solving chronic disease is a long game. There is nothing to be gained if a person with metabolic syndrome loses weight for a few months only to stop treatment and relapse. Longer healthspan and a better health trajectory are the essential goals against which any nearer-term progress must be assessed. Accordingly everything in the system, from the clinician-participant relationship to compensation structures, must be designed to increase the odds of a better long-term outcome, and valued accordingly.

Outcomes should drive how we value and price clinical and preventive care. Very little health care pricing is tied to outcomes. Much of health care relies on interpersonal exchanges of information and care, which makes them inherently less efficient, in productivity terms, than manufacturing. Most success metrics are linked to volumetric inputs including activities and time. That can work in routine and emergency situations. It does not work with chronic disease. Realizing longer healthspans requires new approaches to compensate participants and clinicians over time based on outcomes. It will also enable mechanisms to increase the value attributable to preventive measures.

Measuring Progress

Continuing with that last principle, health systems struggle to assign *current* value to preventive measures. Measures like vaccines against highly contagious or lethal pathogens are straightforward, but few choices in chronic disease prevention are as clear cut when undertaken. Likewise, chronic disease prevention generally requires continual effort rather than a one-and-done solution.

Clinicians and health economists wonder how to price a preventive measure now without knowing future efficacy, without waiting years (or decades) to confirm the outcome. Even then, they wonder, how is it possible to know how much any one measure contributes to a distant result? This line of thinking, premised on the idea that the value of an action or service has to be paid for when the action is taken or the service provided—the approach to all health care pricing—is why efforts to reward preventive medicine get stuck in conceptual cul-de-sacs.

Fortunately, Life for Health provides metrics and a financial mechanism to assess progress against multimorbidity over time. We do not have to guess at the future value now, assign value to individual measures, or wait decades to see if interventions worked. Instead, we can assess progress against multimorbidity continuously using the following three metrics:

- The number of people with multimorbidity in absolute and percentage terms.
- How many people there are at each point along the chronic disease cascade, measured in terms of the number of comorbid

conditions (i.e., how many people have zero conditions, one or two, three or four, and so on).
- The median age of multimorbidity onset.

The first metric tells us if the problem is getting larger or smaller in absolute and percentage terms, overall and in particular age ranges or demographic segments. The second metric tells us whether we are making progress in the *composition* of the chronic disease cascade. Reducing the number of people with multimorbidity (the first metric) is good provided the distribution of people along the chronic disease cascade (the second metric) is also improving. We are making progress if both indicators are going down; however it would be less good if the number of fifty somethings with four plus conditions is going down while the number of thirty somethings with two chronic conditions is going up much faster. That means that a decade from now, the intensity of chronic disease prevalence is likely to worsen. Thus, looking at the first two metrics together helps explain *future* disease risk given *current* levels and trends.

The final metric, median age of multimorbidity onset, tells us how well we are doing to postpone onset of advanced disease. It tells us, in combination with the second metric, whether progression into multimorbidity is slowing down. This is one of the best single metrics of healthspan, and yet as much as US health experts track expected lifespan, no one estimates expected healthspan! For now, entry into multimorbidity is the most reliable dividing line to assess progress. Recent academic studies from England suggest that the current median age of multimorbidity onset in the US is somewhere between 55 and 60.[9] Thus, we will know that we are making progress in delaying multimorbidity onset if the median age starts to ebb upwards towards 65, and then, hopefully, to 70 or above.

Together, these metrics illustrate the total size, distribution, and velocity of chronic disease incidence and prevalence, and, although the metrics are described here in terms of overall multimorbidity, each could also be calculated defined to focus on metabolic syndrome alone, or even specific conditions like diabetes.

ENDNOTES

8 Trang, B. (2024, September 19). Q&A: Former NIH director Francis Collins on a Trump administration, science, and God. STAT. https://www.statnews.com/2024/09/19/francis-collins-former-nih-director-science-congress/

9 A 2019 UK study using one million English citizens' medical records concluded that the median age of multimorbidity is 55, a decrease of 11 years or 17% from a median age of 66 in 2004. Multimorbidity onset was 7 years earlier in the lowest versus the highest socio-economic quintile. See: Head, Anna, Kate Fleming, Chris Kypridemos, Pieta Schofield, Jonathan Pearson-Stuttard, and Martin O'Flaherty. 2021. "Inequalities in Incident and Prevalent Multimorbidity in England, 2004–19: A Population-based, Descriptive Study." The Lancet Healthy Longevity 2 (8): e489–97. https://doi.org/10.1016/s2666-7568(21)00146-x.

3. VISUALIZING MULTIMORBIDITY'S COST

> "Neither a high, even 100 percent, mortality from cardiovascular disease nor sudden death itself are to be regretted, provided they take place at an advanced age after a healthy and happy and useful life right up to the last minute. In fact, this is actually an ideal goal toward which man may strive, for it means the eradication not only of other diseases such as the infections of the past, and the cancers, accidents, and the wars of the present, but also the control of the serious cardiovascular threats ... to the lives of our youth and middle aged."
>
> –Dr. Paul Dudley White, cardiology pioneer, 1957

How much does multimorbidity cost in years and dollars, and how much healthspan could Americans gain by solving chronic disease?

To answer these, we need to visualize current health trajectories and the impact of current multimorbidity trends. Ideally, we would answer this using healthspan curves if reliable US data existed. Unfortunately, it does not, so we have to start by using life expectancy curves (which are rigorously gathered), from which we can approximate the impact of changes in healthspan.

Figure 3.1 illustrates lifespan under three scenarios, expressed as the probability of being alive every year from age 40 onwards.[10] The first scenario (shown by the dashed line) is our current situation. Median life expectancy right now is about 81, the point at which the dashed curve intersects with the line representing a 50% probability of being alive. The second scenario (shown by the dotted line) is where we are headed if multimorbidity prevalence continues to grow. The third scenario (shown by the solid line) is where we *could* be if we curtail multimorbidity.

Figure 3.1. Visualizing Multimorbidity's Cost

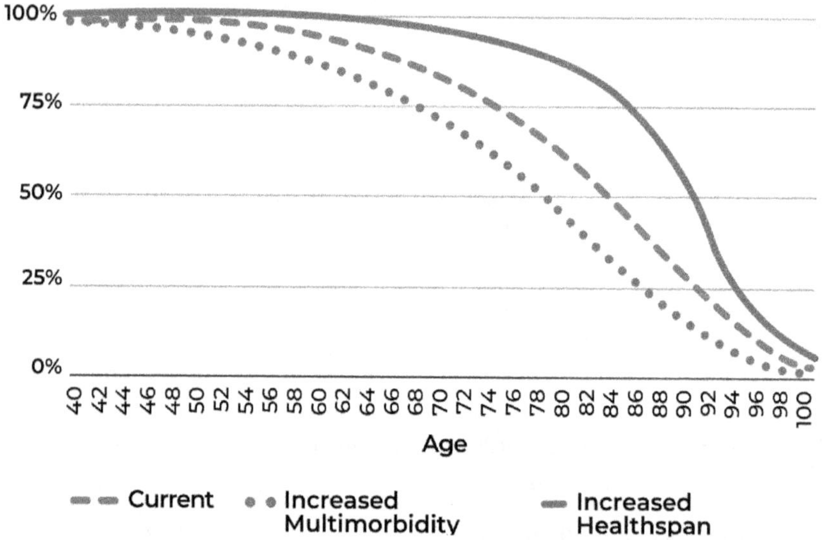

- - Current   • • Increased Multimorbidity   — Increased Healthspan

Starting with the current situation, the chance of being alive declines gradually from age 50 to 65, after which it declines sharply until about age 90, when the decline levels off. The latter group of people are called superagers, exceptionally healthy individuals who have a good shot at becoming centenarians.

The dotted curve shows what will happen as multimorbidity increases. The longevity/healthspan curve will shift left. The big drop in life expectancy will start about five years earlier at age 60 and continue through age 80. The solid line shows the opposite, how ending multimorbidity could shift life expectancy and healthspan to the right. In this scenario, sharp downturns in lifespan and healthspan could be postponed for most people until their seventies. Most Americans could live well into their eighties before experiencing a rapid decline in physical and cognitive capacity.[11]

So that's lifespan, but what about healthspan? To answer that, we add vertical lines to the chart representing the median age of multimorbidity onset in each scenario, as shown in Figure 3.2. In the status quo, the median age of onset is estimated at about 60, but would drop six years to 54 as multimorbidity advances, meaning the median American would spend about 38% of their adult lives in poor health.[12] In contrast, ending metabolic syndrome could shift the age of multimorbidity onset as much as fifteen years into the future, increasing productive years and reducing the portion of life spent in ill health by 40%.

Figure 3.2: Visualizing the Median Age of Multimorbidity Onset

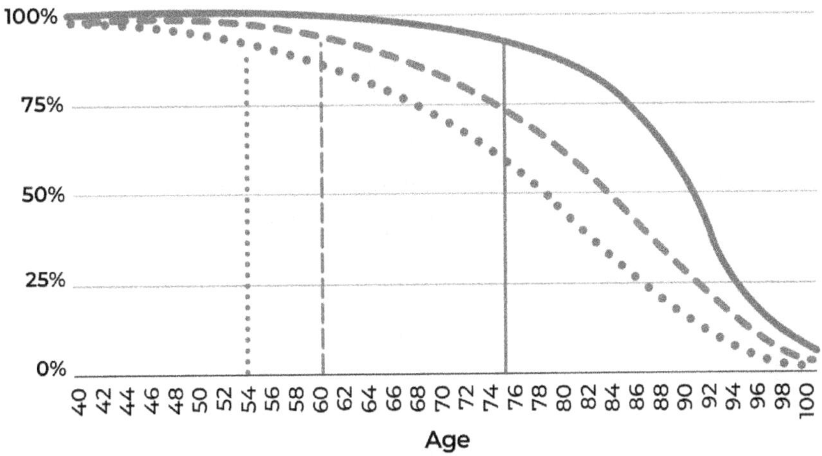

This chart illustrates the non-linearity of preventing disease onset and the importance of acting early. The differences among the curves seem relatively small at age 50 or 55 but in fact represent the start of trends that become much larger over time. Chronic disease pathology conspires with aging forming a feedback loop in which each contributes to the other. The key point is that with so much to gain by forestalling disease until a person is in their sixties or seventies, we have to act much earlier, reversing and preventing disease when people are in their thirties, forties, and fifties.

Figure 3.2 also illustrates the Prevention Paradox, our tendency to prioritize use of newer and more effective therapies for individuals with advanced disease over those who are earlier in the chronic disease cascade. The smaller gaps between the two curves at younger ages suggests that there is much less *current* economic value to invest in preventing disease when someone is young versus spending those same resources on someone older with advanced disease. Which is exactly what is happening today in the debate over prioritizing use of GLP-1 drugs for people with obesity. Health policy experts and insurers are prioritizing GLP-1 use among those with the highest Body Mass Indexes (BMIs) preferring less intensive measures like dietary counseling among those who have earlier stages of overweight or obesity. Yet, we know the only way to forestall advanced disease is to act earlier, and more decisively. That argues for *greater* use of GLP-1s among people with *less* advanced disease. So, which is it? Both answers seem "right." Chapter 25 explains how *Life for Health* resolves the Prevention Paradox by creating a mechanism to encourage simultaneous intervention at *both* ends of the chronic disease cascade, among those with the most and least advanced situations.

The State of Metabolic Multimorbidity

Until now, we have been discussing all forms of multimorbidity. Now, we need to go a level deeper and see how important *metabolic issues* are as a driver of multimorbidity in general. The clearest way to see how quickly metabolic issues have spread is using a map to trace the growing prevalence of obesity and diabetes. In 2019, over 40% of Americans had some form of obesity, and about 12% had been diagnosed with diabetes. That sounds bad, and it is, but even more troubling is the rate of growth of the two *in combination*.

Consider the following maps published by the Centers for Disease Control showing how much the combined prevalence of diabetes and obesity increased from 2004 through 2019.[13] Co-occurrence of obesity and diabetes is shown in deepening shades. The first two maps show prevalence in 2004 and 2009:

2004 & 2009 Obesity/Diabetes Prevalence Maps

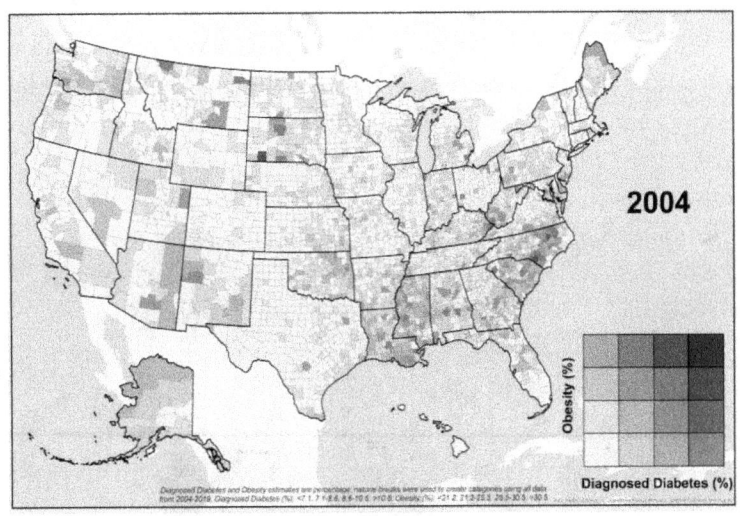

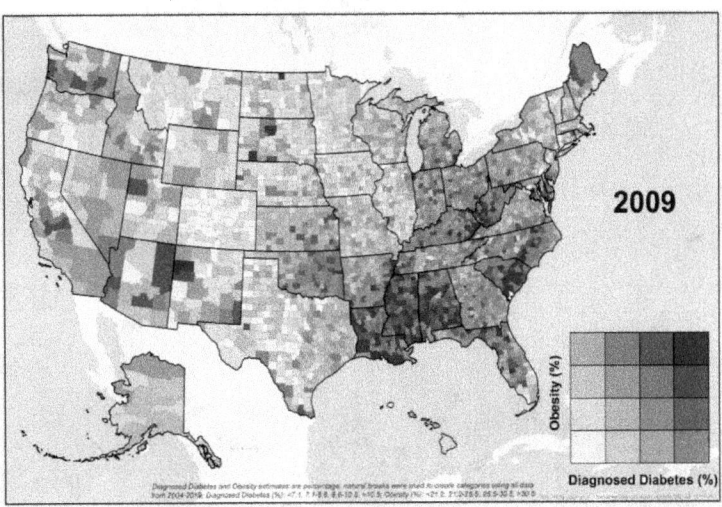

Few counties in 2004 were deeply shaded. Most counties have obesity prevalence below 25% and diabetes prevalence below 8.5%. A thin crescent of dark shading, high overlap of obesity and diabetes, runs from the Virginia/North Carolina border southwest to Georgia and then west into Louisiana. By 2009, the crescent had been replaced by blooms of purple throughout the Piedmont, Deep South, and the Ohio Valley with obesity prevalence approaching 30% and diabetes prevalence around 10%. The pattern intensifies in 2014 and 2019, as the number of purple counties increases throughout the Midwest, spreading into the Great Lakes and Maine, Florida, inland California, the Southwest and the Great Plains.

2014 & 2019 Obesity/Diabetes Prevalence Maps

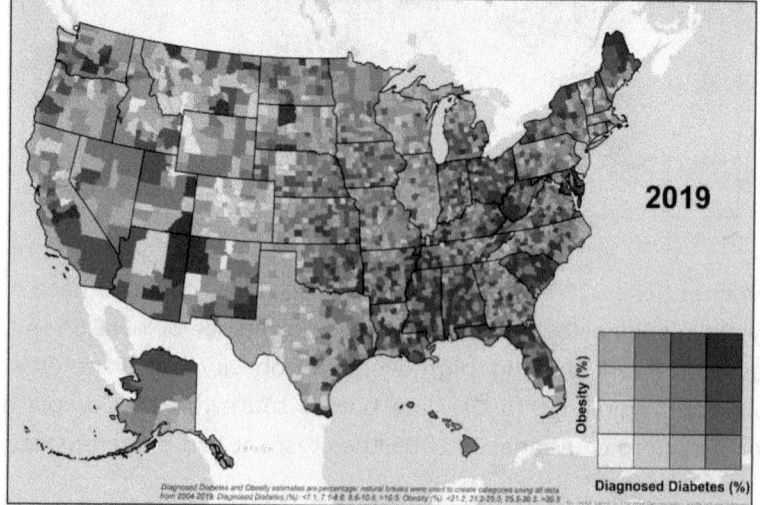

It's little wonder that multimorbidity prevalence among new entrants into Medicare jumped by two-thirds over this period, tipping over 40% before COVID. Tens of millions of working-aged Americans are contracting their third, fourth, or fifth chronic illness in their forties and fifties. Age of onset matters because the longer a person has a metabolic condition, the harder it is to achieve long-term remission. It's not impossible, but it is much harder. The body becomes acclimated to a state of dysfunction, with natural defense mechanisms switching from resistance to acceptance.

The maps show us how much prevalence of both conditions has increased in aggregate, thereby begging the question: how *quickly* are individuals progressing from their first condition to multimorbidity? As with everything in chronic disease response rates vary, but data from a federal agency working to improve the quality of hospital care called the Agency for Healthcare Quality and Research (AHRQ), gives us a good sense. In 2019, the AHRQ tracked the number and type of comorbidities among people admitted to hospital. They segmented this data by the age range of people admitted, breaking each age range into groups based on the number of chronic conditions at the time of admission—either one chronic condition, two, or three or more.

Comparing the composition of chronic disease across age ranges gives us a sense of how quickly people progress from one comorbidity level to the next.[14] The following figure from the AHRQ report is essentially a visualization of the chronic disease cascade, and how it changes over time.

Figure 3.3. Multimorbidity Distribution by Age Range, 2019 Hospital Admissions

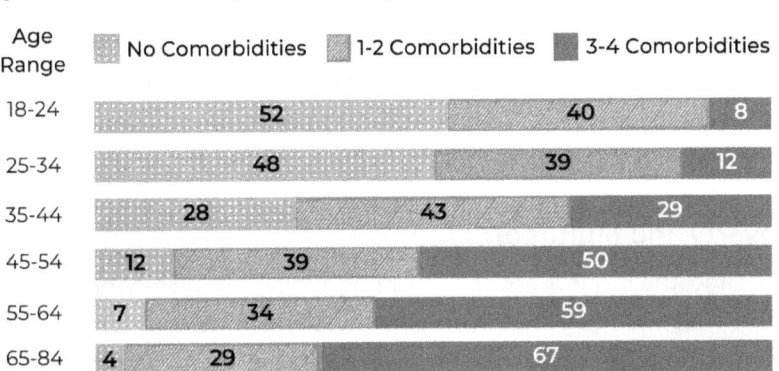

Without doing any math, it's obvious that the biggest shifts in chronic disease onset and progression happen from the early thirties to the mid-fifties, as the dotted bar shrinks to 12% while the solid bar swells to 50%.[15] Now, doing a little math quantifies *how quickly* people can progress from no disease to multimorbidity:

- Forty percent of people with no comorbidities by age 34 have one or two a decade later. Another 40% who already have one or two comorbidities by age 34 enter multimorbidity during the ensuing decade.[16]

Then, as people age, the pace of progression accelerates.

- About 60% of people with no comorbidities at 44 have one or two by the time they are 54. About half of the people with one or two comorbidities at 44 have multimorbidity a decade later.[17]

The AHRQ study is not longitudinal, meaning it does not trace the same individuals' path along the chronic disease cascade over time. However, this population-level snapshot is good enough for our current purpose, which is to get a directional understanding of how quickly chronic disease progresses. About 40% of people escalate one comorbidity category per decade from 25 to 44, with 50% to 60% of people progressing from one level to the next between 44 and 54.

This analysis provides a useful baseline for how we need to look at chronic disease and assess how well we are doing to reverse disease and prevent onset or progression. It underscores that we do not need to wait for the future to have an accurate sense of what it will look like (absent action). Chronic disease progression can be reliably predicted, making it possible to quantify both future disease burden and the value created by preventing that result.

Poverty and Multimorbidity

After age, the biggest driver of multimorbidity is poverty, which is itself, often, a factor of geography, employment, and education. It's often said that the zip code where a person lives is the best single indicator of their health status. When it comes to chronic disease, the shorthand of using zip code as a proxy for health should actually be reconceptualized as a summative score incorporating data about where a person was born, went to high school, and the places they have lived through their thirties and forties. This would provide a better sense of their trajectory over time, reflecting the cumulative nature of chronic disease risk and outcomes.

Still, the association between income and multimorbidity is striking as shown in the following maps. The first map illustrates per capita income by county in 2017. Beige areas represent lower-income areas while darker shading reflects higher incomes. The next map is the same as the one shown earlier depicting county-level obesity and diabetes prevalence in 2019. Looking at the maps, it's easy to see how much low income (shown in lighter shades in the first map) overlaps with higher multimorbidity (shown in darker shades on the second map.)

Income by county map and 2019 Obesity/Diabetes Prevalence Map

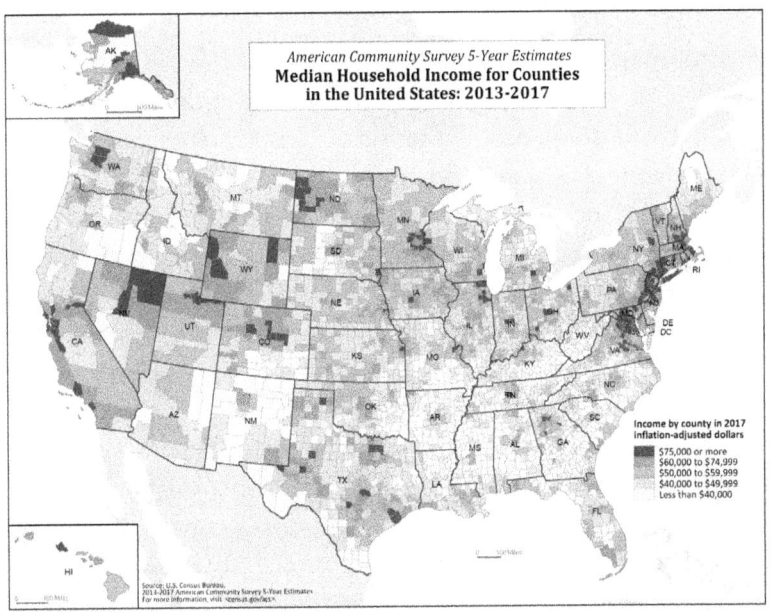

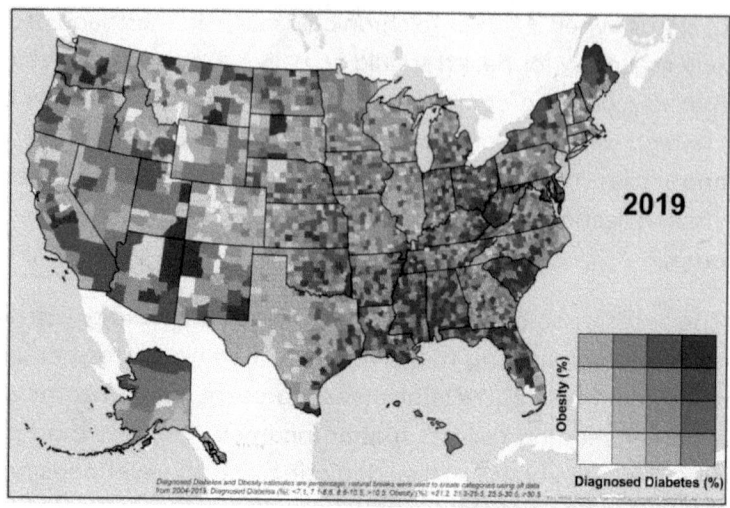

Leaving political ideology aside for the moment, there is no way to end metabolic syndrome and multimorbidity nationally without improving access to treatments and preventive measures in lower-income areas. We can argue about the "how" and "why" of multimorbidity prevalence, but the strength and size of the association is undeniable.

From the mid-1980s until the mid-2010s many health policy experts steeped in financialist thinking explained geographic disparities in health outcomes and costs in terms of healthcare economics. In this view specialist physicians and sophisticated resources gravitated to wealthier areas seeking higher incomes, depriving poorer areas of comparable care. This consensus was challenged by Dr. Richard (Buz) Cooper in 2016 in his book, *Poverty and the Myths of Health Care Reform*. Cooper, a hematologist who led a top cancer center in Philadelphia and a medical school in Milwaukee, showed that the prevailing view about cost and outcomes was backwards. Poorer people were unhealthier throughout their lives evidenced by higher per capita rates of hospitalization at all ages, thereby driving up costs. Cooper illustrated the point by tracing hospitalization rates and per capita spending in neighbor-hoods along the path of a New York City subway line, which passes through wealthy, middle class, and low-income neighborhoods. The less well-off the area, the greater the per capita hospitalization rate, and with it, per capita medical costs. Well-off New Yorkers along Park Avenue undoubtedly accessed some of the priciest specialists in the city, but because they were fundamentally healthier, these infrequent but exorbitant office visits were more than offset by higher hospitalization rates in less wealthy areas.

The takeaway here is that it is impossible to end multimorbidity and increase healthspan broadly unless Life for Health approaches are also adopted within Medicaid. Chapter 19 addresses how this can be done. As in the system overall, it will require governors and state Medicaid leaders to approach routine and emergency issues differently than chronic and life-threatening disease. States will have to invest more to reverse *and* prevent disease among enrollees. People who move in and out of public assistance will need to maintain a continuous relationship with clinicians overseeing their health trajectories regardless of their coverage status. Most controversially, Medicaid enrollees should have the same opportunity as other Americans to be compensated for meeting health goals, and to accrue these awards (up to a point) without invalidating Medicaid eligibility. Solving chronic disease requires a consistent approach to stopping multimorbidity among all Americans regardless of income.

Multimorbidity is not limited to the US

Finally, we need to address the common observation about how poorly the US health system performs compared to other countries especially in spending relative to life expectancy. Unquestionably, the US spends much more for equal or worse outcomes on many measures, especially in prenatal and pediatric care. However, the picture shifts on multimorbidity prevalence. There, the US is very much in the middle of the pack. In fact, the global picture on multimorbidity, across all manner of health systems, is remarkably consistent: no one is doing well.

A 2023 review of multimorbidity in 126 countries—with multimorbidity defined as two or more chronic conditions—found average global prevalence of 37%.[18] Multimorbidity rates were highest in South America, followed by North America, and then Europe. Younger populations in Asia and Africa had rates below the median although India and many Middle Eastern countries are seeing rapid increases in metabolic syndrome. Among Anglophone countries, prevalence in the US and England is higher than in Canada and Australia.

The situation in England is particularly relevant as a comparison to the US, since England's publicly funded health system, the National Health Service (NHS) is often touted as a superior counterpoint to the US's messy public–private hybrid. Actually, the English data underscores why we need separate systems for acute and chronic issues. The NHS may do much better than the US on routine and some emergency services, but it is just as bad as the US on chronic and life-threatening issues.

Multimorbidity prevalence in England has doubled since the early 2000s, from the 20% range then to the 40% range today. As in the US, prevalence in England varies by region, with higher prevalence in more middle- and lower-income areas.[19] Even more troubling, England has seen a dramatic drop in the age of multimorbidity onset. From 2004 to 2019, the median age of multimorbidity onset *worsened* by eleven years, from 66 to 55. That is a massive change in just a decade and a half.

By comparison, Canada is about a decade behind the US and England but is starting to see similar increases in multimorbidity. A 2017 study of Ontario (which includes 40% of Canada's population) revealed large increases in multimorbidity rates since the early 2000s, especially among Canadians aged 35 to 60.[20] The greatest change occurred among those with three or more conditions. The UK and Canadian data underscore the disconnect between common beliefs about the value of publicly-financed versus privately-funded systems when it comes to chronic disease. Science matters more than finance. Multimorbidity prevalence is undoubtedly worsened in the US by our convoluted health care system, but no system is set up to deal with the long-term and variability challenges of chronic disease.

Reframing US Health Spending

Much of the debate about improving US health care comes back to questions of cost, and yet, here too, our current framing is misleading. We are inundated with reports of ever-rising total health spending—$3 trillion, $4 trillion, now over $5 trillion. Even expressed as a percentage of GDP, the numbers are hard to fathom. What is the practical difference between 15% of GDP and 17%? Is there a point at which we should merely be concerned versus another at which point we should run screaming from the theater? Why, even, is a higher share of GDP necessarily bad? And if it is bad, why does total spending keep going up if people who worry so much about cost oversee the system?

The problem with these questions and the data behind them is that they approach health spending as an accountant might, in terms of how money flows *between entities*. Ask a health expert where most of the cost in today's system is and they will tell you, hospitals. Well, sure, but why? Because, you will be told, a greater proportion of older and poorer people have advanced chronic disease and cancer. Right, exactly, spending is a function of disease prevalence and severity, but the way we *account* for spending ignores this reality.

In the accounting view, the "income" portion of the ledger lists entities that inject money into the system including private health insurers; individuals, through out-of-pocket payments; workers' compensation programs funded by companies and public funds; and the biggest entities of all, public health plans including Medicaid, Medicare, and the Veterans Health Administration.[21] The expense side of the ledger lists entities that receive payment including clinicians, hospitals, pharmacies and prescription drugmakers, home health service providers, and makers of medical devices and equipment like wheelchairs and blood sugar monitors. The national health accounts include a final catch-all for administrative costs.[22]

Broadly speaking, according to this view, health dollars get spent in three areas. The first two are hospital care and clinician visits (i.e., doctors, nurse practitioners, physical and behavioral therapists, and dentists), each accounting for about a third of the spending. The remaining third is split among prescription drug costs (about 15% of total spending), home health and nursing care (about 12%), with the rest, about 8%, covering insurer and government administrative costs.[23]

This accounting-centric view works for Washington budgeteers and Wall Street analysts but it tells us little about the *disease prevalence* that drives cost. In particular, how many Americans have various conditions, the severity of their situations, and how disease burden is changing *over time*? The latter perspective is critical because most of the money spent today is to address chronic disease that began years or decades ago. Little is spent on first-time or traumatic injuries. Rather it is old debts, long neglected, that are coming due.

We look at health spending two-dimensionally, like a straightforward math problem, when it is more like a physics problem. Chronic disease prevalence and severity has mass, momentum, and direction. Disease burden accumulates at non-linear rates along with costs. In fact, as we will see, per capita medical spending increases at exponential rates as a function of the number of chronic conditions that a person has.

The green eyeshade view of health distorts policy, leading lawmakers and regulators to conjure financial fixes for problems that are rooted in medical science. When the President or Congress asks Medicare's leaders how to reduce hospital-based spending, their natural response is to change how hospitals or physicians are paid, hoping that reimbursement rate and rules changes will improve chronic disease prevalence. Spoiler alert, it rarely does. It *does* change clinician and hospital behavior but often not in the way policymakers intend.

In fact, incessant tweaking of payment rules increases opportunities for regulatory arbitrage or fraud, creating a game of whack-a-mole. Entities jockey to qualify for higher payments or buy non-profit hospitals to access certain government programs, leading regulators to change rules, leading to another round of financial legerdemain.[24] Multimorbidity prevalence may in fact be the greatest driver of waste, fraud, and abuse since the more conditions people have, the more specialists they see, and the more tests and procedures they undergo. Multimorbidity expands the "opportunity canvas" for dishonest practitioners or criminals to commit fraud. Reduce multimorbidity and the breadth of people and situations subject to abuse will, in turn, shrink.

So, how should we think about costs if the entity specific view of health spending is wrong? We should adopt a *disease severity approach*, tying spending to population segments based on where they are along the chronic disease cascade. This shifts our view from looking at *where* dollars are spent, to *who* they are spent on, and *why*. The left-hand side of the ledger would group people based on the number of their chronic conditions—none, one, two, three, and so on. The right-hand side of the ledger would look at spending for each group. Beneath this top layer, data could be sliced by condition groups like stage of metabolic syndrome, age or duration of diagnosis, locus of care, and all the other standard variables like gender, location, and wealth. Reframing spending in terms of disease severity will also improve our understanding of how much disease prevalence and costs are changing over time. Are we getting better at reversing disease incidence and prevalence, and if so, how is this impacting cost over time?

The good news is that we already have a sense of what health spending looks like reframed in terms of the chronic disease cascade. In 2017, a team at the RAND Institute, a widely-respected think tank, analyzed health spending by chronic disease stage. They divided Americans into four groups—zero chronic conditions, one or two conditions, three or four conditions (i.e., early multimorbidity), and five or more (i.e., advanced multimorbidity).[25]

The list of chronic diseases included metabolic issues like heart disease, high cholesterol, diabetes; respiratory conditions like asthma; and behavioral conditions like depression. The RAND team did not include obesity since it had only recently been classified as a distinct illness. The results, shown in Figure 3.7, paint a starkly different picture of health spending from the usual view. Expense, it turns out, is largely a function of multimorbidity. *In fact, two-thirds of spending goes to treat the 28% of Americans with three or more chronic conditions.*

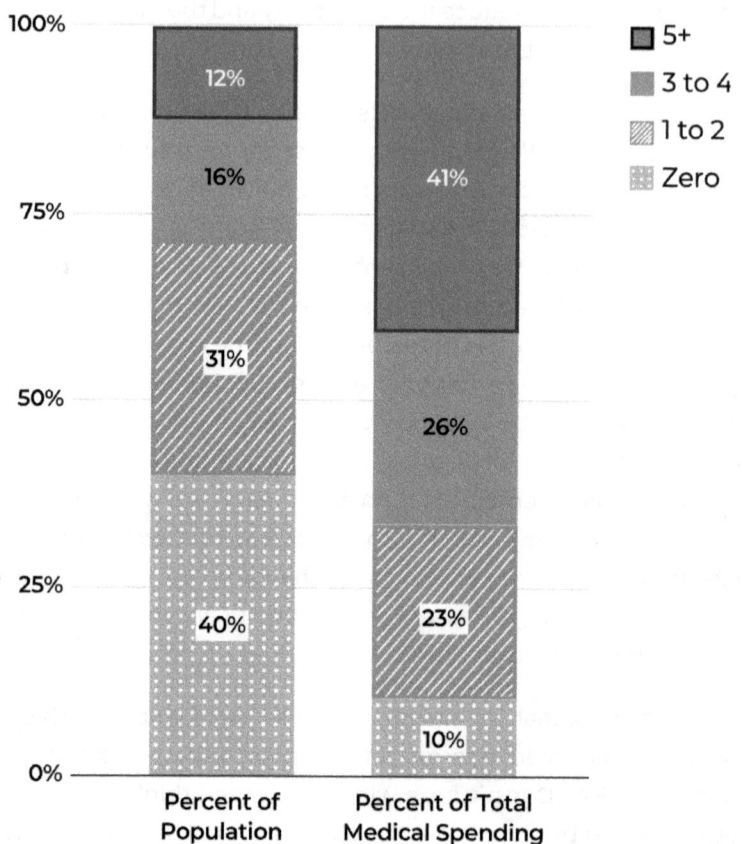

Figure 3.7. Chronic Disease Cascade (as a % of Population and Health Spend)

There is an almost eerie mirroring in the prevalence and spending data between Americans with no chronic disease (at the bottom of each column) versus those with five plus conditions (at the top of each column). Spending on the 40% of Americans with no chronic disease accounts for just 10% of all health costs. In contrast, spending totals 41% for the 12% of Americans with five or more chronic conditions.

Why is this? People without chronic conditions mostly need Routine Medicine and occasionally, Emergency/Elective Medicine. In contrast, people with multimorbidity require an extraordinary amount of treatment including hospitalizations, office visits, prescription drugs, and tests. Early in the chronic disease cascade, drugs to manage blood pressure and high cholesterol forestall life-threatening issues like heart attacks. Later on, however, the opposite is true. Advanced multimorbidity requires an expensive mix of drugs, in-person care, and hospitalizations. Multimorbidity also increases the risk of cancer, meaning that a disproportionate share of cancer treatment is for those who are older and have advanced chronic disease.

Doing some math on the RAND data, it is evident that *costs increase exponentially as a function of the number of conditions*. This is illustrated by calculating a cost to population share ratio, dividing each segment's share of health spending by that segment's share of the total population. The cost to population share ratio is three times higher for people with one or two conditions versus those who have none.[26] The ratio doubles again for those with early multimorbidity (three to four conditions), and then *again* for those with advanced multimorbidity (five plus conditions).

Interestingly, the composition of conditions, population, and spending in the overall population is also directionally true looking at Medicare alone. One might expect that spending among the Medicare population would be more evenly distributed than across all age ranges given the greater odds of hospitalization or serious illness among everyone over 65. Medicare data suggests otherwise.

In 2018, program experts performed a similar analysis to the RAND study on traditional Medicare enrollees except that their groupings along the chronic disease cascade included one more condition in each segment. Thus, RAND's grouping of zero conditions is comparable in the Medicare analysis to beneficiaries with zero or one condition. The RAND study group with one to two conditions becomes two to three in the Medicare study, and so on. This increase in the boundaries of each segment is reasonable given the extremely high likelihood that a person over 65 has at least one chronic condition such as high blood pressure or arthritis. What's remarkable is that the distribution of Medicare recipients along the chronic disease cascade, and the relationship between spending and conditions, are similar to data for the whole population:[27]

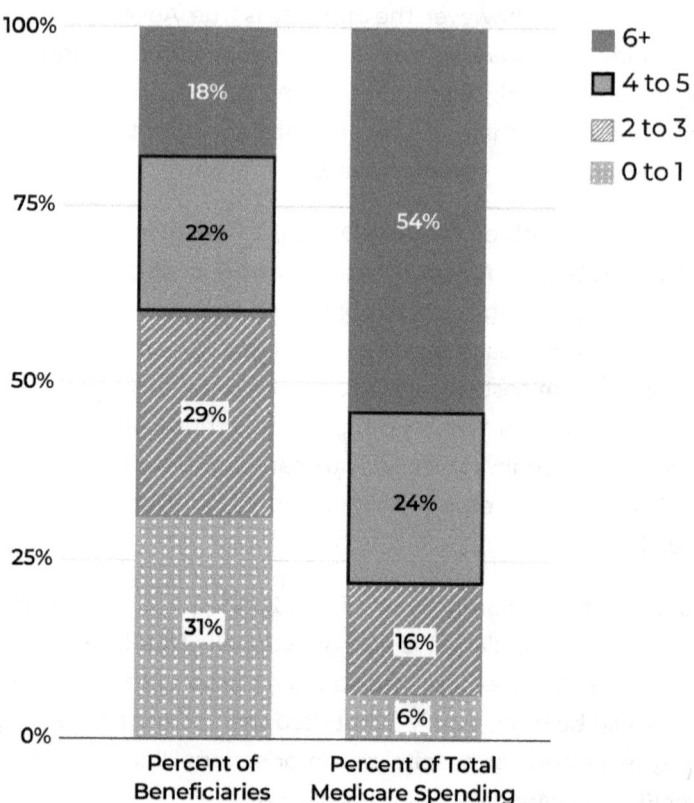

Figure 3.8. Chronic Disease Cascade in Medicare

If fact, the relationship is even stronger at both ends of the cascade. Medicare beneficiaries with the most multimorbidity (six plus conditions) make up a larger share of the population (18%) and spending (54%) than for the population as a whole. However, the 31% of Medicare beneficiaries with little or no chronic disease account for even *less* Medicare spending (6%) than the comparable segment for the total population (10%). In other words, the value of getting someone to Medicare age with zero or one chronic condition is *even greater* than in the population as a whole. Once again, the data is clear. The only way to bend the cost curve down is to push the healthspan curve out.

The exponential relationship between spending and population share by disease stage holds true among older Americans, as it did in the total population. The spend to population ratio is about three times higher for those with two to three conditions than for those with zero or one; it's about twice as high for the four to five condition group as those with two to three, and about twice as high again for those with the most advanced multimorbidity. The consistency between the two population groups is remarkable.

The RAND and Medicare analyses underscore three points. Multimorbidity drives cost, and how people are distributed along the chronic disease cascade is the best predictor of current and future health costs. From this, it is clear that the disease severity view provides much more insight about health care spending. Total dollars and dollars as a share of GDP are useful in some aggregate sense, but what really matters is the composition of the chronic disease cascade. Everything else follows from that.

A world without multimorbidity

Now that we have recast spending in terms of multimorbidity we can ask what the relationship is between multimorbidity prevalence and spending. If we now spend about $4 trillion annually on Americans with chronic disease, how much would multimorbidity need to be reduced, and what would the chronic disease cascade then look like, to lower spending by $1 trillion (25%) or even $2 trillion (50%)?

The answers are illustrated in Figure 3.9. Essentially, multimorbidity prevalence would need to be cut by almost half (from 28% to 16%) to save $1 trillion and by over 80%, from (28% to 5%) to save $2 trillion annually.[28] The current chronic disease cascade is shown in solid columns; slashed columns show disease prevalence to save $1 trillion a year; dotted columns show prevalence necessary to spend $2 trillion a year less.

Figure 3.9: Population Breakdown by Multimorbidity Status

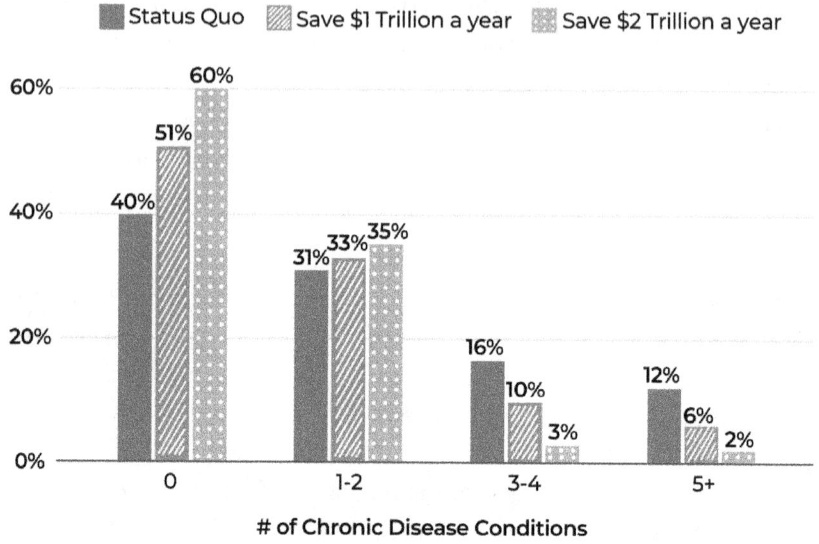

# of Chronic Disease Conditions	Status Quo	Save $1 Trillion a year	Save $2 Trillion a year
0	40%	51%	60%
1-2	31%	33%	35%
3-4	16%	10%	3%
5+	12%	6%	2%

From this we can see that reducing costs is about more than reversing multimorbidity among those who already have it. Rather, we must act along the whole chronic disease cascade. The number of Americans with no conditions will have to grow by almost a quarter, from 40% to 51% to save $1 trillion annually, and to 60% of the population to save $2 trillion. The proportion of Americans in the middle, with one or two conditions, would remain roughly constant, increasing from 31% now to 35% of the population in the $2 trillion savings scenario. In other words, we must work both ends of the distribution at once: reversing multimorbidity where it exists and maintaining those gains as far into retirement as possible, while also keeping as many people with zero conditions from acquiring disease. The longer we wait, the harder it will get.

Multimorbidity reductions would translate directly into reductions in health spending. Unsurprisingly, almost all of the cost savings come from reversing multimorbidity and stopping advancement into it, as shown in Figure 3.10. Spending on people with multimorbidity would decline from the status quo of $2.6 trillion annually, to about $1.4 trillion in the first scenario, and to a third of that level or $0.5 trillion in the $2 trillion savings scenario.

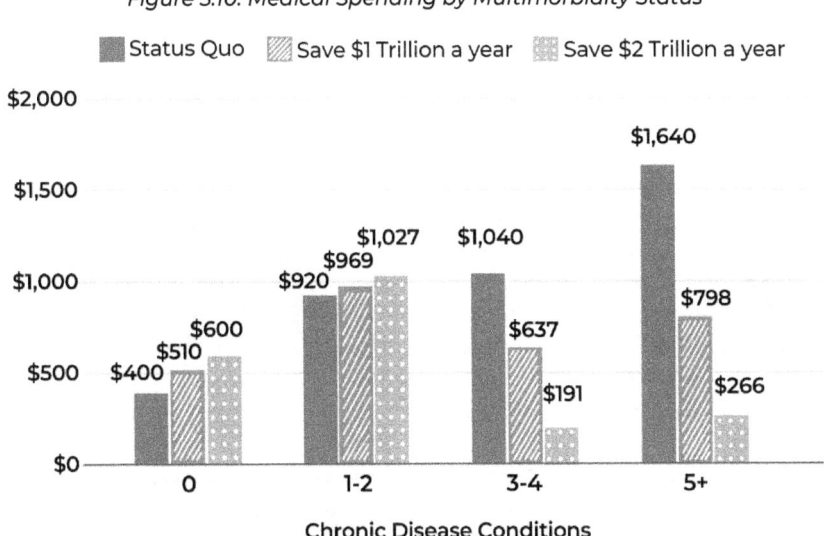

Figure 3.10: Medical Spending by Multimorbidity Status

Spending among Americans with zero conditions would *increase*, reflecting the significant growth in their ranks, which will mean greater use of Routine, Predictive/Preventive, and Emergency/Elective Medicine.

These scenarios illustrate that nothing in health care spending will change significantly until we change disease burden. Multimorbidity "in" will always equal extraordinary cost "out." Conversely, we stand to gain a tremendous amount individually, societally, and scientifically by changing the amount, distribution, and timing of chronic disease.

ENDNOTES

10 Life expectancy varies by ethnicity and gender (higher for women than men), but the curve's shape is fundamentally consistent across each group.

11 One criticism of scenarios like these is what happens if the status quo just shifts to the right? That is, what if multimorbidity onset can be deferred some years but the width of the curve does not shrink? People continue to have long and painful declines that last many years. The short answer is that it is impossible to rule out but it likely that lifespan will not expand by as much as healthspan. This is because the lifespan/healthspan curve is shaped by both disease incidence and progression and aging. We will almost certainly make progress against the first faster than against the second, if for no other reason than we have very good technology to reverse obesity and diabetes but little functional

technology to slow aging. It is likely that there is a lot of overlap between the two. Measures to counteract aging will also improve resilience against chronic disease and vice versa. Likewise, as discussed in Parts IV and V, reductions in one form of chronic disease, especially metabolic syndrome, will reduce risk for others like cancer and neurodegenerative disease. Thus, reducing multimorbidity will naturally reduce the duration and intensity of other, later in life illness. However, even in the worst case, in which lifespan increases as much as healthspan (suggesting as many years of late-in-life illness), the outcome will still be better than the status quo since individuals will have more years of good health to build wealth and savings. See, e.g. Hassen, Céline Ben, Aurore Fayosse, Benjamin Landré, Martina Raggi, Mikaela Bloomberg, Séverine Sabia, and Archana Singh-Manoux. 2022. "Association Between Age at Onset of Multimorbidity and Incidence of Dementia: 30 Year Follow-up in Whitehall II Prospective Cohort Study." BMJ, February, e068005. https://doi.org/10.1136/bmj-2021-068005.

12 This is calculated as the difference between the median lifespan (77) and the median age of multimorbidity onset (54) divided by adult lifespan of 59 (median lifespan less 18).

13 National Center for Chronic Disease Prevention and Health Promotion, Centers for Disease Control, "Age-Adjusted Prevalence of Diagnosed Diabetes and Obesity Among Adults, by County, United States (2004, 2009, 2014, 2019)" Obesity is defined as a self-reported Body Mass Index (BMI) of 30 or more, and diabetes prevalence is based on a positive response to the question "Has a doctor ever told you that you have diabetes?" Data is for adults 20 and over and excludes women with gestational diabetes.

14 Overall, about half the people admitted to hospital had multimorbidity, which is higher than in the total population but not surprising since people admitted to hospital skew older and have more conditions. See Owens, Pamela L., Lan Liang, Marguerite L. Barrett, and Kathryn R. Fingar. 2022. "Comorbidities Associated With Adult Inpatient Stays, 2019." Healthcare Cost and Utilization Project (HCUP) Statistical Briefs - NCBI Bookshelf. December 15, 2022. https://www.ncbi.nlm.nih.gov/books/NBK588380/.

15 Metabolic issues are by far the most common comorbidities in the AHRQ data, especially hypertension, obesity, diabetes, and kidney disease. Chronic respiratory disease is the next most common comorbidity, and can result from smoking, air pollution, asthma, or advanced metabolic issues.

16 The 40% is calculated based on the 20% difference in the proportion of those with no comorbidities between the 25–34 and the 35–44 age ranges, divided by the 48% of 25–34 year olds who have no comorbidities. The 60% equals the 16.8% reduction in those with no comorbidities between the 35–44 to the 45–54 age ranges, divided by the 28% of 25–34 year olds with no comorbidities.

17 The 48% equals the 20% increase in those with three plus comorbidities between the 35–44 to the 45–54 age ranges, divided by the 42.5% of 35–44 year olds who had one to two comorbidities.

18 Chowdhury, Saifur Rahman, Dipak Chandra Das, Tachlima Chowdhury Sunna, Joseph Beyene, and Ahmed Hossain. 2023. "Global and Regional Prevalence of Multimorbidity in the Adult Population in Community Settings: A Systematic Review and Meta-analysis." EClinicalMedicine 57 (February): 101860. https://doi.org/10.1016/j.eclinm.2023.101860.

19. Head, Anna, Kate Fleming, Chris Kypridemos, Pieta Schofield, Jonathan Pearson-Stuttard, and Martin O'Flaherty. 2021. "Inequalities in Incident and Prevalent Multimorbidity in England, 2004–19: A Population-based, Descriptive Study." The Lancet Healthy Longevity 2 (8): e489–97. https://doi.org/10.1016/s2666-7568(21)00146-x.
20. Kone, Anna Pefoyo, Luke Mondor, Colleen Maxwell, Umme Saika Kabir, Laura C. Rosella, and Walter P. Wodchis. 2021. "Rising Burden of Multimorbidity and Related Socio-demographic Factors: A Repeated Cross-sectional Study of Ontarians." Can J Public Health 112 (4): 737–47. https://doi.org/10.17269/s41997-021-00474-y.
21. Even this is not a full revenue accounting, which would entail tying back revenue categories to their original sources such as Medicare payroll taxes, employer and worker premiums for private insurance, and government borrowing.
22. Health spending does not include costs incurred by full or part-time caregivers or transportation to and from medical visits.
23. There are differing views about how to account for prescription drug costs given differences in how they are accounted for in different health settings and whether costs include or exclude rebates by manufacturers or distributors or other fees paid to prescription benefit managers.
24. A classic example is a hospital assistance program called 340B, named after the section of the Public Health Act. Created to help hospitals serving poorer Americans to purchase drugs at discounted prices, the program has grown sevenfold since 2010 as hospital owners figured out how to squeeze into the program or route prescriptions through favorable pharmacy arrangements.
25. Buttorff, Christine, Teague Ruder, and Melissa Bauman. 2017. "Multiple Chronic Conditions in the United States." RAND. May 26, 2017. https://www.rand.org/pubs/tools/TL221.html.
26. To illustrate the calculation, the cost to population share ratio for those with no conditions is 0.25, calculating by dividing the 10% cost share by the 40% population share. The cost to population share ratio for those with 1 to 2 conditions is 0.73, calculated by dividing the 23% cost share by the 31% population share.)
27. Center for Medicare and Medicaid Services, CMS Chronic Condition 2018 Zip Data file. (Note, this file has been removed from the CMS website but was retrieved by the author before its removal).
28. These scenarios assume current rates of spending per capita in each disease segment continue into the future, (i.e., if we spend $10,000 a year now for someone with one to two, constant dollar spending in the future would not change).

4. SOLVING MULTIMORBIDITY ADDS A DECADE OF HEALTH AND TRILLIONS OF WEALTH

Scenarios are one thing, but what does the evidence say about the feasibility of reversing multimorbidity? What can we reasonably expect to gain in terms of healthspan, and how will this translate economically, beyond just health care savings?

To answer these questions, we return in Figure 4.1 to the curves shown at the start of the last chapter. The dashed curve represents current lifespan while the solid curve illustrates gains by ending multimorbidity. The gap between the two curves approximates potential gains in lifespan and healthspan. At the median scenario (the 50% line), people would gain about a decade. Those already at greater risk of dying early (the 75% line) might gain even more, about thirteen years.

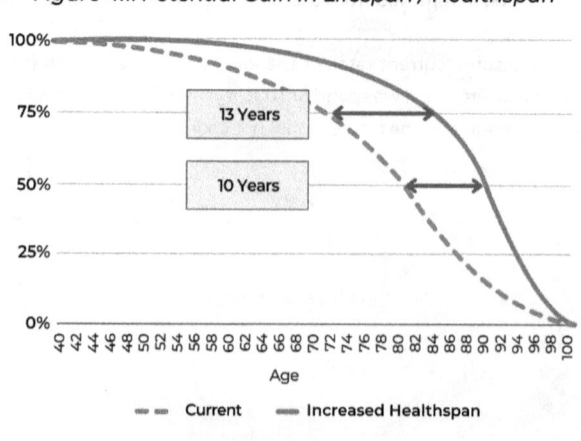

Figure 4.1: Potential Gain in Lifespan / Healthspan

Is this magnitude of gains realistic with current medical technology? Yes, it turns out. There is a rich library of research studies buttressing the case that preventing chronic disease onset and progression translates into a *decade plus of healthspan*. Four large studies published since 2019 laid out the evidence for a decade's gain just focusing on metabolic health.[29] Collectively, they found, people without chronic disease and those with early-stage disease who maintain good diet and exercise levels live *five to ten years longer* than those with more advanced metabolic dysfunction. Importantly, people with good metabolic function enjoy a decade more of good health before chronic disease onset versus those with poor metabolic function.[30] Another study traced long-term health outcomes for 116,000 individuals who were free of chronic disease at age 40, exploring how long people were able to avoid disease onset depending on their levels of smoking, exercise, alcohol intake, and BMI.[31] Women and men with the best health scores enjoyed almost a decade more free of chronic disease than those with the lowest scores. The best outcome is never to get chronic disease, but decade-long gains are still possible by postponing onset beyond the mid-fifties.

Does this mean that longer healthspan is primarily due to behavioral and lifestyle factors? No, it means that the most challenging part of maintaining health after reversing obesity or diabetes is achievable with diet, exercise, and other healthy behaviors. Medications, counseling, and other measures will only increase the odds of realizing a decade more of good health.

Likewise, there is strong evidence to support the feasibility of reversing metabolic syndrome using surgical *or* medical approaches. The most widely practiced surgical techniques consistently yield 20% to 25% weight loss when complimented with postoperative nutritional and behavioral counseling. Three-fourths of surgery recipients with obesity and diabetes achieve healthy blood sugar levels, with many able to stop taking blood sugar drugs altogether.[32] Recent studies have also shown that surgery recipients have significantly lower risk for liver disease, and breast, colorectal, kidney, and gallbladder cancers.[33] A long-term analysis of mortality for surgery recipients showed a six plus years increase in lifespan compared to similarly-situated individuals who did not have surgery. The biggest contributors to longevity were comparatively fewer fatal heart events and diabetes-related complications.[34]

Of course, surgery is a major undertaking and requires lifelong changes in diet and nutritional intake, which is why the emergence of GLP-1 drugs to combat obesity and other metabolic issues is so transformational. Novo Nordisk's first-to-market drug, semaglutide, yielded 10% to 15% weight loss, only to be bested a couple of years later by Lilly's dual-target drug, tirzepatide, which pushed weight loss into the 15% to 20% range. In June 2023, a mid-stage clinical trial for Lilly's three-target drug suggested weight loss on par with surgery, a first for any medication.

Interestingly, both surgery and GLP-1 drugs cause multisystem benefits, although how and why this happens appears to differ. Surgery obviously reduces the volume and types of food consumed, but it also improves insulin sensitivity and gut function. Long-acting GLP-1 drugs affect brain circuits that regulate appetite and addictive rewards as well as drug receptors in the gut. One of the co-discoverers of GLP-1's benefits, Dr. Daniel Drucker believes that GLP-1s may work in part by quieting inflammatory signals inside and outside the brain, opening the door to testing their efficacy against immune-related neurodegenerative disease.

Neither surgery nor medication technology is a silver bullet. Surgery recipients must continuously monitor key vitamin levels, and some people cannot tolerate GLP-1 side effects. As in all chronic disease situations, variability in situation will warrant a range of treatment approaches. Older drug recipients may benefit more from combination therapies that preserve lean muscle even at the expense of less extensive weight loss. Some will find it easier to stay on medication taking pills daily while others will respond better to long-acting injections.

In short, the menu of disease reversal and maintenance options are only going to improve, especially within systems like Life for Health that monitor outcomes and seek to identify why some participants do better or worse. We have safe and effective means to reverse disease and maintain gains, and these will only get better with experience. A decade plus of additional healthspan is very achievable.

Trillions to Gain By Counteracting Multiple Condition Risks

The next question is what is a decade's worth of increased healthspan worth?

The best answer, based on two studies by top health economists, is that Americans could gain *between $10 trillion and $20 trillion of increased wealth* over the next few decades as reduced chronic disease translates into more earnings and savings.[35] That is an immense sum, equivalent to about half of America's annual GDP.

However, these estimates come with an important caveat. It's insufficient to solve diseases one at a time, focusing on heart disease, and then diabetes, cancer, or ADRD. Realizing the benefits of longer healthspan requires parallel progress against multiple conditions. In effect, we need a systemic effort to counteract the full range of chronic and age-related disease. Prior to the two studies referenced above, the seminal analysis of the value of defeating disease, written in 2006 by economists Kevin Murphy and Robert Topel, estimated that gains in life expectancy since the 1970s had added about $3.2 trillion per year to national wealth."[36] Solving cancer—the biggest mortality threat after heart disease in the latter half of the twentieth century—would be even more valuable: "[A] permanent 1% reduction in mortality from cancer has a present value to current and future generations of Americans of nearly $500 billion, whereas a cure (if one is feasible) would be worth about $50 trillion."[37]

It was into this disease specific context that a team of health economists, led by Dana Goldman at USC, David Cutler at Harvard, and Jay Olshansky at University of Chicago, set out to test a new longitudinal model that accounted for multiple disease threats and the economic tradeoffs of increasing lifespan and healthspan. They agreed with Murphy and Topel that postponing lethal illnesses *could* have tremendous value but concluded that sequential progress against individual diseases would yield only marginal longevity and economic gains.[38] The risk of dying from any one of multiple advanced chronic or age-related conditions increases rapidly as a function of age. Solving cancer would eliminate that threat but a person would remain just as susceptible to all the other mortal threats, such as metabolic disease, ADRD, or a lethal infection. Realizing the economic value of living longer would require broad progress against the most common healthspan threats, which they categorized as "delayed aging;"

> "[M]aking progress against one disease means that another one will eventually emerge in its place. However, evidence suggests that when aging is delayed, all fatal and disabling disease risks are lowered simultaneously. Not surprisingly, we see extremely large population health benefits in our delayed aging scenario … The benefits to society of delayed aging would accrue rapidly and would extend to all future generations. Investing in research to delay aging should become a priority."[39]

If scientists and clinicians could delay life-threatening disease—principally multimorbidity, cancer, and ADRD—societal gains (in 2023 dollars) could exceed $10 trillion over the ensuing decades.

In 2020, longevity researchers Andrew Scott and Dr. David Sinclair updated the Goldman analysis, calculating an even greater potential windfall from postponing age-related illness.[40] Their initial estimate was almost three times higher than the Goldman team's, although much of this difference reflected more aggressive assumptions about how quickly health gains would be realized and a lower discount rate on future economic value.[41] Adjusting for these differences puts the Scott/Sinclair analysis closer to $20 trillion in incremental value (in 2023 dollars.)

Setting aside these methodological differences, both teams arrived at essentially the same conclusions. First, it's no good to tackle long-term diseases separately or sequentially. Potential gains have to be enjoyed broadly, and requires systematic work to defer disease and age-related pathology. Second, and even more critically for *Life for Health*, it's useless to try to delay aging by starting to intervene when someone is approaching retirement. Stopping the ravages of age and chronic illness has to start decades earlier, including a continuous effort over many decades.

Both teams were writing as health economists not as scientific experts in the mechanisms of disease or aging. However, their insights have been subsequently validated by researchers studying the interplay between markers of aging and chronic disease risk. In metabolic syndrome, for example, the characteristic indicators of progression, including buildup of fat tissue and insulin resistance is associated with inflammation, leading to diminished liver function and buildup of cholesterol in arteries, eventually causing declines in heart and vascular function. At a cellular level, these breakdowns coincide with increasing signs of aging including diminished cellular function, nutrient sensing, changes in gene expression, and chronic inflammation.

In conclusion, there is much to gain in solving chronic disease but also much to overcome. Our perspective of the problem has been distorted by the health care system that has helped to create it. It is only by taking a fresh look at the nature of the problem, reorienting ourselves around disease severity and chronic disease cascade, that we can see the importance of time and variability, and the complexities that each creates.

But how did we get here? How did a system, well-intentioned and led by individuals with the best of intentions, evolve into the impossible and mistrusted labyrinth that exists today? How much was accident and how much design? Why do we need to undertake something like Life for Health? Is it impossible to reform the system from within? It is to these questions that we turn next.

ENDNOTES

29 See: Li Y, Schoufour J, Wang D D, Dhana K, Pan A, Liu X et al. Healthy lifestyle and life expectancy free of cancer, cardiovascular disease, and type 2 diabetes: prospective cohort study BMJ 2020; 368 :l6669 doi:10.1136/bmj.l6669. Nyberg ST, Singh-Manoux A, Pentti J, et al. Association of Healthy Lifestyle With Years Lived Without Major Chronic Diseases. JAMA Intern Med. 2020;180(5):760–768. doi:10.1001/jamainternmed.2020.0618. Xu C, Zhang P, Cao Z. Cardiovascular health and healthy longevity in people with and without cardiometabolic syndrome: A prospective cohort study. EClinicalMedicine. 2022 Mar 6;45:101329. doi: 10.1016/j.eclinm.2022.101329, and Wang X, Ma H, Li X, et al. Association of Cardiovascular Health With Life Expectancy Free of Cardiovascular Disease, Diabetes, Cancer, and Dementia in UK Adults. JAMA Intern Med. 2023;183(4):340–349. doi:10.1001/jamainternmed.2023.0015

30 Wang et.al.

31 Nyberg et. al.

32 Kirwan JP, Courcoulas AP, et. al., "Diabetes Remission in the Alliance of Randomized Trials of Medicine Versus Metabolic Surgery in Type 2 Diabetes (ARMMS-T2D)," Diabetes Care. 2022 Jul 7;45(7):1574-1583.

33 See: Aminian A, Wilson R, Al-Kurd A, et al. Association of Bariatric Surgery With Cancer Risk and Mortality in Adults With Obesity. JAMA. 2022;327(24):2423–2433. Kristensson FM, Andersson-Assarsson JC, Peltonen M, et al. Breast Cancer Risk After Bariatric Surgery and Influence of Insulin Levels: A Nonrandomized Controlled Trial. JAMA Surg. 2024;159(8):856–863. O. Lovrics, J. Butt, Y. Lee, et. al., "The effect of bariatric surgery on breast cancer incidence and characteristics: A meta-analysis and systematic review," The American Journal of Surgery, Volume 222, Issue 4, 2021:715-722. Feigelson, Heather Spencer PhD, MPH; et. al., "Bariatric Surgery is Associated With Reduced Risk of Breast Cancer in Both Premenopausal and Postmenopausal Women," Annals of Surgery 272(6):p 1053-1059, December 2020.

34 After five years, about 1% of surgery recipients had died versus 2.8% of people with obesity who did not have surgery. See Courcoulas, Anita P.; Johnson, E.; Arterburn, David E., et. al. "Reduction in Long-term Mortality After Sleeve Gastrectomy and Gastric Bypass Compared to Nonsurgical Patients With Severe Obesity." Annals of Surgery 277(3):p 442-448, March 2023. The study included data from 25,000 metabolic surgery patients and over 65,000 people with similar demographics and medical situations who did not undergo bariatric surgery.

35 This value estimate is in 2023 dollars.

36 Murphy, Kevin M., and Robert H. Topel. "The value of health and longevity." Journal of political Economy 114.5 (2006): 871-904.

37 Ibid.

38 Goldman, Dana P., et al. "Substantial health and economic returns from delayed aging may warrant a new focus for medical research." Health affairs 32.10 (2013): 1698-1705.

39 Ibid.

40 Scott, A.J., Ellison, M. & Sinclair, D.A. The economic value of targeting aging. Nat Aging 1, 616–623 (2021). https://doi.org/10.1038/s43587-021-00080-0.

41 Scott et. al. forecast that ending age-related disease across the whole population could generate $8.8 trillion in annual value (in 2023 dollars), totaling between $50 trillion and $65 trillion over ten years.

PART II

BEYOND HEALTH INSURANCE

5. THE MISCONCEPTION AT THE HEART OF THE SYSTEM'S FAILURE

> "If more of our resources were invested in preventing sickness and accidents, fewer would have to be spent on costly cures. If we gave more attention to treating illness in its early stages, then we would be less troubled by acute disease. In short, we should build a true "health" system and not a "sickness" system alone. We should work to maintain health and not merely to restore it."
>
> –President Richard M. Nixon, February 1971

President Nixon's call a half century ago to do more to prevent illness than treating it would garner as much public support today as a half century ago. So, what happened? Why is our health care system incapable of stopping chronic disease?

Many inside and outside the system say the answer is obvious. "Sick care" is more profitable. There's money in treatment for physicians, hospitals, and insurers, so treatment is what the system does. Some on the Left would solve this by creating national health care, removing the profit motive altogether. Others on the Right decry government and insurance rules that stop individuals from shopping for health care. As much as these views are diametrically opposed in terms of *how* the system should work, they agree on the underlying principle that it is possible to design *a system,* singular, to encompass all kinds of health issues.

This belief in the necessity of a single system is so deeply ingrained in how we think about health care as to be almost unnoticeable. There are library shelves stacked with histories of medicine and health care and volumes debating how to finance health care, but on the question of whether one system makes sense, there is silence. Why? Given what we know today about chronic disease, it's apparent that routine and emergency care, and many kinds of surgery, are fundamentally different from conditions that unfold and build up over time. Why does health care, alone among industries, try to solve and value very different kinds of medical challenges using the same structure?

How did the assumption of a unitary system come to be? Before World War II, neighborhood hospitals and physicians started to form citywide and, in some cases, multi-city networks. Local health systems treated every kind of medical issue because most illness was either routine or acutely serious, requiring hospitalization.

After World War II, America's political, scientific and business elites had supreme confidence in the value of building nationwide systems, flush from successfully mobilizing the forces of science, industry, and logistics to defeat the Axis powers. It stood to reason that America's approach to health care should follow a single design, as in transportation, the electricity grid, and telecommunications. So treatments for heart disease and cancer, the two fastest growing postwar health threats, were added to the existing system just as wider use of vaccines and antibiotics vanquished infectious and bacterial disease. From the 1950s onwards, polio and tuberculosis wards shuttered as cardiac, intensive care, and chemotherapy units opened.

The unitary system assigned value to treatments along three dimensions: urgency—how life-threatening an illness or injury was; location—whether care was provided in an office or a hospital; and the specialty of the clinician who provided it. At the top of the value hierarchy were treatments to solve imminently life-threatening issues, delivered in a hospital by surgeons or oncologists. At the bottom were non-urgent treatments to resolve issues that were not life-threatening, most provided by a general practitioner or nurse in a doctor's office.

The system also reinforced professional boundaries as new specializations were created and the lines between primary and specialty care hardened. New professions, including nurse practitioners and physician assistants bolstered primary and in-hospital care. Decades later, the value hierarchy remains essentially unchanged. Treatments delivered by primary care clinicians are lower priced, with clinicians receiving lower pay. Surgical and cancer care is expensive and surgical specialties, cardiologists, radiologists, and oncologists are highly compensated.

Any chance to revisit the suitability of a unitary system disappeared in the early 1970s as policymakers and industry leaders shifted their focus from advancing medicine to rationalizing health care delivery. Americans' desire for new technology, fueled by steadily rising earnings, would make health spending unsustainable. Access to treatment had to be controlled, and so the benefits of a unitary system solidified. Insurers, hospitals, and clinicians cohered around a model that used primary care physicians as gatekeepers to specialty care, while preserving specialists' compensation edge and the central role of hospitals in childbirth, emergencies, and treating life-threatening disease.

From the outside, it looked like the system was making progress. Heart-related death rates were declining thanks to new surgical techniques and equipment, drugmakers were making headway in fighting cancer while blood pressure, blood thinner, and blood sugar medications seemed to help manage metabolic disease. In actuality, the system was making progress *in treatment*. The nature of the disease threat had changed. Chronic disease, especially metabolic, respiratory, and autoimmune conditions were caused by an array of innate and environmental factors, including unhealthy food and greater exposure to pollutants and allergens. Multimorbidity did not adhere neatly to boundaries between medical specialties. In a system structurally organized around treatment, the underlying dynamic was a race between medical technology—new drugs, imaging technology, and safer surgical techniques—and steadily advancing chronic disease. Medical technology surged to an early lead, but by 2010, the slow-building tsunami of multimorbidity began to swamp the system's capacity. Suddenly, like Alice and the Red Queen, everyone was having to run much harder just to stand still. Lost in the decades-long effort to thwart ever more advanced disease was any concerted attempt to make disease prevention as valued as treatment. Prevention made sense, in theory. Politicians and industry leaders could "see" it, but without honestly reckoning with the unique challenges of chronic disease, there was no way to realize preventive medicine as a part of health care equivalent to treatment.

It's possible now to see that the Nixonian ideal equalizing prevention and treatment is achievable, just not within a unitary system. Treatment-centric approaches are well suited for acute, shorter-term challenges including emergencies and well-understood medical and surgical procedures. However, we need a different system to confront multi-decade challenges including abilities to predict disease risk, prevent onset, and reverse pathology once it takes hold. The former system is transactional and episodic. The latter is relational, outcomes-centered, and longitudinal. No system can do both at once. Trying to balance the conflicting payback horizons of short- and long-term issues within a single framework is doomed to fail.

6. THE FOUR TYPES OF MEDICINE

> "What I want to do is to have the medical men and the health plan of this country to keep people healthy, not to cure them after they get sick, or after they get beyond the point where they can be cured."
>
> –President Harry S Truman, May 1, 1948

In the current system, concepts of medicine parallel the value hierarchy and are defined by the type of clinician providing treatment (i.e., primary versus specialty care) and location of care (i.e., in an office or outpatient setting versus in a hospital). Illnesses tend to be classified as either urgent and life-threatening or chronic and life-sapping. Psychiatric, neurodevelopmental, and behavioral challenges fall into a netherworld of poorly understood and hard to solve. Primary care encompasses the routine, with physicians directing individuals up the treatment hierarchy to specialists with deep knowledge of an organ or bodily system. Obstetric care bridges both worlds, with clinicians providing primary and life-saving care along with treatment for long-term issues. Emergency room clinicians occupy a similar role, triaging all manner of issues, sometimes becoming life-saving heroes of trauma victims, but more often, being on the receiving end of issues associated with advanced chronic disease.

The burden of preempting illness falls to primary care clinicians including pediatricians, family and nurse practitioners, gynecologists, and doctors of osteopathy. They are equipped to provide vaccines, family planning and protection against sexually-transmitted disease, heart and cholesterol screenings, and anti-smoking messaging. However, they lack the resources or authority to preempt issues like obesity and diabetes.

Preventive measures for metabolic issues have drifted out of the medical realm and into the marketing-driven world of wellness. Eat better, nutritionists and dietary mavens advise, even as the definition of "better" changes as the food industry sways federal dietary guidelines. Exercise more, sleep eight hours, reduce stress. Of course, yes, if one has the time and the means.

The path out of today's dysfunction begins by redefining medicine based on the time dimensionality of disease challenges and the degree to which underlying science is settled. Applying these standards, the broad concept of "medicine" should actually be divided into four categories—Routine, Emergency/Elective, Serious, and Predictive/Preventive.

Routine Medicine includes situations that are not life-threatening or permanently disabling, where the science of diagnosis and treatment is well established, and a treatment's efficacy can be assessed within hours or days of administration. Think colds and flus, skin infections, regular dental and vision care, minor sprains and fractures. Routine Medicine may be delivered in a medical office, hospital, pharmacy, clinic, or increasingly, at home through mail-in tests, telehealth, or remote monitoring. Measures that originate in Serious or Predictive/Preventive Medicine that are well-validated and can be systematized or commoditized can move into Routine Medicine. For example, childhood and HPV vaccines or prophylactic use of HIV antiretrovirals. Both are products of Serious Medicine, repurposed as preventive measures, and once confirmed to be effective, are widely distributed through Routine Medicine.

Emergency and Elective Medicine includes hospitalization for emergent illnesses, immediate treatment of injuries resulting from accidents or traumas, and services associated with a routine child birth. It also includes elective surgical procedures that have well-established protocols, even if related to an underlying chronic condition. For example, implantation of a cardiac or vascular stent, cardiac ablation to address a heart arrhythmia, a hysterectomy, a cesarean section, appendectomy, or joint replacement surgery.

Serious Medicine includes diagnostics and treatments to reverse, stop, slow, or cure chronic, age-related, and life-threatening disease where the underlying issue is complex or key aspects of risk, pathology, or treatment are unsettled or not standardized. This includes metabolic syndrome, chronic respiratory conditions, autoimmune conditions, mental health and behavioral disorders, all forms of cancer, neurodevelopmental disorders, and neurodegenerative diseases including ADRD, Parkinson's Disease, and ALS. Rare diseases, including those caused by genetic malfunction, are part of Serious Medicine, along with vaccines to address novel infectious diseases and antibiotics to counteract drug-resistant strains. Serious Medicine includes research to develop new drug classes, such as GLP-1s or cancer immunotherapies; regenerative medicine to regrow or fabricate human tissues; new treatment approaches such as gene editing; improved ability to target treatment delivery to some cells or tissues and not others; and devices to augment or remediate sensory perception, speech, or movement. Finally, Serious Medicine encompasses issues relating to fertility, fetal development and treatment, and resolution of issues like preeclampsia that pose serious risk to expectant mothers and the fetus. Likewise, extraordinary measures to treat premature babies or those born with congenital defects are Serious Medicine.

Predictive/Preventive Medicine includes measures within and adjacent to medical care to understand disease risk and etiology and forestall disease onset or progression. In chronic disease this includes an understanding of nutrition, the interplay between innate and environmental factors in disease vulnerability or resilience, and development of a longitudinal understanding of how disease pathology begins and advances in different situations. More broadly, Predictive/Preventive Medicine includes tests, algorithms, biomarkers, and longitudinal evaluations to understand a person's susceptibility to a condition, where they are along the chronic disease cascade, and how likely they are to respond to a particular set of treatments. Predictive/Preventive Medicine also incorporates aspects of functional medicine and wellness that have traditionally been treated as parallel or complementary to treatment. Thus, questions of validating different dietary interventions to prevent disease or maintain restored function fall within Predictive/Preventive Medicine, as well as behavioral supports to encourage individuals to maintain better health trajectories.

An important part of this definition is the connection between prediction and prevention. Selecting the right preventive measures depends on being able to accurately and reliably identify the risk factors that increase the likelihood or speed of disease onset. Conversely, in the absence of predictive power, efforts to prevent onset or progression become overgeneralized or unfocused. This is common in wellness, where we have a general idea of what is probably more or less healthy but lack precision to specify dosage or intensity or measure impact. Integrating predictive and preventive efforts forces clinicians to be more precise in defining the essential aspects of a risk factor, cross-system interactions, the role of environmental factors, and the time frames over which risk may become actual disease.[42]

Predictive/Preventive Medicine for chronic and age-related diseases will need to connect understanding of organ-level or tissue-specific events with observations about cross-system effects and processes. For example, in obesity and diabetes, we need to understand what is happening in the gut, liver, and brain but also the dynamics of gut-brain interactions, immune dysfunction and inflammation, cellular senescence, and protein expression.

Visualizing Types of Medicine in Terms of Risk, ROI, and Outcomes

The central divide between Routine and Emergency/Elective and Serious and Predictive/Preventive is time dimensionality. Routine and Emergency/Elective are short-term. Serious and Predictive/Preventive are longer term. Each of the four types of medicine also differ in terms of the risks involved and the ROI potential.

Riskiness captures the degrees to which a condition or treatment is life-threatening as well as the degree to which underlying science is well understood. A condition may not be immediately life threatening, but a novel treatment may cause serious side effects—thus, it's a lower risk condition but a higher-risk treatment. Conversely, a person undergoing cell or gene replacement therapy for a life-threatening cancer is facing high condition and treatment risks. The term "life-threatening" in the definition of riskiness may not mean *imminently* life-threatening. A person who has suffered a gunshot wound to a vital organ obviously faces an imminent threat. That's not true for a person with metabolic syndrome although their situation is also life-threatening if underlying pathology is not reversed or halted.

ROI potential incorporates two ideas. First, what is the potential long-term value to individuals who have a successful outcome? How impactful is the medical issue and how effective can the treatment be? Second, to what degree can the intervention be deployed widely for large effect? A miraculous treatment that can only be used on a small number of people has limited ROI potential unless something in the underlying science can be replicated in another condition. The first open heart surgeries and organ transplants had high individual ROI but were of limited value societally since they required specialized teams and equipment that were not widely available. Later, as procedures were standardized, and heart-lung machines or anti-transplant rejection drugs could be used reliably, ROI potential increased for individuals and societally. This is why pills or self-administered injections have inherently greater ROI potential than treatments that require administration by a physician or in a hospital. Scale and friction matter.

Outcomes time frame measures how long it will take to know whether a diagnostic or intervention has been successful. Some treatments or tests provide immediate clarity. A drug can be given one-time with proven long-term efficacy. A test can say whether or not a person has a disease-causing gene variant. Conversely, a test measuring changes in brain proteins over years to provide updated one-to-three-year predictive outlooks requires multiple readings over many years.

The following diagram visualizes how each type of medicine lines up along each of these axes:

Figure 6.1: Visualizing the Four Types of Medicine

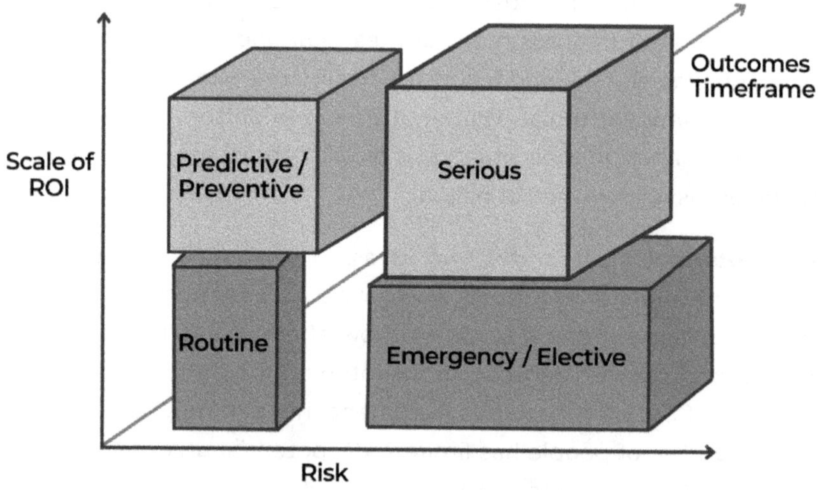

Routine Medicine is the least risky and has the shortest outcomes time frame.

Emergency/Elective Medicine encompasses a wide range of surgeries and interventions from the tried and true, like a stent implant, to the very risky, like surgery to repair a gunshot wound to a vital organ. The ROI potential is somewhat lower than Routine Medicine since surgeries can be life-saving or life-restoring, which has high individual ROI; however, surgeries, by definition, must be done one at a time. Likewise, the time frame to determine a successful outcome tends to be relatively short.

Serious Medicine occupies the largest space, reflecting its inclusion of chronic, age-related, and life-threatening illnesses. However, the time to validate outcomes may take years, even decades to achieve a successful outcome. Likewise, there is a wide variability in Serious Medicine outcomes reflecting the heterogeneity of disease processes, quality of clinical care, and treatment responses.

Predictive/Preventive Medicine can be higher risk initially insofar as newer diagnostics need time (beyond clinical trials) to be refined and validated in large populations. However, Predictive/Preventive measures tend to be broadly scalable especially if they are applied to routine biosamples like blood draws or passive monitoring.

This visualization also helps us see the connections between Predictive/Preventive Medicine and Serious Medicine, and from both of those to Routine and Emergency/Elective Medicine. Risk prediction and prevention informs Serious Medicine and vice versa, driving innovation to fill gaps in knowledge and results. What starts in those realms as bespoke and complex can then, with time and repetition, become standardized, commoditized, and distributed widely within the Routine and Emergency/Elective realm.

Reframing medicine into four categories provides a rational guide to the work ahead to establish parallel systems for acute and chronic issues, slimming down health insurance while expanding life insurance's purpose. Health *is* different but it is not, as many incumbents suggest, *so complex* that it defies first principle rethinking. Incumbents use complexity as a shield to undermine provocative approaches, implying that disrupting current approaches will injure people or cause a systemic breakdown. In fact, reimagining medicine for today's challenges is very much in keeping with the historical record, just as those before us reconceived and reinvigorated medicine for their own times.

ENDNOTES

42 In Outlive, Dr. Peter Attia coins the term "Medicine 3.0" to describe much of what I mean by predictive and preventive medicine. I prefer the admittedly clunkier term "Predictive/Preventive Medicine" because it's important to underscore the interdependency between the two.

7. ROCKEFELLER, ROOSEVELT, AND THE END OF EPIDEMIC DISEASE

"Presumably man's spirit should be elevated if he can better review his shady past and analyze more completely and objectively his present problems."

–Vannevar Bush, 1945

Health policy experts point to World War II and the years immediately following as a critical period in America's adoption of employer-paid health coverage, a decision that many consider to be the original sin of modern American health care. We will come back to what happened in the 1940s but, as a historical matter, the origins of employer-paid care in the US go much farther back, all the way back to America's founding and the restless mind of its genius Treasury Secretary, Alexander Hamilton.

In the early 1790s, Hamilton fretted about the young republic's reliance on import tariffs to pay off newly nationalized Revolutionary War debt. Growing up in the ports of St. Croix, young Hamilton knew firsthand how economically devastating epidemics could be, sweeping in like a hurricane without warning. Hamilton worried that a prolonged epidemic in Boston or Philadelphia could interrupt revenue from trade.

In 1792, he endorsed a petition to Congress by Boston's civic leaders to create a maritime hospital for use by ill sailors and their families. He wanted to contain outbreaks, limiting the need for citywide quarantines and shoring up foreign ship owners' confidence that American ports were not breeding grounds of fatal disease. He proposed that the hospital be funded by shipping companies through a compulsory ten cent per month charge deducted from sailors' wages. Had it come to pass, it would have been America's first payroll tax to fund medical care.

Congress shrugged off Hamilton's proposal but within a year a devastating yellow fever epidemic in Philadelphia, imported by infected sailors, vindicated his concerns. President Washington and Congress fled the city, narrowly escaping the scourge. One in ten Philadelphians perished. Hamilton took ill but, hardened by childhood brushes with seaborne illness, survived. Five years later Congress saw things Hamilton's way, passing the Act for the Relief of Sick and Disabled Seamen. The new law established maritime hospitals in key ports funded by a twenty cent levy per sailor, paid by shipowners. It was the first employer-paid coverage in America.

In this law, we also see the foundational role of hospitals in US public health and treating serious illness. Nineteenth-century medicine was primitive by today's standards but the creation of hospitals funded by cities, religious institutions, or philanthropy, became a mark of social progress. Even if the earliest versions were little more than storehouses for the infirm, hospitals served a need. In time, they expanded into childbirth, and then to treat occupational injuries. The medical profession, surgery and nursing in particular, advanced quickly during the Civil War as physicians tried to keep pace with industrialized slaughter. Serious wounds to the gut or torso were almost always fatal; however, it's estimated that three-quarters of soldiers shot in an extremity who reached a field hospital alive survived a limb amputation.[43]

As America grew, community and private hospitals became signposts of progress. By the Great Depression, America had over 6,000 hospitals scattered across cities and rural towns. Interestingly, even then, a third of hospital revenues came from city and state coffers, with the rest from philanthropy, subscriptions, or direct payments by patients. Physicians and hospital administrators realized they were exposed to Americans' ability to pay; they needed more consistent revenue. Hospitals organized local health insurance schemes, later branded as Blue Cross, collecting premiums from workers at local firms and city governments in exchange for guaranteed inpatient care. Family physicians, under the auspices of their national trade group, the American Medical Association, developed a parallel program for Americans to prepay for medical services, rebranded in 1946 as Blue Shield.

And where, as the medical industry evolved, had efforts to understand and treat infectious disease—Hamilton's animating worry—gone? As the twentieth century dawned, efforts remained localized, even after creation of the US Public Health Service. Although the number of medical schools grew, there was little strategic effort to build institutional research to study disease or development treatments. That is, until a very special four-year-old took to his bed with a scorching fever.

Rockefeller Casts the Philanthropic Mold

Pocantico Estate, Christmas Day 1900. The world's richest man, John D. Rockefeller and his family, gather at their newly constructed family estate in Westchester County. Though still a vigorous 61, Rockefeller's mind is turning to his legacy, with most aspects of Standard Oil's operations now managed by subordinates.[44] Rockefeller's first philanthropic effort, funding the new University of Chicago, has been judged a success. Now he is thinking about medicine, worrying that American scientists lag far behind European counterparts in understanding infectious disease. That summer he had followed a bubonic plague outbreak in San Francisco, poring over daily reports from the West Coast.

By Christmas his worries about epidemics turn closer to home. A month earlier, two of his grandsons had contracted scarlet fever including his favorite, four-year-old John Rockefeller McCormick. When little John's health takes a turn for the worse, Rockefeller reportedly offers a New York doctor $500,000 to save the boy. The bacterial hordes proliferating in the boy are indifferent to their host's lineage or wealth, and on the second day of the new century, the boy dies.

In grief, Rockefeller finds renewed purpose and a focus for his medical philanthropy. He funds a new Institute of Medical Research with a mission to understand "the nature and causes of disease and the methods of its treatment, and to make knowledge relating to these various subjects available for the protection of the health of the public and the improved treatment of disease and injury." Renamed Rockefeller University, the institute goes on to house a remarkable group of researchers, including 26 Nobel laureates. Little John's mother, Edith, and her husband, (an heir to the International Harvester agricultural fortune), create the John McCormick Memorial Institute for Infectious Diseases at the University of Chicago, accelerating work to cure scarlet fever.[45]

Rockefeller's example set the mold, one that continues to this day. In the late 1990s, America's first Information Age Rockefeller, Bill Gates, established a foundation with his wife and father to end communicable diseases worldwide. Paul Allen, Microsoft co-founder, funded landmark research in neuroscience through The Allen Institute. A generation later, the Chan-Zuckerberg Initiative—led by Dr. Priscilla Chan and Facebook co-founder Mark Zuckerberg—is funding research on cell biology, AI in medical diagnostics, and infectious disease. Zuckerberg's co-founder, Sean Parker, donated billions for an institute to advance cancer immunotherapies. Eli Broad, who achieved the rare feat of becoming a repeat billionaire in different industries, and his wife Edythe, funded cutting-edge research centers in Boston and Los Angeles studying cancer, genomics, and neuroscience. David Koch, scion of a Midwestern energy company and known as much for his conservative political advocacy, endowed the MIT Koch Institute, pursuing cancer breakthroughs. The philanthropic model established by Rockefeller of funding medical research is, one might say, timeless.

FDR Fuses Government, Finance, and Science to End Infectious Disease

To Franklin Delano Roosevelt, philanthropy was fine, but scattershot. He knew firsthand, having established a foundation to care for polio victims after being paralyzed by the virus in 1921. FDR wanted results—a cure, not care—and a means to get medicine to the masses. In September 1937 he announced a new National Foundation for Infantile Paralysis, brazenly creating a private entity stamped with the president's imprimatur to eradicate a specific disease. It was just the first step in an even big-ger plan to nationalize solutions to societal threats like polio. In 1938, FDR invited comedian Eddie Cantor to lead a nationally broadcast fund-raiser from the White House. In a stroke of marketing brilliance, Cantor urged Americans to send a dime to the White House, literally coining the name March of Dimes. Within two months, one in ten American families (over 2.5 million total) did just that, amid the greatest economic downtown in history.

What Rockefeller started, Roosevelt finished. He realized that America's potential to lead medical science represented a key weapon to defeat the Axis powers. Do whatever it takes, he told Vannevar Bush, his chief science advisor, to keep soldiers healthy and battle ready. Adapt the scientific and industrial practices of weapons research to develop and manufacture medicines. Speaking on Halloween Day 1940, at the dedication of the National Institutes of Health campus in Bethesda, Maryland, FDR said:

> "The total defense that we have heard so much about of late … involves a great deal more than building airplanes and ships and guns and bombs. For we cannot be a strong nation unless we are a healthy nation. So we must recruit not only men and materials, but also knowledge and science to serve our national strength."

FDR and Bush charged a select group of pharmaceutical and government officials to scale up penicillin manufacturing. In the decade plus since the wonder drug had been discovered, it remained difficult to produce in bulk. Solve it, FDR ordered. A team of academics and private industry experts did as asked, just in time for American troops' departure for Africa, Europe, and the Pacific.

Likewise, FDR directed scientists to scale up production of flu vaccines and develop antimalarial drugs. No one wanted a repeat of the 1918 Spanish flu. Fortunately, in 1938, a team led by Dr. Thomas Francis, including up and coming virologist Jonas Salk, developed the first live attenuated flu vaccine. As war approached, scientists and drugmakers scaled up the process enabling American and British troops to be inoculated before heading to battle. Meanwhile, a team in New York headed by future NIH Director Jim Shannon developed the first antimalarials. Absent these drugs, American Marines slashing paths through tropical rainforests were as vulnerable to mosquito bites as bullets.[46] Fewer infection-related casualties allowed FDR to send fewer troops to battle the Japanese, freeing up troops to help liberate Europe.

Validated by the mobilization of medical know-how during wartime, FDR directed Bush to institutionalize a postwar fusion among government, academic, and corporate researchers. America's wartime gains in medical know-how, FDR wrote Bush,

> "... should be used in the days of peace ahead for the improvement of the national health, the creation of new enterprises bringing new jobs, and the betterment of the national standard of living ... [W]hat can be done now to organize a program for continuing in the future the work which has been done in medicine and related sciences? ... The fact that the annual deaths in this country from one or two diseases alone are far in excess of the total number of lives lost by us in battle during this war should make us conscious of the duty we owe future generations."

FDR and Bush's plans heralded a golden age of synergy among medical researchers, clinicians, drugmakers, and public health experts, buttressed by public and corporate funds, health insurers, and philanthropists. The era's dominant theme was more. More research and discovery. More hospitals in cities large and small, more equipment, more specialized treatment units within hospitals, especially intensive and cardiac care units. It meant more medical professions and professionals: physician specialties to focus on particular organs or systems; new professions like nurse practitioners and physician assistants to supplement physicians in community settings and hospitals; and eventual acceptance of doctors of osteopathic medicine to deliver primary care alongside MDs.

Vaccination, the most successful twentieth century incarnation of preventive medicine, accelerated, helped along by 1950s era rules governing clinical trials and use of new treatments. The first flu shot for public use was released in 1945. The last smallpox case in the US occurred in 1949, a year that also saw the first childhood vaccine for diphtheria and tetanus, followed quickly by a yellow fever vaccine (1953) and in 1955, FDR's dream, the first inactivated virus against polio vaccine. In 1971, the first measles, mumps, and rubella combination vaccine was licensed, seven years after the largest rubella epidemic in US history.[47]

Health Insurance Built On the Science of Routine and Emergency Medicine

In the context of mid-century medical advancements, the widespread adoption of employer-provided health insurance was a good example of finance following science. The economics of health insurance were built around the nature of the medical challenges it covered. Routine treatments were short term and relatively predictable, along with pregnancy and childbirth. Workplace injuries and car accidents were much less common than routine issues, but required immediate treatment and expensive hospitalizations. Health insurance blended the complementary risks and costs of routine and emergency situations. A steady margin on cheap and frequent issues subsidized periodic losses on the expensive and less common. Voluntary insurance associations formed to ensure physicians and hospitals would be paid for house calls or hospital stays. Initially divided between plans covering physicians' services (Blue Shield) and hospitalization (Blue Cross), the approaches were merged after World War II to cover both needs.

Employer-financed health insurance got a critical boost during World War II when factory owners, caught between the desperate need to hire workers and the constraints of wartime salary price controls, petitioned the War Production Board to treat employer-paid health insurance as a non-cash benefit, excluding it from wage controls. This arrangement was institutionalized after the war, with the IRS adding a financial sweetener allowing employers to treat their health premium contributions as a deductible expense.

Separating insurance and care was not the only approach. Early in the New Deal, a competing idea emerged to integrate coverage and treatment. In 1933 Los Angeles, young Dr. Sidney Garfield sensed an opportunity to treat workers building a massive aqueduct to funnel Sierra Nevada snowmelt to fast-growing Los Angeles. With financial help from his father, he built a small hospital on the edge of the Mojave Desert. He originally planned to access workmen's insurance to get paid, but he soon realized that disability insurers had an established practice of resisting payment on claims as long as possible. So he decided to offer insurance *and* treatment, charging the aqueduct's construction company $5 per worker per day for whatever hospital care they might need. Echoes of Hamilton.

Garfield's idea caught the eye of industrialist Henry Kaiser, an FDR ally, whose firm was building the massive Grand Coulee dam. Kaiser recruited Garfield to replicate his Mojave enterprise there. A few years later, when FDR elevated Kaiser to oversee all wartime naval construction, he required participating shipbuilders to adopt the integrated care model. After the war, Kaiser expanded the system, contracting physicians under exclusive arrangements in exchange for access to Kaiser hospitals, salaried positions, and consistent patient flow. Participants (or their firms) paid a flat per member per month price in exchange for agreeing to use Kaiser facilities and doctors exclusively. Today, the entity he created, Kaiser Permanente, is the largest non-profit integrated insurer and health system in the US, and remains the most successful approach to integrated care.

In many ways, all of the various forms of health insurance that have been tried or adopted in the US have their roots in one or the other model. The common thread is a belief in the power of financial controls to govern clinicians and member behavior. In the traditional employer-paid model, the forcing function is the insurer's ability to negotiate lower prices for treatments and services as dictated by employers' and workers' willingness to pay higher or lower premiums for more or less coverage. The Kaiser model uses fixed payment per patient as a forcing function to prioritize care decisions, and hopefully, greater use of preventive medicine. It employs clinicians directly and links their compensation to the enterprise's overall success.

ENDNOTES

43 Reilly RF. Medical and surgical care during the American Civil War, 1861-1865. Proc (Bayl Univ Med Cent). 2016 Apr;29(2):138-42.
44 Rockefeller's wealth is hard to fathom. At the time, it was about 3% of US GDP, the equivalent of about $850 billion today.
45 In a twist of fate that also speaks to the interweaving of Gilded Age wealth and medical philanthropy, the McCormick family's fortune also helped finance development of the contraceptive pill. Edith Rockefeller McCormick's sister-in-law, Katharine Dexter McCormick, married Stanley McCormick, one of John McCormick's younger brothers. Katharine was a pioneer in her own right, becoming the second woman to graduate from MIT, later becoming a leader in the women's suffrage movement. Stanley developed schizophrenia and was institutionalized, freeing Katharine to pursue political and medical endeavors. In 1917 she met Margaret Sanger, and under her guidance became a leading financier of birth control research. When Stanley died in 1947, leaving Katharine a fortune, Sanger introduced her to Gregory Pincus and Min Chueh Chang, researchers who had prototyped an oral contraceptive using synthetic progesterone. Katharine funded their research and a controversial clinical trial in Puerto Rico to demonstrate efficacy. Spurred by the results, pharmaceutical company G.D. Searle acquired rights to the prototype, and after wider trials, won FDA approval for the first commercial version of the pill. McCormick donated close to $25 million (in 2023 dollars) to bring oral contraceptives to the market, an investment that yielded life-changing implications for billions of women thereafter.
46 One of the postwar years' most prolific innovators in heart surgery, Dr. Michael DeBakey, got his start during World War II designing mobile army hospitals, later immortalized in the TV show "MASH."
47 The nature of vaccines and public perceptions of their use has evolved since the 1970s. Increasingly, in the U.S. vaccines were developed to target specific populations, especially older Americans, against shingles or respiratory syncytial virus (RSV). Similarly, shots for teens and younger adults were developed to prevent cervical and other cancers caused by human papillomavirus. In the 21st century, public trust in vaccines has been under pressure due to demonstrably false -- but widely reported studies -- linking childhood vaccines with autism spectrum disorders. Public discomfort with vaccine requirements was further inflamed during COVID when public health and government officials required workers in health professions, public sector jobs, and members of the armed forces to be vaccinated or risk losing their positions

8. ENDING HEART DISEASE: THE GOOD, THE BAD, AND THE UGLY

> "The point to be made about ... the real high technology of medicine is that it comes as the result of a genuine understanding of disease mechanisms, and when it becomes available, it is relatively inexpensive, relatively simple, and relatively easy to deliver ... The price [of medical technology] is never as high as the cost of managing the same diseases during the earlier stages of no-technology or halfway technology. If a case of typhoid fever had to be managed today by the best methods of 1935, it would run to a staggering expense."
>
> –Dr. Lewis Thomas, *The Lives of a Cell*[48]

In 1955, when President Dwight Eisenhower suffered a major heart attack, he received state of the art care. At the time that included morphine, an oxygen tank, anticlotting drugs, and bed rest. In other words, not much, and he was lucky to escape with his life.[49] Eisenhower was not alone in his plight. In 1950, heart-related death rates approached the peak death rate of the 1918–1919 flu epidemic. While flu deaths quickly fell, heart death rates reached similar levels and stayed there.

Six decades on, the age-adjusted heart disease death rate had plummeted by 70%, an incredible success. It is the foremost example of how Serious and Predictive/Preventive Medicine can work hand-in-hand, as surgeons and drug developers achieved a string of surgical and medical breakthroughs (within Serious Medicine), informed by—and informing, in turn—researchers' efforts to understand heart disease causes and risk factors (within Predictive/Preventive Medicine). Collectively, these advances in knowledge and technology enabled much more effective surgeries for a range of cardiovascular issues, cheap and highly reliable predictive risk assessments, a decades-long effort to reduce smoking, and some of the most valuable drug classes developed. Recalling the 1966 Clint Eastwood movie mentioned in the chapter title, that was the "good" of what happened.

Unfortunately, many of the insights developed within cardiology remained there even as the heart disease risks increased in tandem with rising obesity and diabetes. After a multi-decade decline in heart disease death risk, progress stagnated during the 2010s, even ticking up in 2020 and 2021 among older men.[50] Clinical specialties became siloed and care fragmented. No one had the big picture, or if they did, no one exerted authority to solve it. That's the "bad."

Finally, advances in predicting, preventing, and treating heart disease have been, like much of American health care, unevenly distributed. Disease burden is still disproportionately shouldered by Black and Native Americans and those from less wealthy areas. That's the "ugly."

In this sense, the fight against heart disease provides a valuable case study of what it takes to end multimorbidity. It illustrates how much progress can be made by integrating Serious and Predictive/Preventive Medicine, but also the criticality of a system purpose-built for chronic disease, including to eliminate silos between medical specialties, fragmentation in solving and preventing interrelated conditions, and inequities in access to treatments and preventive measures.

Curbing Premature Heart Deaths

From the Great Depression to 1960, heart disease death rates almost doubled, making heart disease both the leading cause of death overall, and the leading cause of *premature* death. More than a third of deaths among middle-aged Americans (45 to 54) were caused by heart disease, far outpacing accidents, cancer, or infectious disease. The term "widow maker" was not for nothing. Premature heart deaths happened among men at three times the rate as among women.[51] Yet, from the late 1960s onwards, heart disease death rates plummeted, as shown in Figure 8.1.

Death rates among 45–54 year-olds halved. The gains were even greater among 55–64 year-olds with death rates dropping by two-thirds.[52]

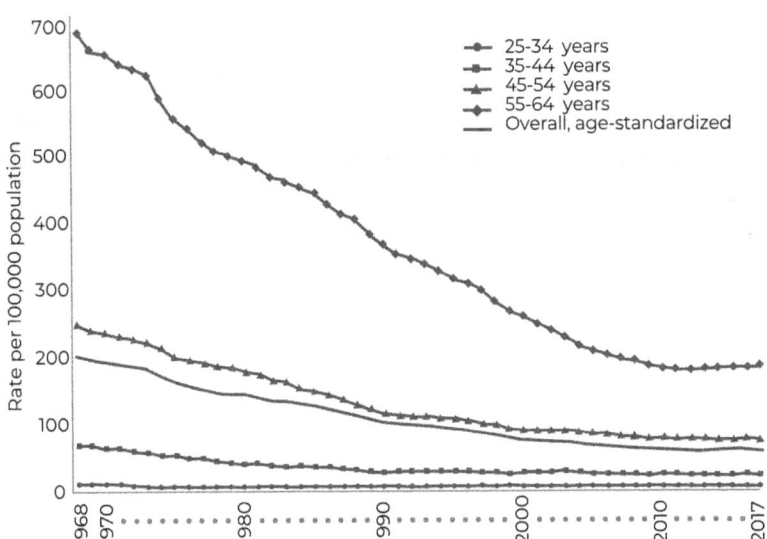

Figure 8.1: Decline in Heart Death Rates by Age Group, 1968 - 2012

Data Source: Centers for Disease Control, National Center for Health Statistics[53]

This happened because of a full-court press across research and clinical practice. The forces of Serious Medicine, first personified by heart surgeons like Michael DeBakey, mobilized to develop life-saving surgeries to save heart attack victims, eventually developing ways to prevent arrhythmias and heart valve failures. Drugmakers translated insights from surgery and research into more effective and eventually ubiquitous drugs to halt or prevent buildup of harmful lipids, arterial inflammation, and stroke-creating blood clots.

In parallel, epidemiologists undertook a decades-long effort to understand the nature of heart disease, how and when it developed, and why. Public health advocates translated findings about smoking's harmful effects into the most effective public relations and behavioral change effort of the last century. Throughout the postwar period, cardiologists committed to a profession-wide flexibility to adopt and integrate the latest findings into clinical practice, shortening the runway from research to results.

None of this happened overnight. Rapid surgical advances in the 1960s built on decades of work to perform surgery on a beating heart. In 1929, a young German physician, Werner Forssman, threaded a catheter from his elbow to his heart, creating a new route to perform cardiac procedures. It was a daring and foolhardy act, but it ultimately won a Nobel Prize. Open heart surgery proved a much harder problem until surgeons and engineers invented the heart-lung machine to divert circulation from the heart while a blockage was repaired.

Still, surgical success was bloody and slow. Mortality rates were high, at first. As often as not with a new technique, as many patients died on the table as survived.[54] Pioneering surgeons persevered, learning how to maintain oxygen and blood flow, perfecting arterial bypasses, transplants, pacemaker implants, and valve surgery. Post-surgical recovery was arduous but surgeons and care teams improved protocols, getting patients back onto their feet sooner. In the 1980s, surgeons began using implantable balloons, called angioplasty, and then wire mesh stents to re-inflate clogged passages. A decade later drug-eluting stents were added to counteract blood clots, only to be supplemented within a few years by statin drugs to delay the lipid buildups that require surgery.

Looking back, it's amazing to see how quickly each generation of technology replaced earlier ones. Bypasses evolved from being risky and rare to being safe and accessible within two decades. Angioplasty and stents made preventive and restorative surgery safer, more accessible, and much cheaper. Fifteen years later, all surgical interventions (bypasses *and* stents) declined as statin use delayed need. Although the number of Americans in the prime age for cardiac surgery (those over 65) increased in the aughts, bypass volume dropped by half, while stents dropped by over a quarter.[55] The rapidity with which new and cheaper approaches replaced earlier ones, even as death rates continued to decline, is illustrated by the following chart showing heart procedures in the United Kingdom from 1981 to 2011.

Figure 8.2: UK Cardiac Procedure Volume and Heart-Related Death Rate

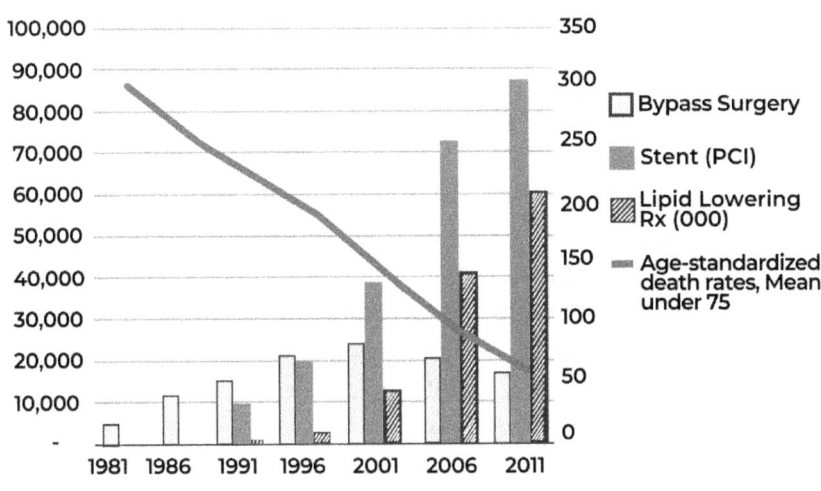

Data Source: British Heart Foundation

From 1981 to 2001 in the UK, bypass surgeries increased fivefold, only to decline 44% as stents and statins achieved widespread use. Including the decade to 2011, the age-standardized heart disease death rate for men under 75 dropped by more than four times in three decades.

Predictive/Preventive Medicine and Efforts to Stop Heart Disease

As impressive as advances in Serious Medicine were, the decisive measures to curb heart-related death came from Predictive Medicine, as cardiologists developed easy-to-administer tests and diagnostics to identify those at greatest risk. This effort began after World War II, as leaders in the U.S. Public Health Service realized that they needed to know more about events and breakdowns that led to heart attacks. Influenced by Dr. Paul Dudley White, who helped treat President Eisenhower after his heart attacks, Public Health Service officials decided to run a multi-decade longitudinal study in a representative community, hoping to isolate confounding geographic factors. In 1948 they settled on Framingham, Massachusetts, a sleepy Boston suburb of 25,000 as the site of what would become one of the most impactful epidemiological studies in history. Initially, the study would track 5,000 residents from their twenties to sixties for a couple of decades, but as the years passed the Framingham Study was repeatedly extended, eventually gathering data from four generations of residents and their descendants.

At the outset, study architects faced similar challenges in understanding heart disease that we face today with multimorbidity. Critically they made the development of reliable risk assessments a key study goal, realizing that "specific and unambiguous tests for precise diagnosis of the early stages of [cardiovascular] diseases are lacking."[56] Longitudinal studies invariably take time to yield actionable results, but a decade after starting, a deluge of studies using Framingham data opened new vistas into heart disease risk and the roles of hypertension, high cholesterol, and smoking. As shown in Figure 8.3, the steady drumbeat of findings, aided by surgical and drug advances, contributed to a one-third drop in heart-related death rates from 1957 until the mid-1970s:

Figure 8.3: Key Framingham Heart Study Dates and Heart-Related Death Rate

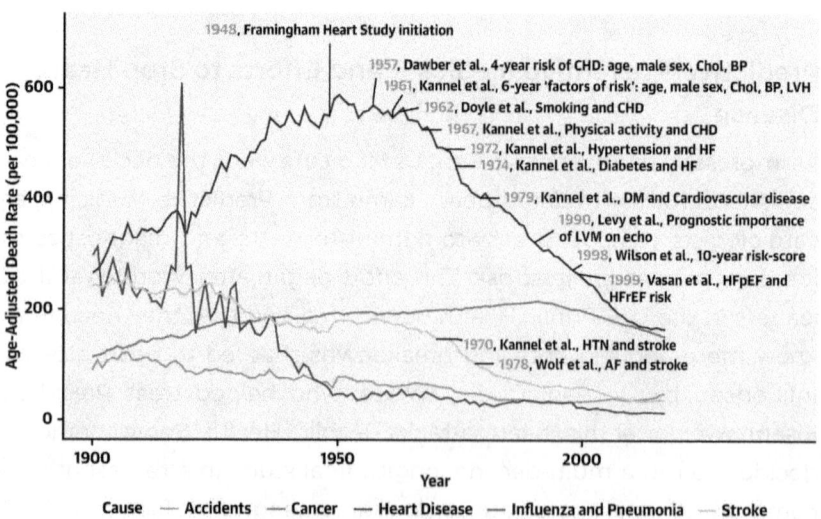

Andersson, C. et al. J Am Coll Cardiol. 2021;77(21):2680-92.

Study data helped bust a lot of myths. Before Framingham, some cardiologists theorized that high blood pressure was actually a beneficial adaptation to degenerating cardiac muscle. With study data they could see that the opposite was true, along with the danger posed by enlarged left ventricles. They deciphered relationships between hypertension and atrial fibrillation in strokes and connected the dots between diabetes and heart disease. Once reliable risk metrics were validated, Predictive/Preventive Medicine was moved quickly into Routine Medicine with primary care physicians engaging people earlier about heart health, and intervening proactively along with cardiologists to prevent heart attacks.

The Framingham data also provided key ammunition in the battle against cigarette makers. In January 1964, in a legendary Saturday press conference held to avoid spooking Wall Street, Kennedy's Surgeon General, Dr. Luther Terry lowered the boom. Fortified by Framingham data, he issued a damning indictment of smoking. Within six years, cigarette ads were banned from television and radio, and by the mid-1990s from all sporting events. Later, data about the harmful effects of secondhand smoke led to bans on smoking in public, first on domestic air travel and then later in restaurants and workplaces.

The decades-long fight against heart death illustrates that it is possible to reduce disease prevalence dramatically by blending Serious and Predictive/Preventive Medicine to halt or reverse disease and intervene earlier to prevent onset. The thought experiment in Chapter 3, suggesting that we need to reduce multimorbidity by 50% or more may have seemed wildly ambitious, even delusional. Yet, we see, it has been done. The template exists, if we have the will to update and apply it. Surgical and medical technology to restore function, the right clinical and financial alignment to maintain gains, longitudinal data to predict and prevent, cultural change within medical professions to lean into adoption and iterative improvement, and sustained public education to change attitudes about harmful products. It is all very doable.

Inconsistent Outcomes and Specialty Silos

So, what of the bad and ugly? Despite much progress, progress against heart death rates stagnated after 2010, even increasing following COVID. The threat has changed. There are many fewer midlife heart attacks but much greater prevalence of "late-stage" disease in the form of heart failure—characterized by a significant reduction in the heart's pumping ability.

The lack of recent progress illustrates how much the battle against heart death has been subsumed by the rising tide of multimorbidity. Still, the aperture of heart disease treatment remains narrowly focused on cardiac issues rather than the growing importance of obesity. General practitioners and cardiologists were ill-prepared or unenthusiastic about taking on responsibility to treat all aspects of metabolic syndrome. A 2020 survey of cardiologists treating heart failure concluded that most specialists surveyed "believe that weight loss did not fall within their purview, and they reported that they did not frequently prescribe anti-obesity medications."[57] Only 40% of cardiology specialists and 60% of heart failure experts considered it their responsibility to actively contribute to their patients' weight loss efforts. Overall clinicians estimated only 20% to 30% of patients were capable of losing weight, although over 80% of cardiologists said they had received no formal training in weight management outside of medical school and clinical practice. The gap between awareness and action continues even in practice guidelines. New standards for managing heart failure issued in 2022 include obesity as one of many comorbidities but provide no guidance on treating it, unlike for heart-specific situations like atrial fibrillation or atherosclerotic disease.[58]

Efforts to create interdisciplinary practitioners or expertise across specialties have been slow to gain traction. A decade ago the American Board on Obesity Medicine began offering a specialization in obesity medicine, specifically for clinicians most likely to treat individuals with metabolic syndrome. By 2024, about 8,100 clinicians had been certified, representing about 1% of prescribing physicians. New certificants had been growing over 20% a year but it still translated to fewer than one obesity medicine specialist per 40,000 Americans *with obesity*.

The overwhelming majority are general practitioners. A measly fifty-six are cardiologists, representing less than 1% of all obesity medicine specialists and 0.2% of prescribing cardiologists, a ridiculously small number given the overlap between cardiovascular issues and obesity. This is not to denigrate a whole speciality but to emphasize how pervasive fragmentation is. Cardiology has been one of the most aggressive and progressive specialties in terms of incorporating cardiovascular risk diagnostics and new treatments into practice. Yet, it is also one of the least aggressive in terms of broadening practitioners' exposure to help resolve underlying conditions that hasten heart failure.

A similar kind of siloing plays out in the way drugs are developed, approved, and reimbursed. The FDA approves drugs to treat individual conditions, or specific aspects of a condition called indications. Physicians have broad discretion to prescribe approved drugs for another purpose; however, insurers often deny coverage for these "off-label" uses.

Although metabolic syndrome is a recognized diagnosis with clear diagnostic metrics, the FDA does not recognize it as an indication, and therefore drugs are approved for underlying manifestations like high cholesterol, but not for the overall condition. This requires drugmakers to run separate trials to test a drug's impact on specific issues like heart function, blood sugar, or weight loss, demonstrating the drug's impact in isolation even if it is used in combination with others in the real world. As a result, cross-system benefits (or risks) are slow to emerge, delaying wider use of more effective drugs while perpetuating overuse of multiple therapies which may have offsetting effects. Polypharmacy, defined as individuals taking five or more prescription drugs, doubled among adults from 1999 to 2018, with the largest increases seen among Medicare recipients with heart disease or diabetes.[59]

The second major failure in fighting heart disease is our inability to close outcome gaps for Black Americans. The heart-related premature death rate for Black Americans has halved since 1968—which is good progress—but it is still twice as high as in other ethnic and racial groups. The age-adjusted heart disease mortality rate for Black women under 65 is double that of White women.[60] Closing outcomes gaps is inherently important to ensure equal opportunity, but it is especially critical, scientifically, to understand multimorbidity in all of its manifestations. Equity in risk assessment, prevention, and treatment is inseparable from good science, enabling researchers and clinicians to identify factors that are more or less important in sub-groups and refine treatment approaches. The more people who are engaged and able to access best-in-class diagnostics and treatments, the faster we learn what does or does not work, when, and why. Multimorbidity is a constellation of challenges. It requires us to think and work outside of professional silos and preconceived notions. The battle against heart disease demonstrates it's possible but it requires a system that aligns science, clinicians, and financial arrangements to achieve better long-term outcomes.

ENDNOTES

48 Thomas is a pathologist and former dean of the Yale School of Medicine. This quote is from a chapter in Lives of a Cell titled "The Technology of Medicine," first published in 1974.
49 Dr. Paul Dudley White, quoted at the start of Chapter 3, consulted on Eisenhower's case and persuaded him to stop smoking and start a more vigorous exercise program.
50 Mehta, N. K., Abrams, L. R., & Myrskylä, M. (2020). US life expectancy stalls due to cardiovascular disease, not drug deaths. Proceedings of the National Academy of Sciences, 117(13), 6998-7000.
51 Ritchey MD, Wall HK, George MG, Wright JS. US trends in premature heart disease mortality over the past 50 years: Where do we go from here? Trends Cardiovasc Med. 2020 Aug;30(6):364-374.
52 Ibid.
53 Ibid.
54 One early study concluded that of the first 18 operations with a heart-lung machine, 17 patients died. See Stoney, William S. 2009. "Evolution of Cardiopulmonary Bypass." Circulation 119 (21): 2844–53. doi.org/10.1161/circulationaha.108.830174.
55 Weiss AJ, Elixhauser A. Trends in Operating Room Procedures in U.S. Hospitals, 2001–2011. 2014 Mar. In: Healthcare Cost and Utilization Project (HCUP) Statistical Briefs [Internet]. Rockville (MD): Agency for Healthcare Research and Quality (US); 2006 Feb-. Statistical Brief #171. Available from: https://www.ncbi.nlm.nih.gov/books/NBK201926/
56 Dawber, Thomas R., Gilcin F. Meadors, and Felix E. Moore Jr. "Epidemiological approaches to heart disease: the Framingham Study." American Journal of Public Health and the Nations Health 41.3 (1951): 279-286.
57 Butler, J., Shah, S. J., Magwire, M., Campos, C., et.al. Treatment pathways in patients with heart failure with preserved ejection fraction and obesity: perspectives from cardiology specialists and patients. Global Cardiology 2024, 2(2).

58 Heidenreich, Paul A., et al. "2022 AHA/ACC/HFSA guideline for the management of heart failure: a report of the American College of Cardiology/American Heart Association Joint Committee on Clinical Practice Guidelines." Journal of the American College of Cardiology 79.17 (2022): e263-e421.

59 Wang, X., Liu, K., Shirai, K. et al. Prevalence and trends of polypharmacy in U.S. adults, 1999–2018. Global Health Research & Policy 8, 25 (2023)

60 Kyalwazi AN, Loccoh EC, Brewer LC, Ofili EO, Xu J, Song Y, Joynt Maddox KE, Yeh RW, Wadhera RK. Disparities in Cardiovascular Mortality Between Black and White Adults in the United States, 1999 to 2019. Circulation. 2022 Jul 19;146(3):211-228.

9. 1973: THE SCHISM OF SCIENCE AND FINANCE

On July 30, 1965, President Lyndon B. Johnson traveled to Independence, Missouri to sign Medicare into law. He went there as a tribute to former President Harry Truman who had tried and failed to pass national health insurance after World War II. Now, two decades on, the former New Deal warriors were enjoying a measure of retribution. If not national coverage, Medicare and Medicaid at least promised much greater protection for elderly and impoverished Americans.

President Lyndon B. Johnson signing the Medicare Act in Independence, Missouri on July 30, 1965, flanked by former President Harry S. Truman

"Through this new law, Mr. President," Johnson said, addressing the eighty-one-year-old former president, "every citizen will be able, in his productive years when he is earning, to insure himself against the ravages of illness in his old age." In words that both resonate with and haunt Americans in the prime of their working lives, LBJ added: "No longer will young families see their own incomes, and their own hopes, eaten away simply because they are carrying out their deep moral obligations to their parents, and to their uncles, and their aunts." After signing the bill, Johnson turned to Truman and handed him a card making him Medicare beneficiary number one.

To its supporters, Medicare represented a natural extension of New Deal principles fusing government's equalizing power with medical science. Many in Washington assumed that it was just a matter of time until Medicare would be extended to all. Five years later, Nixon's advisors considered it, as they triangulated among competing strains of liberalism and conservatism. Ultimately they put the White House's prestige behind environmental issues rather than universal coverage, backing the creation of the Environmental Protection Agency and bills to improve air and water quality.

Undeterred, powerful Democrats in the Senate and House of Representatives decided to push forward with universal coverage, announcing a series of hearings to build support. Sensing opportunity, a small but vocal group of Americans suffering from fatal kidney disease seized the moment to argue for a dramatic expansion in government-financed care, if only for their specific need. What followed changed American health care forever and unintentionally hastened the schism between finance and science.

End-Stage Renal Disease

November 4, 1971 was an unseasonably warm day in Washington DC, as Rep. Wilbur Mills, Chair of the House Ways and Means Committee, gaveled a hearing on national health insurance to order. The agenda was full, and Mills moved quickly through a series of witnesses. Late that morning he recognized a slender, forty-three-year-old, Shep Glazer, to begin his testimony. Glazer had terminal kidney disease, placing him among an unfortunate group of about 100,000 Americans living under a veritable death sentence. Their only hope was to live long enough, relying on hemodialysis, until they could receive a kidney transplant. Testifying on behalf of the National Association of Patients on Hemodialysis, Glazer argued that the government should pay for dialysis and transplants.

Invented decades earlier, hemodialysis became safe and reliable enough to enable wide use in the early 1960s. Yet a decade on, only a few dozen US hospitals had machines and the process took hours, constrained by shortages of equipment and technicians. Federal support, Glazer argued, would allow dialysis recipients to get in-home systems. At the time, the cost for home care seemed prohibitive, about $90,000 in today's dollars plus $50,000 a year for ongoing care. The possibility that the government would agree to anything like that level of support seemed delusional, but Glazer had a plan. Next to him at the witness table was a washing machine sized contraption mounted on a cart. Glazer had arranged to have a dialysis machine brought from Georgetown University's hospital into the hearing room. He planned to receive dialysis while delivering his statement, showing as vividly as possible that kidney failure patients could be productive citizens.

Glazer's shirtsleeves were rolled up, a tube in each arm. As he began speaking, an attending nephrologist activated the machine, initiating dialysis. After describing the plight of kidney failure patients and the lack of accessible dialysis centers, Glazer ended with an emotional plea:

> "I am 43 years old, married for 20 years, with two children, ages 14 and 10. I was a salesman until a couple of months ago until it became necessary for me to supplement my income to pay for the dialysis supplies. I tried to sell a noncompetitive line, was found out, and was fired. Gentlemen, what should I do? End it all and die? Sell my house for which I worked so hard, and go on welfare? Should I go into the hospital under my hospitalization policy, then I cannot work. Please tell me, if your kidneys failed tomorrow, wouldn't you want the

opportunity to live? Wouldn't you want to see your children grow up?"

Glazer's decision to undergo live dialysis was a massive risk. Some in the dialysis community who caught wind of his plan were horrified. What if he had a medical emergency? By all appearances, the gamble paid off. Chairman Mills later called it one of the most compelling pieces of testimony he ever witnessed. Years later, the nephrologist overseeing Glazer's dialysis confided to a peer that his detractors' worst fears almost came true. During the testimony, Glazer had gone into ventricular tachycardia but the physician quickly clamped the blood lines, halting the process. Committee members were none the wiser.[61]

The hearings ultimately came to naught in terms of a bill guaranteeing health coverage and momentum for national health insurance faded during the 1972 election campaign. That December, however, just before adjourning, Congress passed a set of Medicare changes including a provision that created the End-Stage Renal Disease (ESRD) program. It was the answer to Shep Glazer's call, the first Medicare benefit granted to Americans of all ages, and it guaranteed any American with end-stage kidney disease to receive dialysis as long as they lived, or until they received a kidney transplant.

The program was envisioned as a bridge to buy time until a fortunate few could receive a transplant. At worst it provided humanitarian support for those succumbing to a terminal disease. Both assumptions proved wrong. The number of Americans who qualified for coverage was far greater than expected, swelling in the 1990s and beyond with advanced metabolic syndrome. Program outlays exploded fifty times in real terms, from just over $1 billion (in 2021 dollars) in its first year of operations to $52 billion in 2021.

Even more so, ESRD came to represent the victory of near-term symptom management, in the form of hemodialysis, over investments to refine and democratize access to transplants. Instead of putting the government's resources behind advancements to increase functional lifespan, the program devolved into an even more expensive way to manage late-stage illness. When ESRD began, transplant surgery was still very dicey and not ready to be done at scale. There was a limited supply of matching organs and experienced clinical teams. Managing post-transplant anti-rejection drugs was tricky.[62] This changed in the 1980s as transplant outcomes and technology improved, especially advances in immunosuppressive regimens that allowed end-stage patients to receive organs from unrelated donors.

ESRD policies, however, continued to discourage transplants. Although recipients had to take immunosuppressive drugs for life, Medicare rules stopped paying for drugs three years after transplant. Thereafter, recipients had to find private coverage, even though many insurers routinely denied coverage for preexisting conditions like being an organ transplant recipient.[63] In addition transplant recipients were ineligible for ESRD coverage of dialysis, should they need it, while their transplanted organ functioned. The number of kidney transplants grew much slower than ESRD enrollment, increasing from just 5,000 a year in the early 1980s to about 9,000 a year a decade later.

Meanwhile, a highly profitable business of outpatient dialysis centers and in-home treatment services developed, creating commercial constituencies with a large financial stake in symptom management. By 2005, outpatient dialysis centers had capacity to serve 80,000 people. Vastly more federal resources poured into dialysis than scientific work to improve transplants. From 1985 to 2015, the NIH awarded an average of $10 million a year in transplant research grants, a pittance compared to the $40 billion spent annually on dialysis from 2005 to 2015.[64]

So why was the choice between dialysis and transplants one of finance over science? Because transplants cost much more up front than dialysis. Medicare officials trying to manage to annual spending targets focused on near-term outlays instead of long-term returns. Expanding the ROI horizon changes the math dramatically since post-transplant, recipients cost Medicare about half as much annually as dialysis recipients. As early as 1991, Medicare studies showed that transplants saved money compared to dialysis.[65] The crossover point happened after five and a half years, leaving aside transplant recipients' better quality of life, ability to work, and lower out-of-pocket spending on other health needs.

But here's the kicker. Transplant recipients also live longer than dialysis patients, much longer. Today, those over 65 live more than seven years longer than people on dialysis; transplant recipients like Shep Glazer, in their late forties, live about fourteen years post-transplant, twice as long as similarly aged dialysis recipients.[66] The five year survival rate for individuals starting dialysis 65 or older is about 25%, meaning that the vast majority of recipients do not even live five years.[67] From a budgetary perspective, this makes transplant recipients a double whammy, costing more in the year of surgery and more over time, since recipients *live much longer*. It's crazy, but it's a pattern that plays out again and again in the current system.

A half century on from ESRD's inception, there are just 25,000 kidney transplants a year, about 4% of the roughly 550,000 Americans who receive dialysis. None of the congressional leaders who shepherded ESRD into existence imagined that it would lead to massively higher spending and little numeric progress on transplants.[68] Yet, that's exactly what has happened, and continues to happen, in a system biased towards short-term financial goals instead of investing more, earlier, to realize longer healthspan.

The Schism of 1973

Most people would not rank 1973 as one of the most consequential years of the twentieth century. It is remembered, if anything, for coverage of the Watergate break-in and the OPEC oil embargo following America's support of Israel in the Yom Kippur War. It is also the year that a mobile phone was first used, when a Motorola engineer called his Bell Labs counterpart to crow about winning the race to build a working product.

Yet 1973 was one of the most decisive years in American medical history, signaling a schism between the previously allied worlds of medical science and health care. From 1973, the alliance of science and finance that had fueled a quarter century long medical golden age was over. As the ESRD program ramped up, Congress created a new health insurance model called Health Maintenance Organizations (HMOs), establishing cost control as the organizing principle of health delivery. It combined deep skepticism about medical technology with a belief in using financial rules to limit access to expensive care and payments to clinicians. Intended as a way station to the Nixonian ideal balancing treatment and prevention, HMOs ultimately reinforced sick care, and the interlocking relationships among insurers, hospitals, and clinicians.

That year also provides a plausible answer to the question, "When did obesity start to take off?" Changes to agricultural policies in 1973, occasioned by Nixon's policy of detente, caused a decisive shift in the use of corn, artificial sweeteners, and seed oils in food, making it much more economic to create ultra-processed ingredients and engineer food for taste and texture. Obesity rates had been declining through the early 1970s but, from 1976 onwards, reversed course and have continued steadily upwards ever since.[69]

Medical science underwent something of a mini-big bang in 1973, with development of magnetic resonance imaging (MRI), a breakthrough in diagnostic imaging; new understandings about the accumulation of cholesterol in blood vessels; proof that drugs could be manufactured to target specific cells; and validation that genes could be predictably reengineered. These discoveries enabled some of the most meaningful advances in recent medical history including immensely greater power for clinicians to visualize internal organs and brain activity non-invasively, without radiation; statin drugs to prevent cholesterol buildup; and monoclonal antibodies—a mainstay in treating cancer and autoimmune conditions.

Within five years of proving the feasibility of genetically engineered drugs, Genentech became the first biotech to earn FDA approval for a drug created with the technology. Fortuitously, it was synthetic insulin, a product soon to see a boost in demand as the number of insulin-dependent diabetics began to increase.

The schism between finance and science was not absolute. When existential perils like HIV/AIDS emerged in the 1980s or COVID in 2020, financialists stepped aside to let researchers and drugmakers lead. Despite the political vitriol stirred up by COVID, the pandemic's early months brought unprecedented cooperation among infectious disease leaders and drugmakers to speed up vaccine development. Much of the early work to develop mRNA technologies used in the two most successful COVID vaccines had been underwritten by federal defense and health agencies. The federal government doubled down in 2020, making massive commitments to ensure drugmakers could build sufficient manufacturing and distribution capacity. FDR and Vannevar Bush would have been proud. However, moments like these became the exceptions rather that the rule. From 1973 on, financialists were firmly in charge of American health care.

Health Maintenance Organizations (HMOs) and the Financialist Delusion

The early 1970s were a time of intellectual ferment in Washington. Just a few years removed from the upheavals of 1968, there was growing wariness among political and cultural elites about materialism and environmental destruction. Channeling Thomas Malthus's eighteenth-century prediction that population growth would soon exhaust food stocks, 1970s era neo-Malthusians preached a steady drumbeat of "less" in all things—fewer people, fewer goods, less consumption. Multinational corporations and industrialists were so powerful, activists argued, that planners and regulators would have to actively regulate conglomerates and constrain their growth. So scarcitarianism fit right in.

Health policy experts already harbored a deep mistrust of economic forces to control demand for medical care. Nobel Prize winner Kenneth Arrow laid out the case in the early 1960s.[70] Health care and traditional market forces, he argued, were incompatible. Physicians and insurers have superior information to consumers. Sometimes physicians make economically suboptimal decisions, using more expensive treatments than necessary in deference to patients' wishes, or to fulfill their own sense of an ethical obligation. Other times, treatment choices were motivated by clinicians' or hospitals' economic self-interest. Unreliable individual choices had to be constrained. The best way to deal with this,

Arrow concluded, was to link insurers, hospitals, and clinicians within a single entity, forcing a reckoning among competing interests.

To Arrow's critique, the neo-Malthusians added a deep suspicion of medical technology, believing it increased costs and demand while providing little value or better outcomes. Hospitals particularly abused the system, investing in diagnostic and surgical equipment that encouraged physicians to boost treatment volumes beyond what was necessary. Medical care was a superior good, they argued, and the wealthier Americans became, the more of it they would want. For-profit entities and clinicians, in their view, would be only too happy to oblige.

These critiques were catnip to health insurers, regulators, and budget minders. It gelled with their sense that the system needed someone "above it all" to keep competing interests in check. Experience with Medicare and Medicaid cost growth seemed to confirm this; even in the first few years of the program, costs were growing much faster than originally expected. Less closely examined was whether the original forecasts captured the breadth and depth of medical need around the country, especially in the South where Black Americans, denied access to segregated hospitals, had been systematically underserved.

Instead of pushing for national health coverage, Nixon put his weight behind a new insurance model called HMOs, an idea that fused Arrow's theories about mismatched incentives with Henry Kaiser's vision of integrated physician-hospital networks. The main idea was to integrate insurance and treatment, with coverage provided at a fixed rate per person, hoping that a fixed amount of revenue per capita would drive treatment efficiencies and greater reliance on preventive medicine.

At the time, HMOs represented a radical departure from the way traditional health insurance worked, controlling both consumer demand and clinician access. HMO members (i.e., consumers) received cheaper coverage than under non-HMO plans, including regular access to primary care and hospital treatment in case of severe injury or illness. Between the two ends of this care spectrum, members would need permission from their primary care physician to see a specialist and would have to make out-of-pocket payments for specialist visits. Higher co-pays, it was assumed, would make people think twice before going to a specialist.

The supply side would be managed as well. As in the Kaiser model, physicians entered into exclusive contracts with the HMO, and agreed to treat only HMO members, make referrals to other HMO-contracted physicians, and abide by HMO-set fee schedules. In theory, this would provide certainty about patient flow, in-network referrals, and revenue. HMO entities also agreed to constraints including to run annual open enrollment periods and accept all applicants regardless of pre-existing conditions. At the time, traditional insurers could pick and choose when to take in new members and could deny coverage or hike premiums based on an individual's health status.

Today this list of member, clinician, and insurer requirements might elicit a shrug. Isn't that pretty much how *all* health insurance now works? Yes, it is, which is why HMO's creation in 1973 was so important. Plan members pay more to be treated by out-of-network clinicians or at an out-of-network facility. While they may not have to get a referral to see a specialist, insurers exert control over pricier treatments using prior authorization, letting them deny coverage for measures recommended by clinicians. HMO principles also drove the ACA's requirements that health insurers price coverage for smaller employers using community-wide cost metrics rather than the risk profile of individual companies' workers. It has taken four decades, but every key aspect of HMOs is now a given in private and public health coverage.

Ironically, HMOs got off to a rocky start in the 1970s, unable to compete with traditional insurers who did not have to follow the same constraints on enrolling members, pricing plans, or physician contracts. After a few years, Congress relented, amending the original law to loosen constraints on clinicians and plans. In their new guise, with physicians able to take HMO member patients and others, the arrangements grew. Looking back, it's clear that HMOs succeeded in providing the superstructure of financialism but failed in their original goals of increasing preventive medicine and outcomes while slowing cost growth. It might have worked had HMOs confined their services to primary and catastrophic care, but enmeshed in a unitary health system with traditional insurers, they too succumbed to multimorbidity's slow boil.

When Food Got Sweet and Ultra-Processing Took Off

While technosceptics gained the upper hand in health care, food production embraced abundance, with leading minds working to increase crop productivity as much as possible, thereby reducing famines. Agronomists like Nobel Prize winner Norman Borlaug confronted neo-Malthusian skepticism about population growth and food shortages with better seeds, fertilizers, and farming practices, evangelizing new ways to increase crop yields. They succeeded beyond expectations, lifting hundreds of millions of people worldwide out of starvation.

Pesticide makers developed increasingly effective products, swatting aside potential effects on animal and human health. Advances in genetic engineering (hastened by discoveries published in 1973) led to drought and pest resistant crops. International supply chains and widespread adoption of refrigerated transport enabled producers to engineer food for longer shelf lives and lower costs. Food marketers applied science in less helpful ways, creating new ways to make products addictive, optimizing color, taste, and texture. Ad campaigns and packaging targeting children and time-pressed working parents reinforced demand.

All of these forces were building that year as President Nixon attempted a high-wire act of defusing nuclear tension with the Soviet Union while trying to draw China out of its communist alliance and to open itself to the US. In 1972, the Soviets were in a difficult spot agriculturally, suffering through the second straight year of disastrously low grain yields, triggering fears of food shortages. Sensing an opportunity to advance detente, Nixon and his Agriculture Secretary Earl Butz agreed to sell the Soviets a quarter of US grain production. Soon, Butz realized, the US had oversold and now faced the prospect of food shortages of its own.

Butz, like Nixon, knew how to work multiple agendas at once. Since coming to Washington his main policy goal had been to change American land use policies, including how farmers were paid. Since the New Deal, farmers had been shielded from crop price drops through price supports. Butz wanted to change the formula, calculating income-support payments based on differences between actual market and target prices rather than fixed payment amounts. This, he reasoned, would increase land productivity, with market-based pricing encouraging farmers to use more of their land to grow higher-yielding crops.

With a grain shortage looming, Butz decided to kill two birds with one stone. In early 1973, he urged farmers to plant more land with faster-growing corn and soybeans, hoping to replace wheat headed overseas. Nixon embargoed soybean exports while Butz introduced a Farm Bill to change the crop payment formula.[71] Once enacted, there was no going back. What was presented as an emergency in 1973 became the established norm. Crop production jumped as Butz had hoped, and as shown in the following chart, settled into a long-term shift towards higher yield crops like corn and soybean:[72]

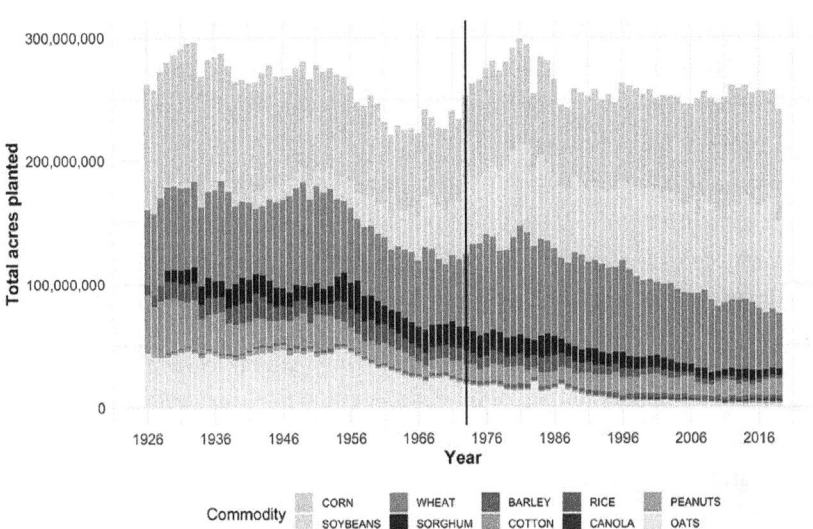

Figure 9.1: US Grain Production by Crop Type, 1926 – 2020

Corn production got a further boost in 1974 with the introduction of a powerful, and now highly controversial pesticide: glyphosate. From 1973 to 2005, corn yield per acre increased by 60% while acres farmed increased by a fifth. In 1973, about two-thirds of grain and oilseeds came from corn and soybeans. Two decades later it was 80%.

This shift was a boon for packaged food companies. More corn enabled cheaper corn-based sweeteners—replacing beet and cane sugar—and emulsifiers, which improved food texture and taste. Soybean production translated into an abundance of vegetable oils, a key ingredient in ultra-processed foods. Over time, higher corn and soybean production lowered the cost to feed livestock, improving the economics of beef, hog, and poultry production, while increasing consumption of processed meat.

As food inputs changed, so too did national dietary recommendations. In 1977, a Senate Select Committee on Nutrition issued a report urging Americans to almost double intake of carbohydrates while reducing saturated fats from meat and dairy products.[73] The committee tried to caveat the carbohydrate advice, urging Americans to eat complex carbohydrates instead of processed sugars. The nuance got lost in translation and an upsurge of splashy packages and advertising. Carbohydrate intake increased, along with obesity rates.

It is hard to pin the blame for obesity and metabolic syndrome on food producers alone. As in the Agatha Christie mystery "Murder on the Orient Express" (also filmed in 1973), a number of sectors had a hand in it. However, the 1973 changes in crop production came at a key moment. Just as health care was separating science from finance, packaged food makers were drawing them together, shortening the time from field to product reengineering to pantry to insulin resistance.

National health survey data provides unmistakable evidence of this association, as shown in Figure 9.2.[74] Obesity rates started to trend upwards in the late 1970s and continued rising at a near constant rate through the late 2010s.

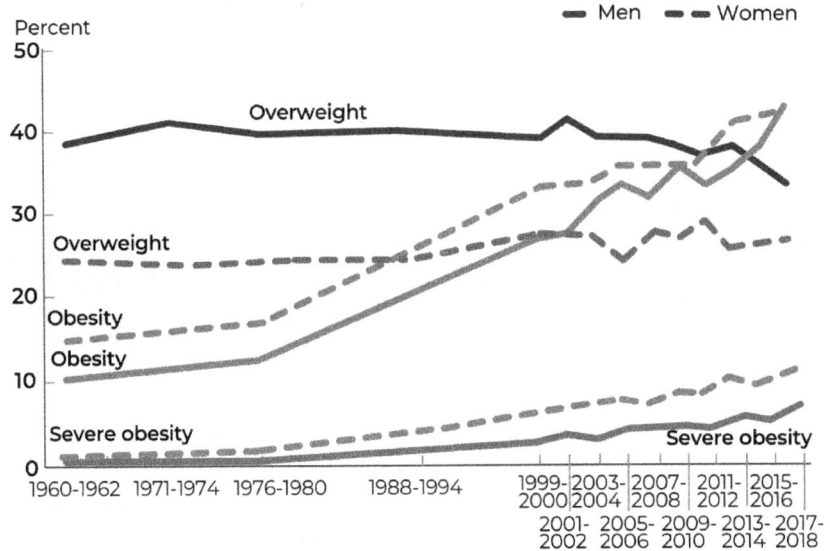

Figure 9.2: US Obesity and Overweight Rates Over Time[75]

Over the four-decade rise, male obesity (defined as a BMI between 30 and 39.9 kg/m²) grew faster than that of women, in part because severe obesity among women (defined as a BMI of 40 kg/m2 or greater) outpaced that of men. Interestingly, the proportion of Americans who are overweight (defined as a BMI between 25 and 29.9 kg/m²) remained relatively steady. Before 1980, most Americans with overweight did not progress to obesity. After 1980 they did, and in keeping with the chronic disease cascade, began to be replaced by an equally large number of people entering the first stage of metabolic syndrome.

Transformative Breakthroughs

While the health care industry changed direction in 1973, increasingly focused on managing symptoms instead of solving disease, medical R&D exploded. Four transformative discoveries in diagnostics, drug design, and manufacturing laid the groundwork for the biotech industry, statins, gene editing, and monoclonal antibodies. Two of the discoveries eventually won Nobel Prizes while a third paved the way for a future Nobel.

Paul Lauterbur's first images of soft tissue generated by magnetic resonance imaging (MRI) prototype were greeted with much skepticism. Using a complex mix of physics and math, he realized he could construct a meaningful image of internal organs and tissues by varying magnetic fields, creating a spatial map of signals emitted by different body tissues. It seemed unbelievable, literally the stuff of science fiction, to image tissues without radiation. Yet, within a decade, Lauterbur's Nobel-Prize winning invention entered commercial use, transforming non-invasive diagnostics along with computed tomography (CT) scanners, which relied on low-dose radiation to image tissues. Since then, MRI resolution has improved by orders of magnitude, making them indispensable in diagnostics, especially breast mammograms and in charting brain activity.

The second Nobel Prize-winning work, by Michael Brown and Joseph Goldstein, explained how low-density lipoprotein, one of the bad cholesterols, finds its way into cells. They discovered a protein on cell surfaces called an LDL receptor, which bound floating LDL, facilitating its uptake by the cell. Their findings were a triple whammy, explaining cholesterol transport, advancing techniques to identify other cell surface receptors, and revealing the liver's critical role in cholesterol processing. Their work paved the way for statin drugs fifteen years later, among the most valuable classes of drugs ever developed.

Another research duo, Jerrold Schwaber and Edward Cohen demonstrated how to make monoclonal antibodies (MAbs), compounds engineered to interact with a particular antigen expressed on cell surfaces. Until then, drugmakers had to go through a painstaking trial and error process to fashion a drug to interact with certain cells and not others (where they would create toxic side effects). Others theorized about building MAbs but Schwaber and Cohen showed both how to do it, and how to repurpose cells to become reliable MAb factories. Their approach led to breakthrough drugs against cancer and autoimmune diseases including rheumatoid arthritis, psoriasis, ulcerative colitis, and Crohn's Disease.

In the final, and perhaps most far-reaching breakthrough in a commercial sense, Herbert Cohen and Stanley Boyer demonstrated the first use of genetic engineering to modify a gene, a capability that revolutionized molecular biology, enabling genetic modification in living organisms and plants. Soon after publishing their breakthrough, Boyer left academia to co-found Genentech, the first biotech company to get FDA approval of a drug made using recombinant DNA.

Each discovery, by itself, is historic but collectively they underscore how critical medical technology proved to be in fighting chronic disease, even as prevalence and severity steadily advanced. Without these discoveries, it would not have been possible to develop foundational understandings about brain function, produce insulin at scale, or create statins and life-saving drugs for autoimmune disease and cancer. Scientifically speaking, it was a landmark year.

After 1973

There is a bitter irony in the arguments that insurers, hospitals, and physicians deployed to defeat national health coverage in 1945, 1970, and 1993. They argued that "government-run" health care would lead to suffocating clinical and financial micromanagement; subpar patient care if physician and hospital prices were capped; and an exodus of clinicians from the system, worsening access to care. Fast forward to now and it's weird to see how much insurers, hospitals, and many specialists have embraced everything they once reviled. Those who shoulder the burdens of multimorbidity and financialism, especially primary care practitioners, may rue the Faustian bargains that enabled the status quo, but it was their own representatives, including the American Medical Association, that helped bring it to fruition.

So, what comes next? Is it possible to reform the post-1973 system and remake it to solve chronic disease? Can the swarms of disruptive health startups overthrow the status quo, as earlier insurgents remade airlines, telecommunications, consumer retail, computing, and software? Today's health startups and their venture investors are betting that it is possible. New care models, price transparency, congressional scrutiny of big insurers, and consumer disgust will eventually bring a revolution. Alas, if only it was true.

ENDNOTES

61 Massry, S.G. (ed.) "The First Forty Years," National Kidney Foundation, 1990:21.

62 By 1980, one-year kidney transplant survival rates approached 80%; a decade later it was above 90%. See "Kidney Failure and the Federal Government," Richard A. Rettig and Norman G. Levinsky, Editors; Committee for the Study of the Medicare End-Stage Renal Disease Program, Division of Health Care Services, 1991.

63 The preexisting condition Catch-22 remained in place until 2010 when the ACA barred coverage denials based on preexisting conditions. The three-year limit on immunosuppressive drugs was changed in 2023.

64 Chandrabhatla AS, Narahari AK, Mehaffey JH, Schaff DL, Kron IL, Brayman KL. National Institutes of Health Funding for Abdominal Organ Transplantation Research Has Declined: A 30-year Analysis. Transplantation. 2022 Oct 1;106(10):1909-1911. doi: 10.1097/TP.0000000000004082. Epub 2022 Feb 16. PMID: 35175240; PMCID: PMC9378811.

65 Kidney Failure and the Federal Government, US Institute of Medicine Committee for the Study of the Medicare End-Stage Renal Disease Program; Rettig RA, Levinsky NG, editors. National Academies Press (US); 1991. 8, Access to Kidney Transplantation.

66 NIDDK, NIH, 2022 Annual Data Report, End-Stage Renal Disease Mortality. Note: NIDDK survival data quoted here includes transplants from live and deceased donors. Results for live donors only are even better. Americans of all ages who received live-donor kidneys over the last decade can expect to live two decades post-transplant, with longer survival durations for younger transplant recipients. See: Poggio ED, Augustine JJ, Arrigain S, Brennan DC, Schold JD. Long-term kidney transplant graft survival-Making progress when most needed. Am J Transplant. 2021 Aug;21(8):2824-2832. doi: 10.1111/ajt.16463. Epub 2021 Feb 8. PMID: 33346917.

67 Ibid, Figure 6.8.

68 At the time ESRD was passed, one of the pioneers of liver and kidney transplant surgery, Dr. Thomas Starzl, argued that many in the medical establishment wanted to do just that, to suppress transplants, seeing it as a kind of unethical arrogance and overreach. While Starzl may have been right about his peers, there is no evidence that members of Congress felt this way. The record suggests everyone thought they were creating a bridge to transplantation rather than a replacement of it.

69 Kranjac AW, Kranjac D. Explaining adult obesity, severe obesity, and BMI: Five decades of change. Heliyon. 2023 May 19;9(5):e16210.

70 Arrow, K. "Uncertainty and the Welfare Economics of Medical Care," The American Economic Review, LIII, 5, December 1963, 941-973.

71 Interestingly, the 1973 Farm Bill also introduced Food Stamps.

72 Spangler, K., Burchfield, E., Schumacher, B., 2020. "Past and Current Dynamics of U.S. Agricultural Land Use and Policy." Frontiers in Sustainable Food Systems 4 (July), and Zulauf, C., G. Schnitkey, N. Paulson and J. Colussi. "Concentration of US Crops in Corn and Soybeans: Importance to Increasing US Production of Grains and Oilseeds." farmdoc daily (13):173, Department of Agricultural and Consumer Economics, University of Illinois at Urbana-Champaign, September 22, 2023.

73 Dietary Goals for the United States, Second Edition, US Senate Select Committee on Nutrition and Human Needs, 1977
74 Fryar CD, Carroll MD, Afful J. Prevalence of overweight, obesity, and severe obesity among adults aged 20 and over: United States, 1960–1962 through 2017–2018. NCHS Health E-Stats. 2020.
75 "Products - Health E Stats - Prevalence of Overweight, Obesity, and Extreme Obesity Among Adults Aged 20 and Over: United States, 1960–1962 Through 2017–2018." n.d. https://www.cdc.gov/nchs/data/hestat/obesity-adult-17-18/obesity-adult.htm.

10. THE ROCK, PAPER, SCISSORS VORTEX

> "When disruptive innovators attempt to commercialize their innovations within the established value network in their industry that system will either reject it ... or co-opt the potential disruption, forcing it to conform to the existing value network in order to survive."
>
> –Clayton Christensen et. al. *The Innovator's Prescription: A Disruptive Solution for Health Care*

In 1981, federal budget analyst Gordon Adams wrote a stinging critique of US defense procurement called *The Politics of Defense Spending: The Iron Triangle.* In it, he explained how the Defense Department, congressional committees overseeing the department, and the defense industry had formed an interlocking triangle of interdependence. With time, the complex prioritized its own financial interests over the public's interest. Adams's book gained wide attention a few years later as whistleblowers and investigative journalists reported on military procurement outrages including $7,000 coffee makers and $600 toilet seats.

An Iron Triangle exists in health care as well, with the triad of interlocking special interests including clinicians, hospitals, and insurers. The latter group, including public and private insurers, controls how much revenue circulates through the system by setting premiums, pricing care, and controlling access to treatments. In this system, employers are an extension of insurers by paying directly for workers' health care or approving the parameters of premiums and benefits. Hospitals, as the premiere locations of care control the largest component of health spending. Clinicians, especially specialist physicians are integral in determining treatments, limit the supply of labor coming into the profession, and effectively bargain for compensation increases.

The power dynamics among insurers, clinicians, and hospitals are in constant flux. Each holds decisive power in some situations against the others, but each, in turn, is vulnerable in other situations to being overridden by others. Mostly they joust over issues of control, including autonomy over treatment decisions, and how system revenue is distributed.

It amounts to an endless game of Rock, Paper, Scissors, the childhood game in which players make hand shapes representing a rock, a flat sheet, or scissors. Like health care, it is a zero sum game in which each element can defeat one of the others but can be defeated by the other. Players win individual rounds but no one can win the game. Thus, too, in health care. At any given time, insurers try to reduce the price of treatments charged by hospitals or physicians. Clinicians link forces with hospitals to change billing practices to offset lower prices with higher value billing codes or increased activity volume. Insurers then retaliate with tighter prior authorization rules or leverage ownership of PBMs and other parts of the value chain to recapture revenue lost elsewhere. And so it goes.

The constant churn, finger-pointing, and alliance shifting creates a formidable barrier to change, forcing would-be disruptors to play by the incumbents' rules while trying to siphon enough business to survive. Ultimately, the internal forces are too strong and even the most well-meaning insurgents succumb to status quo forces. I call this whirlwind of competitive codependence the RPS Vortex (where RPS stands for Rock Paper Scissors). It is an all against all competition among the three dominant constituencies combined with a tacit alliance to repel efforts to force meaningful change.

After 1973, the financial and scientific realms sorted into parallel camps, as shown in Figure 10.1, with the RPS Vortex dominating health care delivery (i.e., system financials) while researchers and the R&D arms of product makers focus on understanding biology and developing technologies and treatments.

Figure 10.1: The Financial and Scientific Realms of Health Care

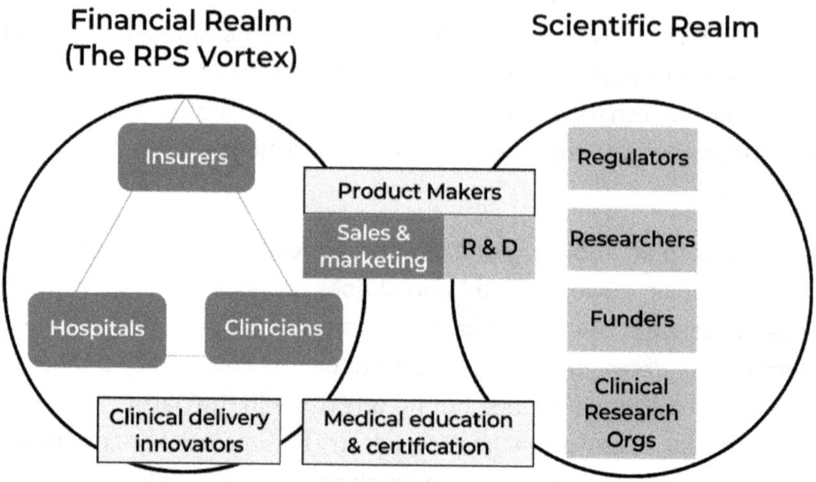

Financial Realm (The RPS Vortex)   **Scientific Realm**

- Insurers
- Hospitals
- Clinicians
- Clinical delivery innovators
- Product Makers (Sales & marketing | R & D)
- Medical education & certification
- Regulators
- Researchers
- Funders
- Clinical Research Orgs

The financial realm faces a continual challenge from would-be disruptors offering new care delivery models focusing on specific conditions (e.g., obesity medicine or mental health), demographic groups (e.g., the elderly or middle-aged women), or delivery modalities (e.g., virtual primary care or physical therapy). However, disruptors' prospects are precarious since they rely on RPS Vortex entities to gain customers and revenue while trying to become self-sustaining. Very few achieve this goal. Many either reach a growth ceiling or end up being acquired by an RPS Vortex entity. It is the definition of being caught between a rock and a hard place.

The scientific realm, shown on the right of Figure 10.1, focuses on research and development, including everything from basic science and development of new methods and research capabilities to applied and translational science developing drugs, surgical capabilities, diagnostics, and devices. It includes regulators who review and approve products like the FDA; public and private entities that fund research and development such as the NIH, academic research centers, venture capital investors, biotechs and large drugmakers; and clinical research organizations, entities hired by drug developers to conduct lab work and run clinical trials.

Bridging the two circles are product makers including pharmaceutical and biotech firms, diagnostics companies, and data and AI vendors. These entities have a stake in each realm, relying on the RPS Vortex to generate revenue even as they focus within the scientific realm on innovation. These entities live a Janus-like existence, influencing the rules and arrangements in each realm, maximizing revenue in the RPS Vortex to underwrite R&D and compensate investors.

It may be controversial not to include drugmakers as coequals with insurers, hospitals, and clinicians, but I think this perception, shaped by the commercial arms of drug companies, obscures drugmakers' essential dependency on RPS Vortex entities to generate revenue. Drugmakers influence, ultimately, is a function of the quality of their products, which come and go over time.

Other entities that bridge both realms include clinical education and certification which involves both academic medical centers and universities that train clinicians and the arms of professional associations that administer board examinations or issue credentials.

How the RPS Vortex Resists Change

Having described the status quo, let's return to the question posed at the end of the last chapter: can the RPS Vortex be sufficiently reformed from within to take on multimorbidity? Unfortunately, no. RPS Vortex entities were designed to meet one kind of challenge and in chronic disease, now face something very different. Complicating matters, the chronic disease cascade guarantees continual revenue growth for the main players, so long as they do not overplay their hands politically. This reinforces the way RPS Vortex entities behave, hardwiring the system to stifle change.

The non-negotiables of institutional behavior in the RPS Vortex can be distilled to the following:[76]

- Systemic accountability for outcomes is impossible and must be resisted at all costs.
- When in doubt, cloud it out. That is, make everything about the way the system operates as opaque as possible—treatment and coverage rules, contracts, decision processes, governance. All of it. Complexity, to the RPS Vortex, is a competitive moat.

The greatest proof of the lack of systemic accountability is its absence. Think about it this way: if systemic accountability *was* a core principle of RPS Vortex entities, what would it look like?

Compensation in the system would be linked in part to changes in policyholders' and patients' health situations. Entities involved in fighting chronic disease would include reporting on the prevalence and severity of multimorbidity of the people they served. There would be incentives to increase remission rates for obesity or diabetes or penalties for failing to do so. Ideally analysts inside the RPS Vortex would track and report on changes in actual or expected healthspan. Leaders of large enterprises would have their compensation tied to patients' long-term outcomes. The US government would enforce systemic accountability if it existed, even adjusting corporate tax rates or hospitals' tax-exempt status based on outcomes metrics. Imagine if the amount that insurers could hike premiums each year was tied to their success in slowing or reversing multimorbidity among people they cover?

Unsurprisingly, none of these performance-based standards exist. In fact, leaders of RPS Vortex entities would dismiss the very idea as laughable: "How can we be held responsible for so many factors that are outside our control or take years to unfold?" Yes, how indeed?

Another argument that insurers voice: "People move in and out of insurance every few years or their employers change insurers." As we will see, coverage switching is much less of a problem than insurers claim, but even then, it is a problem that insurers could solve with risk pools or transfer payments if they put their minds to it.

Or this one: "How can we ensure that people actually *follow* their clinicians' directives or take their medication as prescribed?" Yes, blame Americans for their ignorance or laziness while switching coverage rules and co-pays for medications as insurers see fit. Too often, the excuse that something is "too hard to solve" is a shield or excuse to not even try.

Insurers' unwillingness to tie compensation to longer-term outcomes is, in effect, an admission that they exist to optimize financials, not improve Americans' health. Their value add in managing chronic disease is purely transactional, a product of how well they wring concessions from hospital systems, clinicians, and drugmakers, or get more proficient and efficient at denying claims.

Some might argue that I'm overstating things, overlooking, for example, Medicare's efforts to grade Medicare Advantage plans using a "Star Rating" system. These ratings assess plans based on a mix of customer satisfaction metrics and adherence to good clinical practices like encouraging breast and colorectal cancer screening or counseling people who have consistently high blood sugar. It is a start but look closer and you see that the clinical metrics are really about inputs not outputs. For example, the clinical standard for managing cholesterol is met when a member fills a statin prescription, rather than whether the person experiences an actual improvement in lipid levels.

Another Medicare initiative encourages doctors and hospitals to form Accountable Care Organizations (ACOs), which coordinate seniors' care for a fixed price in exchange for a share in any savings realized by Medicare. Like Stars Ratings, ACOs are a step in the right direction but again fall well short of real accountability. Payments to ACOs are adjusted upwards based on the number of conditions that a person has. The more they have, the higher the payment. It makes sense on one level. The health needs of someone with multimorbidity are more complex than someone with one or two conditions. But here's the rub: no one gets paid more to *reduce* the number of conditions a person has. In fact, if ACOs cannot reconfirm that a person still has a set number of conditions every couple of years, their payment for that person goes down. As a result there has been an epidemic of "up-coding," some of it potentially fraudulent, in which Medicare Advantage plans maximize the number of conditions a person is said to have. Real systemic accountability works the other way, rewarding entities and clinicians for reversing disease or slowing progression, *increasing* payments when a person's health trajectory improves, not when it gets worse.

This leads to the RPS Vortex's second core principle, making intra-system relationships and payments as opaque as possible.

- *Everything is driven by one-year budgeting cycles.* Annual open enrollment periods and budgeting cycles create a perpetual merry-go-round of contract renegotiations, putting the whole system in a constant state of flux. It's roughly akin to having a professional sports league in which all the players and coaches are perpetual free agents. It becomes impossible to build farm teams or sustain franchise value.

- *Financially driven billing languages make health care incomprehensible.* The RPS Vortex relies on a Tower of Babel-like jumble of diagnostic and billing codes. Hospitals and insurer software map conditions and treatments against a triple-layer cake of codes, investing massive energy into optimizing hospital and clinician payments. Likewise, billing and coding practices vary from one hospital system to another, making it very hard to understand the rationale behind treatment choices even after parsing clinicians' notes. In theory, AI should help, except that the data used to train AI is itself unreliable since it builds on past coding decisions.

- *Payment rules serve the needs of people making the rules.* The rules governing what conditions or activities are reimbursed are written behind closed doors, often to benefit those in the room. Responsibility to develop or update diagnostic and payment codes is delegated to the American Medical Association, the chief lobbying organization for physicians. Others have a seat at the table, but they too are card-carrying members of the RPS Vortex. Consequently, rules serve financial needs, measuring activities and inputs instead of outputs.

A great example occurred in early 2024 when the AMA committee that approves billing codes reviewed a proposal to pay physicians to read data from continuous glucose monitors (CGMs)—devices used by diabetics to track blood sugar levels. Until now, physicians were not paid to review CGM data, so clinical practice varied. Some doctors paid close attention, others did not. The way to standardize behavior in a financially-fixated system, physicians reasoned, is to pay clinicians to do it. Naturally, the next question was volumetric. How many times does a clinician have to read the data and over what time frame are they paid? Some wanted a low number, requiring doctors to review only two days of data, while others wanted a floor of two weeks.

In terms of improving outcomes, this is ludicrous. By definition, a *continuous* glucose monitor should be monitored *continuously*. Airline pilots do not get paid more if they check engine fuel flow five times a flight instead of only once; they're paid to operate the plane safely. What matters is that humans pay attention *when it matters and then make the right decision based on the information presented, and their training and experience.*

Humans do not have to do the constant monitoring; that's what software is for, to alert wearers and clinicians when values deviate from desired ranges. The key for the individual and the system is what happens next? If a clinician gets five alerts in two days, calls or meets with the person, they agree to change diet, activity, or medication; and then in the following months other apps confirm behavioral change and no alert is triggered, that's a win. The clinician has added value. The concept of rewarding time spent on high-value decisions and outcomes is not only alien in the RPS Vortex, it's discouraged *by design*.

- *Turn a blind eye to data deserts and gaps.* A final operating principle that inhibits meaningful change is the system's tolerance of data gaps that stop longitudinal performance measurement. The system captures events (if they are billable) but unlike in coloring books, it is impossible to connect the dots across systems or time. Standards vary from state to state and among hospital systems, clinicians, and insurers.[77] Medical claims tell one story, prescription data another; textual commentary (if it exists) a third. This makes it very hard to build a fact-based understanding of what has happened and why over time, a precondition to know which interventions truly work. The RPS Vortex likes it this way. Obfuscation is a feature not a bug. Entities that control the data control the narrative and each RPS Vortex constituency has their story to tell, whatever the truth may be.

Value-Based Care and the Limits of Reform from Within

So the RPS Vortex is wired to resist change, but does this mean the system is beyond repair? Might it be possible to pull all that financial wiring out, and with it, some of the RPS Vortex's power? After the ACA's passage in 2010, a determined band of reformers inside and outside government decided to find out. They wanted to prove that the system could get better outcomes at lower costs by ending payments for specific procedures or treatments, also known as fee-for-service. One hospital CEO turned reformer, Dr. Vivian Lee, calls fee-for-service the "fundamental flaw" in health care.

Reformers were emboldened by an ACA provision that gave the Center for Medicare and Medicaid Innovation (CMMI) extraordinary power to test new payment approaches. CMMI was allowed to waive existing statutes or rules that conflicted with payment tests. They wanted to create a system called Value-Based Care, inspired by the Kaiser Permanente model, to pay clinicians and hospitals a fixed amount to manage a person's overall health. The idea was to shift incentives from doing any number of things to doing the right things necessary to solve a health challenge. As a sweetener, clinicians and hospitals could share in Medicare's savings through bonuses.

For example, CMMI started to pay hospitals the same lump-sum amount when a Medicare beneficiary was hospitalized for heart failure whether or not the person went home in two days or ten days. It was up to the hospital to do as much or as little as possible to restore the person's health, with one catch. The hospital would be penalized if a recently discharged patient had to be readmitted within a month. CMMI applied a similar approach to bundle payments for a number of chronic disease treatments including ESRD.

By 2020, they had enough data to report on eighteen different payment experiments. The results were disappointing, to say the least. Two-thirds of the payment tests had no impact on spending or caused it *to increase*.[78] After factoring in bonus payments to participants, *all* of the experiments lost money compared to the status quo. So, not good.

Meanwhile CMMI tried to push the other side of the RPS Vortex, insurers, to see if they could get them to care more about outcomes. Under a program called Value-Based Insurance Design (VBID), insurers could earn bonuses or penalties based on better care metrics, similar to those used in the Medicare Stars Rating system described above. After a few years, CMMI contracted with the RAND Institute to assess results. Again, the data showed no gains:

> [B]ased on data available and the outcomes we considered, we have yet to find any evidence of overall improvements in health status or cost outcomes. In fact, VBID implementation was associated with increases in risk scores, inpatient stays, beneficiary premiums, and costs to CMS in some years.[79]

Ouch. Undaunted, CMMI tried another tack, testing value-based approaches in cancer care, an area that accounts for a disproportionately large amount of Medicare spending. Reformers worried that clinicians were over-using expensive radiation therapies or targeted therapies where use had little or no benefit to patient survival.[80] Under the Oncology Care Model (OCM), they wanted to see if oncologists would use cheaper treatments where doing so would make no difference, while continuing to use cutting-edge treatments among those who would benefit. The program touched a quarter of traditional Medicare enrollees with cancer. Alas, here again, there was little change in treatment choices or costs. Oncologists increased use of cheaper generic drugs in some cases, but cost savings were very small.

The failure of value-based payment approaches in chronic disease and cancer has been a hot topic on the health policy conference circuit. Why did something that made so much sense on paper come up short in practice? The explanations sound like the usual suspects. Health is "big" and "complex." Health is hard. It's difficult to scale a change that works in one area to others. It takes time to change clinical practice. It's an issue that requires generational change.

Well, maybe. A much simpler explanation is that using financial levers to solve advanced disease is doomed to fail. Financial structures can reward or penalize good science, but getting the science of reversing or preventing disease right is the threshold problem. Changing how clinicians and hospitals get paid within a system that instinctually resists early, more decisive or expensive interventions, is bound to have marginal value.

An equally simple answer is that trying to change systemic behavior in Medicare, years or decades after beneficiaries entered the chronic disease cascade is often too little, too late. To have impact at scale, interventions and systemic change must start much earlier. In the words of the RAND study evaluating VBID, insurance systems must be designed "to stave off costly, downstream complications of chronic disease that might unfold slowly over a beneficiary's lifetime."[81]

Sociologist Peter Rossi published a paper in 1983, initially intended to be somewhat humorous, establishing an Iron Law of program evaluation, "that the expected value of any large scale social intervention is zero." A couple of decades later he refined the maxim to say that most large interventions were poorly designed. So too with value-based approaches, which are not inherently flawed, they're just being implemented in a system that is bound to reject them. Value-based care requires continual assessment of outcomes over longer timeframes. That requires a system built to solve long-term issues. In other words, Life for Health not the RPS Vortex.

Case Study: How the RPS Vortex Suppressed Metabolic Surgery

Everyone recognizes the potentially transformational value of GLP-1 drugs, setting aside their current cost. However, long before GLP-1 drugs there was another very effective treatment, metabolic surgery, that insurers also successfully resisted. I mentioned this in Chapter 1, discussing an embryonic version of Life for Health designed to underwrite broader access to surgery.

What health insurers did to stifle surgery reimbursement and access is a case study in how the RPS Vortex works, suppressing treatments with higher upfront costs even if they have much better long-term returns for patients and, as we will see, insurers as well. They were too nearsighted to see that possibility, focusing instead on the simple math of how much surgery cost up front versus continuing to pay much less to manage symptoms with medications. They could not say this out loud, of course. Instead, they embarked on a three-pronged strategy, contending that frequent coverage changes (whether caused by workers or employers) prevented them from earning a return on surgery costs. Next, they created barriers to access and played to cultural biases about obesity and willpower focusing on primary care physicians (as gatekeepers to specialty care.)

Until GLP-1 drugs became widely available, about a million Americans a year expressed an interest in undergoing metabolic surgery, but actual surgeries totaled about one-fifth that level, about 200,000 per year. The standard insurer math is that if surgery costs between $20,000 and $25,000, it takes more than five years to recoup the cost in terms of lower, future medical expenses. Overall employment data seems to buttress this claim, with median tenure for workers over 25 of 4.8 years. However, people seeking metabolic surgery tend to be in their forties or older, where the median tenure ranges from five to ten years.[82] Almost half of women between 35 to 44 have job tenure more than five years, rising to 60% for women 45 to 54. Job tenure among public sector employers, including teachers, police, and firefighters, is about 70% greater than in the private sector. In short, job switching among those who get metabolic surgery is greatly overstated.

What about the problem of companies changing insurers? This, too, is a red herring. Most workers are employed at self-insured companies, where employers pay health costs directly. In these arrangements, companies, not insurers, ultimately decide which risks to cover. Given surgery candidates' longer job tenures, surgery coverage is a net positive on financial returns for self-employed insurers and public sector employers.

What about smaller companies and those that have traditional insurance coverage? Concerns about employer switching was a real issue until the ACA; however, that risk has gotten much smaller as state insurance markets have become much more concentrated. In forty states, the top three insurers have a combined 80% market share.[83] This means that insurers have about a one-in-three chance of regaining a worker who they previously covered within five years, and a 50/50 shot of covering them again within a decade.[84] This data suggests that insurers' short-termism is actually self-defeating since they are now much more likely to inherit someone later in their career when their metabolic syndrome is more advanced. If anything, insurers should be increasing access to metabolic surgery.

Even if trends in job tenure and coverage switching data were not true, insurers could have figured out a creative way to share the risk that people who undergo surgery switch to a different insurer. One way is to buy reinsurance against the risk of job or coverage switching among metabolic surgery recipients, which would represent a small percentage of all workers covered. Alternatively, health insurers could have created a risk pool to share switching risk, with companies that funded surgeries receiving some compensation from insurers who added workers. We know how financially creative insurers can be when it suits their purposes, and yet on metabolic surgery they have shown little ingenuity.

Instead, insurers have channeled their energies into limiting access, requiring potential recipients to undergo months of supervised diet plans, only to deny coverage to those who show progress losing weight.[85] Barriers to access disproportionately impact lower-income Americans, suppressing their rates of metabolic surgery despite their elevated risk of obesity and metabolic syndrome.[86] Coverage barriers exist in Medicaid, as well. States that copy private insurers' an impose onerous rules have lower surgery rates among groups with higher obesity rates, especially Black and Latino enrollees.[87]

The final battle line for insurers came down to winning the hearts and minds of the medical establishment. Does metabolic surgery work? Unlike heart bypass surgery which was embraced by the medical establishment from the outset, metabolic surgery was dismissed as a last resort, to be used sparingly and only among people with the most severe obesity. As a number of early weight loss drugs failed in clinical trials or were withdrawn from the market, metabolic surgeons focused on surgery safety and training. Realizing that the medical establishment and insurers remained skeptical, the specialty society for metabolic surgeons created a surgery outcomes database, and required members to report deidentified data about recipients' long-term results.

By 2014, longitudinal data showed that metabolic surgery was, by far, the most effective way at that point to reverse obesity and diabetes. Researchers showed that surgery recipients tended to lose 20% to 24% of their pre-surgery weight while reducing waist circumference by 15%, an important metric since abdominal fat is especially problematic for diabetes and liver disease.[88] Surgically induced weight loss coincided with sizable changes in other key, metabolic markers. Bad cholesterol (LDL) levels dropped 15% while good cholesterol (HDL) increased by 35%. Almost three-fourths of surgery recipients with diabetes were able to restore and maintain healthy blood sugar ranges for at least three years. In contrast, just 5% of those who used then-available weight loss drugs or lifestyle interventions achieved or maintained healthy blood sugar. Surgery recipients cut the average number of daily blood sugar and cardiovascular drugs from five to about two.[89]

Eight years later, an even larger study pooling data from multiple trials confirmed surgery's long-term benefits, and for the first time included participants in the non-surgery group who had taken first generation GLP-1 drugs like liraglutide to manage diabetes. Average weight loss among surgery recipients exceeded 25% and three-fourths of recipients with obesity and diabetes achieved healthy blood sugar levels.[90] Parallel studies also showed that surgery recipients had significantly lower risk of liver, colorectal, kidney, and gallbladder cancer.[91] Surgery also reduced women's breast cancer risk.[92]

In 2023, Dr. Anita Courcoulas, a top surgeon and pioneer in long-term outcomes research quantified surgery's benefits in terms of longer lifespan, calculating that surgery led to a 2.7x improvement in all-cause mortality. Much of the longevity gain was due to surgery recipients having fewer fatal heart events and diabetes-related complications.[93] The mortality gap between surgery and non-surgery recipients was evident within five years post-operation and persisted for decades. Two decades after surgery, fewer than one in ten surgery recipients had died for any reason versus one in five people with obesity who did not undergo surgery. Metabolic surgery, she and her study partners concluded, adds more than six years of lifespan.

Notwithstanding increasingly strong outcomes data, insurers realized that the road to surgery generally led through primary care physicians. Reinforcing their skepticism about surgery's benefits and recipients' ability to achieve long-term weight loss would suppress demand. A 2012 survey of primary care physicians nationwide provides a helpful baseline of attitudes towards surgery, since it was conducted before the 2014 long-term outcomes study was published. The survey found almost 60% of primary care physicians agreed with the statement that long-term weight management is impossible, and just a quarter felt strongly that they would recommend surgery to a person with advanced obesity.[94]

A decade later these doubts persisted, despite volumes of evidence about the treatment's value. In 2020, a top Chicago-area hospital system found that one-third of its primary care physicians "almost never or never" referred someone with obesity for surgery even if they thought the patient would qualify. One in five questioned whether surgery yields significant weight loss.[95] In 2022, Mayo Clinic—a leading metabolic surgery provider—found that fewer than one in ten of its own primary care doctors even talked to patients with obesity about a surgery referral, most questioning whether patients would qualify for coverage.[96]

In sum, health insurers successfully suppressed demand and access to surgery during potential recipients' working years. Their near-term gain became policyholders' long-term pain, leaving Medicare to pick up the costs of advanced disease. One of the most common downstream issues of excess weight is arthritis in hips and knees. Most joint replacement surgeries are performed on Medicare beneficiaries. Unsurprisingly, then, about two-thirds of knee replacement recipients have obesity, and these recipients have higher post-operative complication rates.[97] The net result is that there are three times as many joint replacements among Medicare recipients with obesity as there are metabolic surgeries among working-aged Americans. Instead of making metabolic surgery more accessible during prime working years, private insurers created barriers to treatment knowing that Medicare, years later, would pick up the costs of advanced multimorbidity including joint replacements.

ENDNOTES

76 RPS Vortex entities include millions of people, especially clinicians, who care very deeply about the work they do and improving Americans' health. However the system in which they work has been organized to act very differently. In many ways, the increase in clinicians retiring early or leaving practices owned by insurers or hospital groups reflects a growing desire to work for entities that actually work to realize better patient outcomes.
77 As we learned during COVID, even the way deaths are tracked varies state by state.
78 CMS. 2020. "Synthesis of Evaluation Results across 21 Medicare Models, 2012-2020" p.1
79 RAND Health Care, "Evaluation of Phase II of the Medicare Advantage Value-Based Insurance Design Model Test First Three Years of Implementation (2020–2022)." Echoing the potential for insurers to game the system, RAND found that some insurers increased prescription drug premiums in Medicare Part D plans, offsetting risk under the VBID performance metrics.
80 Abt Associates, Matthew Trombley, Sean McClellan, Andrea Hassol, Qing Zheng, Morgan Michaels, Lauren Davis, et al. 2023. "Evaluation of the Oncology Care Model Executive Summary." Abt Associates. https://www.cms.gov/priorities/innovation/data-and-reports/2023/ocm-evaluation-pp1-9-exec-sum.
81 Khodyakov, Dmitry, Christine Eibner, Erin Audrey Taylor, Rebecca Anhang Price, Christine Buttorff, Matthew Cefalu, Brian G. Vegetabile, et al. 2022. "Evaluation of Phase II of the Medicare Advantage Value-Based Insurance Design Model Test: First Two Years of Implementation (2020–2021), and Appendixes." RAND. October 19, 2022. https://www.rand.org/pubs/external_publications/EP69043.html

82 Employee Tenure in 2024, Bureau of Labor Statistics, September 26, 2024. Among those 35 to 44 years old, men have a median tenure of 4.9 years while women's tenure is 4.3 years.

83 This is market share for private-sector employers and individually-purchased plans. See Kaiser Family Foundation (KFF), "Market Share and Enrollment of Largest Three Insurers – Individual Market," 2021 data.

84 Fang H, Frean M, Sylwestrzak G, Ukert B. Trends in Disenrollment and Reenrollment Within US Commercial Health Insurance Plans, 2006-2018. JAMA Netw Open. 2022 Feb 1;5(2):e220320

85 One insurer's guidelines to describing coverage conditions runs to 150 pages. See Aetna Obesity Surgery Clinical Policy Bulletin, 4/25/2023.

86 Matthew Martin, Alec Beekley, Randy Kjorstad, James Sebesta, Socioeconomic disparities in eligibility and access to bariatric surgery: a national population-based analysis, Surgery for Obesity and Related Diseases, Volume 6(1), 8-15.

87 This was true even in states that expanded Medicaid coverage after the ACA was passed. See Hanchate AD, Qi D, Paasche-Orlow MK, et al. Examination of Elective Bariatric Surgery Rates Before and After US Affordable Care Act Medicaid Expansion. JAMA Health Forum. 2021;2(10):e213083.

88 Schauer, Philip R., Deepak L. Bhatt, John P. Kirwan, Kathy Wolski, Stacy A. Brethauer, Sankar D. Navaneethan, Ali Aminian, et al. 2014. "Bariatric Surgery Versus Intensive Medical Therapy for Diabetes — 3-Year Outcomes." New England Journal of Medicine 370 (21): 2002–13. https://doi.org/10.1056/nejmoa1401329.

89 Schauer, et.al., 2014.

90 Kirwan JP, Courcoulas AP, et. al., "Diabetes Remission in the Alliance of Randomized Trials of Medicine Versus Metabolic Surgery in Type 2 Diabetes (ARMMS-T2D)," Diabetes Care. 2022 Jul 7;45(7):1574-1583.

91 Aminian A, Wilson R, Al-Kurd A, et al. "Association of Bariatric Surgery With Cancer Risk and Mortality in Adults With Obesity." JAMA. 2022;327(24):2423–2433.

92 See, e.g. Kristensson FM, Andersson-Assarsson JC, Peltonen M, et al. Breast Cancer Risk After Bariatric Surgery and Influence of Insulin Levels: A Nonrandomized Controlled Trial. JAMA Surg. 2024;159(8):856–863; O. Lovrics, J. Butt, Y. Lee, et. al., "The effect of bariatric surgery on breast cancer incidence and characteristics: A meta-analysis and systematic review," The American Journal of Surgery, Volume 222, Issue 4, 2021:715-722; Feigelson, Heather Spencer PhD, MPH; et. al., "Bariatric Surgery is Associated With Reduced Risk of Breast Cancer in Both Premenopausal and Postmenopausal Women," Annals of Surgery 272(6):p 1053-1059, December 2020.

93 After five years, about 1% of surgery recipients had died versus 2.8% of people with obesity who did not have surgery. See Courcoulas, Anita P.; Johnson, E.; Arterburn, David E., et. al. "Reduction in Long-term Mortality After Sleeve Gastrectomy and Gastric Bypass Compared to Nonsurgical Patients With Severe Obesity." Annals of Surgery 277(3):p 442-448, March 2023. The study included data from 25,000 metabolic surgery patients and over 65,000 people with similar demographics and medical situations who did not undergo bariatric surgery.

94 Foster, Gary D., Thomas A. Wadden, Angela P. Makris, Duncan Davidson, Rebecca Swain Sanderson, David B. Allison, and Amy Kessler. 2003. "Primary Care Physicians' Attitudes About Obesity and Its Treatment." Obesity Research 11 (10): 1168–77. https://doi.org/10.1038/oby.2003.161.

95 Conaty, Eliza A., Woody Denham, Stephen P. Haggerty, John G. Linn, Raymond J. Joehl, and Michael B. Ujiki. 2019. "Primary Care Physicians' Perceptions of Bariatric Surgery and Major Barriers to Referral." Obesity Surgery 30 (2): 521–26. https://doi.org/10.1007/s11695-019-04204-9.

96 Interestingly, Mayo also asked its primary care physicians about their own weight, finding a slightly higher prevalence of obesity among their physicians than in the US population overall. Ouni, A., Khosla, A.A. & Gómez, V. Perception of Bariatric Surgery and Endoscopic Bariatric Therapies Among Primary Care Physicians. OBES SURG 32, 3384–3389 (2022).

97 A 2022 study in the Journal of Knee Surgery showed that from 2009 to 2016, knee replacements for people with obesity increased almost 80% versus just 4% for those without overweight or obesity. Individuals with obesity had longer hospital stays and higher costs, and significantly higher mortality and complication rates. See Mohamed, Nequesha S., Wayne A. Wilkie, et. al. 2020. "The Rise of Obesity Among Total Knee Arthroplasty Patients." The Journal of Knee Surgery 35 (01): 001–006. https://doi.org/10.1055/s-0040-1710566.

11. HASTENING A RECKONING

"Markets can remain irrational a lot longer than you can remain solvent."

–John Maynard Keynes

"If something cannot go on forever, it will stop."

–Herbert Stein

What will it take to force a reckoning for the RPS Vortex? Will the system continue, as Keynes cautions, much longer than we would like, or will it hit a wall? Some look to rising consumer disgust about the system epitomized by the vitriol directed against insurers after United Heath's CEO was murdered in December 2024. Others look to the political arena, including President Trump's Make America Healthy Again initiative and congressional action to curtail insurer denials and the role of PBMs.

Loss of public trust in a system is a necessary ingredient to force change, but it is seldom sufficient. Change requires new coalitions often ones uniting formerly opposed groups. It also requires the existence of a viable alternative. The tipping point happens when all three are true.

Two constituencies now pitted against each other by the RPS Vortex are in fact the two greatest sources of funding for the status quo, CEOs and CFOs of larger employers and their workers. Rising health costs have been a flashpoint between the two groups as corporate leaders raise premiums or trim benefits, but might it be possible to bring them together?

Let's start with the corporate chieftains. Since the Great Financial Crisis, large company leaders have complained about health costs but confronting insurers head-on has taken a backseat to more immediate shareholder concerns like building sales and margin, expanding globally, and beefing up internal technology and customer-facing mobile experiences. Benefits are managed by heads of human resources, who in turn rely on benefit consultants to advise on industry norms. The default mode is to try and do better than peers, but like executive compensation, indexed to peers, this creates a slow burn of rising rates. When CFOs or CEOs reject proposed cost increases, the benefit heads and consultants tweak co-pays or coverage levels, effectively shifting risk or costs onto workers. Left unchallenged is the insurers' perpetual inability to slow underlying medical dysfunctions.

The insurers were able to deflect criticism during a decade plus of near-zero interest rates and low inflation, but the world changed after COVID. Yesterday's aggravation is now a perpetual absurdity. Corporate leaders see progress on costs and outcomes in every area of their business except health costs and rightfully wonder why. Some company leaders are so exasperated that they have begun exploring whether they could get out of much of the hassle of health benefits by shifting coverage choices, and the financial risk associated with them, to workers. These plans, called Individualized Coverage Health Reimbursement Arrangements, or ICHRAs (pronounced ICK-rahs), allow companies to cap their contributions towards an employee's health care, transferring up to that amount to workers to reimburse for premiums or out-of-pocket costs. Workers can select from a menu of company-sponsored plans or craft their own.

It is an appealing idea, especially for younger and healthier workers who, in effect, subsidize health costs for older workers, who have greater chronic disease costs. For those who hold that employer-paid coverage is the original sin of American health care, ICHRAs offer a path out. They are also appealing to value-based startups providing primary or behavioral care, for example, which struggle to get included on larger insurers' preferred vendor lists. Going direct to employees as an a la carte offering is more appealing.

Two problems with ICHRAs, at least as deployed within the status quo, is that they will leave older or sicker workers more exposed, invariably increasing their out-of-pocket or premium costs. In addition, they do not alter the core problem in the status quo, the reliance on one system to address both acute and chronic issues. Workers might do better crafting their own coverage for routine and emergency needs, but without information about their long-term disease risks, will be at greater risk to manage these challenges down the road.

This will leave the leaders of larger companies in a quandary. They will find themselves in a world where younger workers are taking their dollars to shop elsewhere, meaning coverage costs for workers in the latter half of their working years will grow even faster.

For workers, the situation is equally bad. Health premiums represent, in effect, a huge stealth income tax. Whether or not employers pass higher premiums costs onto workers on a dollar-for-dollar basis, the worker is still hurt insofar as their wages grow more slowly. The net effect on earnings and savings is the same.

Health premiums now account for 18% of average annual family earnings, a level that has more than doubled as a share of income since the late 1980s.[98] In 2024, a team of health economists calculated that the health premium stealth tax amounted to $125,000 in lost earnings for the average worker from the late 1980s until 2019.[99] That is about half the average home price over the same period, a massive loss of potential future wealth.[100]

As a point of comparison, a worker at one of Henry Kaiser's shipyards paid about 4% of their weekly wage for health coverage.[101] Over the following four decades, premiums doubled as a share of income, accounting for about 8% of wages in 1988. However, this doubling coincided with a steady increase in lifespan and healthspan and a massive expansion in health care quality including life-saving surgeries and drugs. Since then, the more than doubling of premiums share of wages from 8% to 18% has coincided with flat-lining life expectancy and decreasing healthspan.[102] In other words, double the price for less value. Adding insult to injury, the health insurance wage tax is highly regressive, hitting middle and lower-income workers the hardest. In 2019, insurance premiums accounted for about 30% of compensation for families in the lowest earnings quintile versus only 4% for those in the top 5%, *a ninefold difference.*[103]

So here is the potential coalition that could hasten a reckoning—senior leaders of large employers, especially those at self-insured firms, plus their workers. There is no way for this to happen in the context of the RPS Vortex since the financial structure inevitably puts workers and managers at odds. The only way to bring their interests together is around a system that allows senior leaders and company owners to share alongside workers in better long-term health trajectories. Align everyone in a system to solve the science, and the financial benefits will naturally follow.

As for the RPS Vortex, insurers are confident that they will survive, even prosper, whatever reforms emerge. Their confidence rests on the assumption that health insurance will continue to cover all types of medicine and that in the worst case, if insurers become regulated like utilities, they will still prosper.

Good. Let them underestimate the possibility of an alternative to a unitary system. Amid the darkest days of the 2009 global financial crisis, Treasury Secretary Timothy Geithner dismissed critics of his recovery package who declined to offer one of their own by saying: "plan beats no plan." His point holds. Insurers have no real plan except self-preservation. The last thing they will expect is something that actually solves chronic disease. It may be the end of health insurance as we know it, but that's okay: *Life for Health* awaits.

ENDNOTES

98 AHRQ, STATISTICAL BRIEF #543: Trends in Health Insurance at Private Employers, 2008-2021.

99 Hager K, Emanuel E, Mozaffarian D. "Employer-Sponsored Health Insurance Premium Cost Growth and Its Association With Earnings Inequality Among US Families." JAMA Netw Open. 2024;7(1):e2351644. doi:10.1001/jamanetworkopen.2023.51644. Much of the premium increase happened in the 1990s and early 2000s as insurers adopted HMO-like practices. However, even after the ACA's passage, premiums grew 23% faster than wages.

100 The $125k in lost earnings represents the difference between what the average worker would have made had insurance premiums as a percent of compensation remained at 1988 levels versus what actually happened. Average house sales price data from St. Louis Federal Reserve Bank, "Average Sales Price of Houses Sold for the United States" data series.

101 US Department of Labor, "War and Postwar Wages, Prices, and Hours 1914-23 and 1939-44,"https://fraser.stlouisfed.org/files/docs/publications/bls/bls_0852_1946.pdf, and Kaiser Permanente, "Health care coverage for workers' families didn't come easy," January 5, 2011

102 In 1988, when insurance premiums accounted for 8% of family compensation, a 40 year old could expect to live to 82, about 6 years more than their expected lifespan at birth, or about an 8% gain in lifespan while alive. Three decades later, when insurance premiums consumed almost one-fifth of family compensation, a forty year old could expect to live to about 85, gaining just 4½ years or 3% in lifespan compared to their life expectancy at birth.

103 Hager, et.al. 2024

PART III

LIFE FOR HEALTH

12. LIFE FOR HEALTH—A ROADMAP

> "The ideal entity that puts together the disruptive value network is one whose dominant profit formula makes money by keeping us healthy, not just by making us well. It must be one whose tenure with us is long enough that it would be willing to spend more now, when necessary, in order to save even higher costs down the road. It must be a system whose participants are motivated to spend what is needed—so that neither money nor health is wasted. And it must be capable of acting with considerable speed."
>
> –Christensen et al. *The Innovator's Prescription: A Disruptive Solution for Health Care*

We turn now to realizing *Life for Health* in practice. What it is and how it works.

- Chapter 13 describes the entities in a Life for Health system, what each does, and how the structure differs from the current system.
- Chapter 14 explains the Life for Health experience from the participant's perspective. What happens after someone joins? What are participants' roles and responsibilities in the process of regaining and maintaining metabolic health? How do they work with clinicians, and how does the life insurance policy work?
- Chapter 15 paints a picture of success a decade from now. How big will Life for Health need to become, and what kind of participant outcomes will it need to generate to have a meaningful impact on multimorbidity?

- Chapter 16 turns to the trillion dollar question: how can Life for Health be established alongside health insurance? What would total spending in both systems look like over time? What would it mean practically to have two systems instead of one?
- Chapter 17 goes deeper on Life for Health's economics, explaining how revenue and risk are shared across the system. What do each of the key stakeholders—participants, employers, clinicians, and insurers—contribute, and what do they receive?
- Chapter 18 focuses on the enormous opportunity for life insurers to help solve chronic disease. How does Life for Health create new growth for life insurers and address complex risks like adverse selection in new ways?
- Chapter 19 outlines how Life for Health can be extended to Medicaid, and adapted, to ensure its benefits are available to all regardless of income.

My hope is that this progression from a birds' eye view of the system and participants' experience of it provides a tangible sense of how Life for Health works and how it differs from health insurance. With this experiential foundation, it's possible to explore the system's economics, how it can be built alongside the status quo, and how to shift existing premium revenue from health insurance to Life for Health offerings.

One way to approach Life for Health is to think about it in terms of the four-part strategy to solve chronic disease described in the Introduction. This included four key actions—*reversing* disease and *maintaining* health while *predicting* risk and *preventing* onset or progression. Part III focuses on the first two, reversing and maintaining health, using Serious Medicine. Part IV focuses on the latter two, predicting risk and preventing disease using, of course, Predictive/Preventive Medicine.

Although the four activities are explained sequentially, in practice they occur in parallel and are mutually reinforcing. Everything done to reverse disease and maintain health informs work to predict and prevent, and vice versa. Data, biosamples, and health narratives provided by participants and clinicians in "reverse" and "maintain" activities are reused (with participants' permission) to demystify disease processes, and hasten development of new treatments and predictive and preventive capabilities to use in frontline care.

The first phase, reversing metabolic syndrome, is essentially a challenge to expand access to existing medical and surgical treatments, along with dietary and behavioral counseling. There is much room to improve surgical and medical treatments, but there is very strong evidence for the efficacy of GLP-1 drugs and metabolic surgery. Improving both, over time, and developing more targeted approaches will naturally evolve from greater and more consistent use. The key is to provide these treatments as part of a larger, holistic, set of medical and non-medical services, rather than as standalone prescriptions or interventions. Treatment approaches will evolve as participants and clinicians gain data and experience. Fortunately, much of the clinical infrastructure to deliver more holistic care is starting to develop, including comprehensive weight management, women's health, and behavioral and primary care startups.

The second phase, maintaining health, is more uncertain at present than the ability to reverse disease simply because no playbook to induce long-term success has been developed given health insurers' focus on episodic care. There's no mystery about what it takes to maintain metabolic health. Eat nutritious food, exercise consistently including strength and aerobic activities, get seven or more hours of sleep daily, and limit inflammation and stress. Reality is much messier given work and home life demands, people's financial resources, environmental impacts, and fluctuating motivation. Concierge medicine and subscription-based longevity products are fine for the well-to-do but remain out of reach, financially and practically, to most middle income and poorer Americans.

Life for Health's contribution is an economic and clinical framework to democratize access and increase the likelihood of a person's motivation over time. Here too, as in upfront treatment, consistent data gathering and sharing about which approaches work (or fail) in which situations will help clinicians match and mix interventions over time as participants' situations and outcomes evolve.

Built into *Life for Health* is a recognition that participants' results will vary widely, both across the participant population and on an individual level at different points in time. This is to be expected given all that we know about how engagement and motivation fluctuates. The key to counteracting this in Life for Health begins with the quality of the participant-clinician relationship, and beyond that, opportunities for participants to join or form communities to help each other stay on track or rebound from setbacks without shame.

These relationships will require a new kind of clinician, part physician, part counselor, part coach and teacher, and part scientist. Many clinicians approach their work with this mindset or aspire to do so but for the RPS Vortex's rules. Life for Health offers clinicians an alternative to the status quo, along with the kind of longitudinal data to recognize and reward highly effective practitioners. Life for Health is an opportunity for clinicians who entered medicine to solve disease and help people thrive to realize those ideals in practice.

In sum, Life for Health translates the first principles enumerated in Chapter 2 into practice: using scientific needs to inform longer-term financial structures; rewarding earlier, more decisive interventions; making long-term outcomes the measuring stick to quantify and apportion value over time; and centering clinicians' role and compensation around participants' needs.

13. LIFE FOR HEALTH STRUCTURE AND ENTITIES

"The inevitability of medical uncertainty, to me, is a clarion call to fight all other kinds of uncertainty within health care. That means naming and defining fragmentation as the central issue it is. Making this distinction matters so deeply because fragmentation ... is not a by-product of the complicated nature of human beings. It is by design, it is a product of choices, and it can be changed."

–Dr. Ilana Yurkiewicz, *Fragmented: A Doctor's Quest to Piece Together American Health Care*

Structural Overview

The key entities in a Life for Health system are illustrated in Figure 13.1.

Figure 13.1: Key Entities in Life for Health System

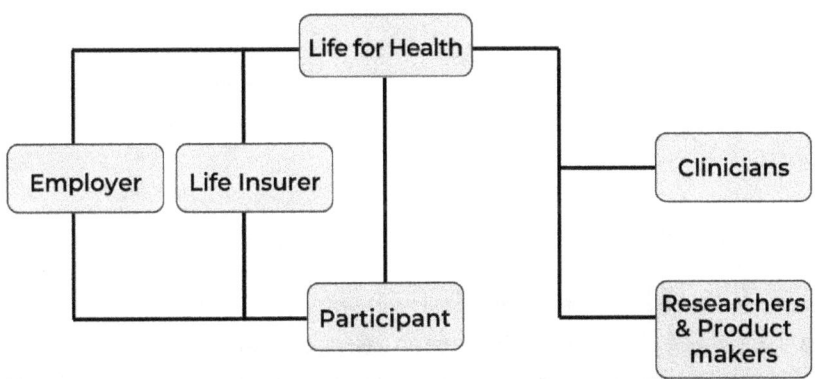

Most of the names are familiar. Individuals or employees are recast as participants. The biggest difference is that the health insurer's role is split between two entities, a life insurer and a Life for Health entity. What's this about?

The central goal of Life for Health's structure is to share the risks and value of realizing better health outcomes over time. Initially, most of the risks are held by entities that underwrite disease reversal, primarily life insurers, employers, and the Life for Health entity. Gradually, risk shifts to clinicians and participants, the entities that are primarily responsible to maintain and prevent health. Outcomes are improved in all periods by researchers and product makers who provide data, insights, and new interventions to improve the efficacy of predictive, preventive, and treatment interventions. Therefore, each entity contributes to the system's finances and shares in its results (for better or for worse) in proportion to the risks they assume and manage.

In today's world, health insurers, often part of larger health conglomerates, occupy a dual role. They assume year-to-year financial risk for total health care utilization and cost in addition to managing the clinician network and the terms under which services or treatments are provided. This combinatorial role works for routine and emergency issues where usage and costs are predictable but falls apart in dealing with chronic issues. There is no incentive to manage long-term health risks, to trade off greater near-term investments to realize larger long-term returns. In addition, there is an inherent conflict of interest in being on both sides of the health market, being able to both set revenue coming into the system and control usage and expenses through policies like prior authorization. The system is optimized for the insurers' risks and returns, not participants.

In Life for Health, questions of financial risk are flipped. The system optimizes for long-term outcomes over near-term returns, an actuarial and risk management challenge for which life insurers are especially well-suited. A Life for Health entity then takes on health insurers' second function, overseeing the network of clinicians and services provided to reverse and prevent disease, and maintain long-term health. Critically, however, the *way* this network is built and operated is centered around participant outcomes, rather than intricate oversight of day-to-day clinical decision-making. Thus, the Life for Health entity, clinicians, and participants are aligned around doing as much or as little as possible at any given point to increase healthspan, emphasizing the likelihood of a good outcome over the nature of a particular input/intervention.

Expectations for health improvements are set using periodically updated health outcomes goals, and participants' success in achieving these are rewarded through health outcomes payments. The life insurance policy provides the long-term framework and connective tissue among insurers, the Life for Health entity, and participants, with Health Outcomes Payments earned by participants deposited into the life insurance policy's savings account where it grows on a tax-deferred basis.

Initially, Life for Health will only be eligible to people with one or more metabolic dysfunctions like obesity or diabetes, who have progressed to metabolic syndrome, or who have a significant genetic risk of developing metabolic issues. Over time, Life for Health eligibility will expand to include chronic respiratory, autoimmune, and behavioral conditions. In addition, as part of Life for Health's mission to improve healthspan, all participants have access to screening, diagnostics, and treatment for high-stakes issues including reproductive health, cancer, and neurodegenerative issues.

Now, let's take a closer look at each of the entity's roles.

Participants join Life for Health as individuals. They agree to receive treatment for metabolic issues from Life for Health-affiliated clinicians and buy a life insurance policy issued by a top-rated insurer affiliated with Life for Health. Participants join Life for Health through an employer-sponsored arrangement or directly, just as they can purchase health or life insurance through their workplace or directly.

The term "participant" is used purposefully, rather than words like customer or policyholder. Life for Health participants join with the understanding that they will have an active role in improving their health situation, including undergoing extensive diagnostics and treatment, making treatment choices with their clinicians, setting health goals, and sharing in the results. Life for Health is not just another diet plan or wellness benefit.

As with any health-related issue, participants are not obligated to undergo any particular treatment. However, coverage terms are structured with the expectation that participants are motivated to reverse disease and maintain their health. Participants who meet health goals earn payments. Conversely, participants who are consistently unable to achieve health goals, despite changes in treatment approaches, and absent extenuating circumstances like a medical crisis, are subject to pay more for coverage.

The **Life for Health entity** is responsible for helping participants regain and maintain metabolic health. It oversees each participant's intervention plan and assesses participants' progress. Life for Health personnel create and manage the alliance of clinicians, counselors, dieticians, and therapists who agree to work with each other on participants' behalf. They also ensure that participants understand and agree to treatment plans, desired outcomes, and any attendant treatment risks.

Each participant's plan and progress is overseen by a Clinician in Charge, employed by or contracted to the Life for Health entity. This clinician is responsible for the participants' experiences and outcomes, including setting and revising treatment plans and ensuring participants have access to Serious and Predictive/Preventive Medicine that they need. The Clinician in Charge also confirms that the participant and members of their treatment team know what is being done, why, and to what ends. They are ultimately accountable for Life for Health's and participants' success.

The Life for Health entity also collects and manages participants' longitudinal health data for use within the system and (with participants' consent) externally as part of datasets licensed to vetted researchers and product developers. Importantly, participants who opt to share their data are compensated for doing so, sharing in data licensing and product royalties received by the Life for Health entity. (Data gathering and use is discussed at length in Part IV).

Clinicians include medical and non-medical practitioners who provide diagnostics, treatments, or counseling to participants. In affiliating with Life for Health entities, clinicians agree to share participant data with anyone else on the treatment team regardless of whether they work for the same entity. Some portion of clinicians' compensation—or that of their practice—is tied to participant outcomes.

Life for Health represents an alternative path outside the RPS Vortex for disruptive health startups to achieve commercial success. Life for Health will be able to grow more rapidly by incorporating and integrating services from health startups focused on particular issues such as metabolic, women's health, or behavioral issues.

Life Insurers issue universal life policies to participants, either as individual policies or as part of a group life arrangement. They help underwrite investments to restore metabolic health and maintain a better health trajectory. Insurers earn a return through premium revenue and fees to manage policyholders' savings. Premiums are paid by participants (in individual arrangements) or employer sponsors (in group life settings). Insurers invest and manage policyholders' savings as they would for any other life policy with a capital accumulation feature.

Employers offer Life for Health as a benefit combining chronic disease treatment and prevention coverage along with a group universal life policy. Initially, eligibility would be limited to employees who have some form of chronic metabolic disease including cardiovascular disease, diabetes, or obesity, or those who have a genetic predisposition to develop metabolic conditions. Workers who qualify for Life for Health are not required to join and could continue to be covered under traditional health insurance arrangements.

Employers help finance Life for Health by shifting a portion of funds now spent through self-insured or traditional health insurance arrangements over to cover metabolic health treatments provided through Life for Health plus group life premiums. Employers benefit from Life for Health by sharing in a portion of savings generated by workers' lower, future medical costs.

Life for Health will be especially appealing to companies that self-insure, which now employ about two-thirds of US private-sector workers. These entities will be able to realize the benefits of lower health spending on workers (after the initial disease reversal investment) very quickly, improving these firms' competitiveness and attractiveness to future hires. Life for Health approaches will also be valuable to state and local public employers, especially school districts, which have longer-tenured workforces. Chapter 17 includes a detailed discussion of Life for Health's economics and the benefits to employers.

Separating Life Insurers from Treatment Decisions

Life for Health's key structural innovation is to separate the insurer, in this case the life insurer, from overseeing treatment planning and decision-making. This is done for both practical and conceptual reasons.

On the practical front, life insurers operate under different statutes and regulations than health insurers. Life insurers have some rights and responsibilities that health insurers do not, and vice versa. A key difference is that life insurers are not allowed to have information about policyholders' health situations after a policy is issued, except in very limited circumstances. Life insurers have a lot of leeway to determine a policy applicant's health status *before the policy is issued* but not afterwards.[104] That's why life insurers ask detailed questionnaires about applicants' health and credit histories, often requiring a blood draw or in-person physical exam. Obviously, this standard is problematic in Life for Health if life insurers are involved in participants' post-underwriting treatment decisions or have access to health data on an identifiable basis. Moving these responsibilities to the Life for Health entity solves this regulatory issue.

The second practical issue is that many life insurers look at the health insurance industry with a skeptical eye, concluding thanks, but no thanks! They want no part of the nitty gritty of health insurance, like contracting with clinicians and overseeing treatment decisions. That is far outside of life insurers' core competencies. Thus, Life for Health's structure lets life insurers focus on what they do best—pricing long-term risks and managing policyholder savings—while Life for Health entities oversee improvements in participant/policyholders' health trajectories.

Another reason to keep either life insurers or Life for Health entities from being treated as health insurers is that under the ACA, traditional health insurers are subject to an annual calculation called the Medical Loss Ratio (MLR). It requires insurers to spend at least 80% of premiums on treatment. It was intended to make sure that premium dollars were not being wasted by insurers on administrative costs or siphoned into non-treatment activities. Once again, the MLR is a classic example of a measure that reinforces short-term focus, encouraging insurers to conduct care planning and measure treatment ROI over annual windows. In this sense, the MLR is antithetical to everything that Life for Health is intended to do.

A natural question at this point is, how can life insurers, holding some of the risk of long-term outcomes, be certain that Life for Health entities and clinicians are making good clinical and financial decisions? This is where the alignment among insurers, Life for Health entities, and participants, expressed through the setting of health goals and continuous measurement, pays off. Life for Health and life insurers have, in effect, a shared equity stake in participants' success. Life for Health entities only make money as participants' health improves and spending over time goes down. The value is less about results in any one year but rather in the consistency of health gains relative to what they would have been absent disease reversal or preventive measures. Life insurers will have a real-time read on how well Life for Health entities (and clinicians and participants) are doing by looking at health outcomes goals and the degree to which participants (in aggregate) are meeting them. Goals that are too lenient are bad for Life for Health entities since it means potential health improvements (and savings) are going unrealized. Goals that are too stringent are also sub-optimal since participants who consistently fail to earn outcomes payments may leave Life for Health. Maintaining a balance in setting goals, interventions, and payments provides the optimal glidepath in terms of healthspan improvement and financial returns for everyone.

Life insurers' ability to see de-identified health outcome goals and results eliminates the need for them to oversee the treatments offered through Life for Health or micromanage clinicians through processes like prior authorization. Both Life for Health entities and life insurers will be able to see how much participant outcomes are improving and the predictability of outcomes over time. Which segments are consistently able to regain metabolic health within two years versus three years? Which interventions are most effective working with which participants or situations? Everyone is aligned to reduce the variability of outcomes for similarly situated participants, providing insurers, employers, and participants greater confidence about Life for Health's efficacy.

The Boundary Between Life for Health and Health Insurance

Separating Serious and Predictive/Preventive Medicine from Routine and Emergency/Elective requires clarity for participants and employers about which aspects of health treatment and prevention are covered under Life for Health versus health insurance. Speaking in the language of the status quo, Life for Health will cover treatment of all aspects of metabolic syndrome including diagnosed conditions like obesity, diabetes, or cardiovascular, liver, or kidney disease. Treatments covered include diagnostic testing and monitoring devices or apps; dietary, behavioral, or therapeutic counseling; and pharmaceutical or surgical interventions.

However, a person does not need to be diagnosed with a particular condition to qualify for Life for Health. Eligibility is based on objective metrics of metabolic function such as waist circumference or blood pressure, blood sugar, lipid, and lipoprotein levels, rather than pre-existing diagnoses. Eligibility standards will evolve as our understanding of disease risk improves. Future metrics might use new or better measurements of fat composition or deposition, lipoprotein levels, polygenic risk scores, inflammation levels, or other biomarkers that prove to be reliable indicators of future metabolic health risk.

Having established Life for Health's eligibility criteria and scope, health insurers next concern will be to define who pays for what? One way is to apply health insurers' existing value hierarchy, defining financial responsibility based on the locus of care and the types of clinicians involved. By this standard, health insurers would be responsible for treatments or hospitalizations associated with emergencies while non-emergency issues associated with metabolic health are paid by Life for Health, including treatment in a hospital or surgery center.

For example, if a Life for Health participant has a heart attack, treatments provided from the moment of cardiac arrest until the person is discharged from the hospital would be covered by health insurance since these procedures fall within Emergency/Elective Medicine. Life for Health's payment responsibility resumes once the participant is discharged from inpatient care.

However, Life for Health is on the hook if a surgery or hospitalization is undertaken as part of the person's treatment plan or as a proactive measure, for example, metabolic surgery or plastic surgery to remove excess skin after weight loss. Today, skin removal surgery, for example might be seen as an elective procedure, but in the context of achieving metabolic health should be viewed as a natural follow-on to success in reversing obesity, validating the participant's success and motivating them to maintain progress.

A final area of overlap may occur when a clinician is contracted to a traditional health insurer as well as Life for Health, and treats the same individual in each system. This seems like an unlikely event, but should it occur, payment responsibility will follow treatment intent, as determined by the Clinician in Charge. If treatment is provided to improve or maintain metabolic health, payment responsibility resides with Life for Health not traditional health insurance.

ENDNOTES

104 An exception to this is when a life insurance policy includes a rider, or feature, allowing the policyholder to withdraw some of their cash balance or take a loan against it, or receive an advance against their death benefit if they are diagnosed with cancer or are deemed to have a terminal illness. In these cases, life insurers require a physician's certification or access to diagnostic information to prove that a triggering event allowing an advanced withdrawal or loan is warranted.

14. THE PARTICIPANT'S EXPERIENCE

> "The doctor isn't seeing you to collect data—he or she is seeing you to talk to you. The best doctors will act as health coaches and sleuths. They will work with you to help you feel better, or be more productive, or maybe just play better tennis. If something is wrong, they will have the time to dig deep and diagnose it … Based on your data, the doctor can help formulate a plan, and set up data-driven goals so you will know if you're staying on track. The doctor becomes the human in the middle as your online data meets your offline physical and mental status."
>
> –Hemant Taneja, Stephen Klasko, & Kevin Maney, *UnHealthcare: A Manifesto for Health Assurance*

We turn now from the structural to the individual, exploring Life for Health from the participant's perspective.

Meet Frank. He is 42, married with two children. He is 5'8" and has obesity and diabetes. He played football through middle and high school, but now weighs 265 pounds. He has a BMI just over 40 and a waist circumference of 41 inches.[105] He was diagnosed with diabetes at 36 and has high blood pressure and elevated levels of bad cholesterol and triglycerides. He takes a statin, a high blood pressure medication, and two medications to control blood sugar.

Frank applies to join Life for Health through an employer-sponsored program and has discussions with Life for Health personnel to understand the program, its benefits and requirements. He receives information about the life insurance policy and how Life for Health coverage works alongside his existing health insurance. Upon becoming a participant,

Frank is matched with a clinician to develop an initial treatment plan. This includes a review of his health history and goals, a physical exam, whole genome sequencing, and relevant blood panels. His metabolic health assessment includes a DEXA scan (or equivalent) to assess his body composition and distribution of fatty tissue. All this diagnostic data is used by Frank and his Clinician in Charge to determine the initial set of interventions to restore metabolic health. Initial conversations also assess participants' motivations to achieve a better health trajectory, and ensure participants are comfortable with the requirements and trade-offs of the initial approach.

The initial treatment plan may include medication, surgery, or a combination of approaches. Frank might choose to go onto a GLP-1 therapy, working with an obesity medicine specialist to initiate therapy and adjusting dosage or medication based on response, along with nutritional, behavioral, and exercise counseling. Alternatively, he might decide to undergo metabolic surgery, which would be performed by an experienced board-certified surgeon affiliated with Life for Health, including travel and accommodations, if needed.

During treatment, Frank receives apps or tools such as a continuous glucose monitor to help track key metrics and capture daily life events or reflections on how he is feeling. Life for Health requires and facilitates data interoperability between proprietary apps or devices to ensure all clinicians and the participant have a consolidated view of their situation and progress.

After starting treatment, Frank undergoes regular virtual or in-person checkups, including blood draws or other diagnostics, as necessary. Check-in frequency is adjusted based on how well he is doing but is frequent enough to review or adjust treatments. Readings are taken at least quarterly during the disease reversal stage to ensure consistent gathering of longitudinal data.

A key part of Life for Health is the process of setting health outcome goals and assessing progress. These goals impact treatment choices and the value of health outcome payments. This sets up a helpful dynamic balancing the magnitude and speed of potential gains. Everyone wants progress as quickly as possible, but gains must be reasonably achievable. It does no long-term good to chart a course of aggressive weight loss if it will increase the odds of other nutritional or health deficits. However, if goals are too modest, the health and financial gains for participants (and clinicians) will be smaller. Over time, Life for Health clinicians will have access to treatment recommendations from similarly situated individuals to help chart pathways for participants to regain and maintain metabolic health.

Life for Health participants share in the value of improved health by receiving Health Outcome Payments based on their achievement of health goals. The potential value of future payments could be set when participants join based on their age and metabolic health situation. Participants would begin to receive payments once they achieve initial milestones to reverse disease with payouts increasing over time based on the participant's consistency in maintaining metabolic health. Participants who achieve and maintain metabolic health might receive $2,000 a year or more during their first decade in Life for Health, with partial payments awarded if they achieve some, but not all, goals.

Participants might also be required to pay higher premiums if they consistently fail to achieve health goals (excluding, of course, if their failure is due to a situation outside their control such as a traumatic health event). Potential premium increases and the conditions under which they would apply would be fixed, and acknowledged by the participant, when the policy begins. This mechanism reinforces the seriousness of the shared undertaking among insurers, participants, and Life for Health, and helps motivate participants to follow through on their commitments to do their part. Life for Health entities will be responsible for determining if participants meet health goals and calculating health outcome payments, not life insurers.

Throughout his time in Life for Health, Frank is surrounded by concentric circles of guidance and support. At each stage of the path to restoring health, clinicians ensure he understands the goals and desired outcomes of treatment. In addition, Frank will have access to insights from participants who are farther along the treatment journey about medical and "living with" questions.

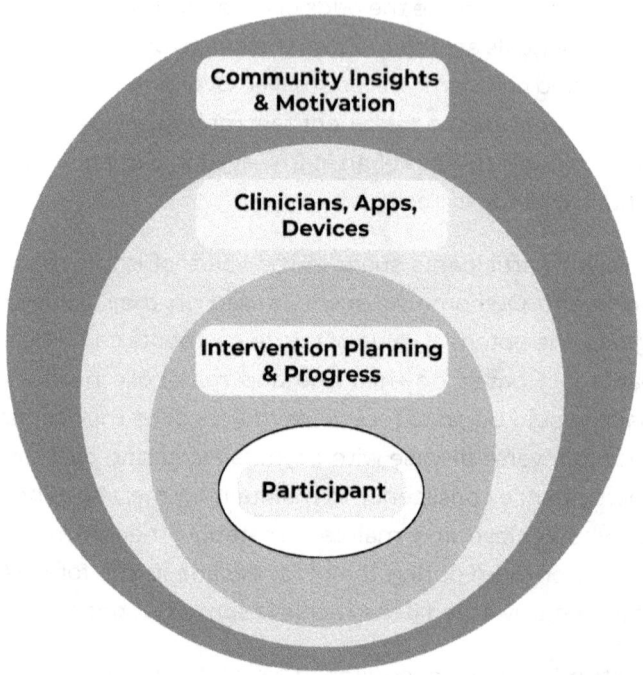

In many ways, the participant's relationship with their Clinician in Charge is akin to developing a retirement financial plan, including periodic discussions about a participants' goals over different time frames and their risk appetite. Tactical choices about treatments and preventive measures are then made in the context of the larger plan, with health goals and treatment choices visible to all clinicians involved in the participant's care.

Once a person regains metabolic health, the focus shifts to maintaining a better health trajectory. Although success in the initial phase establishes a pattern of goal setting, assessment, and continuous improvement, the key challenge going forward is maintaining engagement and motivation. Successful clinicians will help participants stay focused on the tangible and intangible benefits of improved health, reinforcing their sense of self-efficacy, and understanding about which interventions work better for them and why. Financial rewards in the form of health outcome payments provide additional motivation and reinforcement.

Clinicians will need to be attuned to how participants' needs, goals, and motivations change over time, and develop expertise in crafting health goals in tangible but non-medical terms. A participant's desire to "look good" for a family event, to join a pickleball league, to have the stamina for a ski trip, or to run a 10k—all of these can be powerful goalposts to drive healthy behavior. Assessment of health status will always use validated biometric or diagnostic standards, but often the drive to get there will come from something more tangible. Here, too, longitudinal data and participant feedback will be important to uncover which supports (such as community) or goals are most effective in maintaining good habits and motivation. Grit, of a kind, for life.

The Life Insurance Policy

Upon joining Life for Health, participants receive a universal life insurance policy providing standard mortality coverage, with a fixed payout if the participant dies, plus coverage of treatments associated with metabolic health. Life for Health policies also provide coverage for cancer detection and treatment, genetic counseling, and other predictive diagnostics suggested as a result of the participants' initial exam or subsequent medical events. Some coverages may be structured as a primary benefit, accessible directly, or as backup coverage to existing health insurance, in which case the participant could access coverage through Life for Health if a diagnostic or treatment is denied by their health insurer.

As a universal life policy, participants can pay in amounts above premiums to build up savings to be invested by the life insurer, with gains accumulating on a tax-deferred basis. Health outcome payments earned by participants would be treated similarly, adding to the policy's cash balance.

Participants could receive life insurance as part of a group life plan sponsored by their employer, or join directly, as an individual. In a group life arrangement, employers offer Life for Health along with a group life policy. Coverage levels would increase from the current standard of $50,000 to $250,000 or more, enabling insurers to collect a sufficient premium for coverage. In a group life arrangement, employers would exclude metabolic health treatments from existing health insurance benefits, shifting a commensurate portion of employer and employee premiums to cover costs incurred under Life for Health. (This issue is discussed at greater length in Chapters 16 and 17).

Moving premium dollars from health insurance to Life for Health is more straightforward for self-insured employers since these firms already reserve funds and pay directly for workers' health costs directly. However, even companies that are fully insured, where health insurers take on the risk of actual costs, could make this switch by carving metabolic health costs out of existing insurance arrangements. This will reduce health insurance premiums, freeing up funds to cover Life for Health costs and group life premiums.[106] Workers who change employers could convert group life coverage into an individual plan if their new employer does not offer Life for Health.

In the direct purchase case, participants who join Life for Health would pay premiums directly to Life for Health, covering both metabolic health treatments and the life insurance policy. Individuals joining Life for Health directly might need to purchase a high-deductible health insurance plan to free up premium dollars to offset Life for Health costs. Alternatively, Life for Health entities could work with health insurers to offer a bundle of traditional health insurance and Life for Health, with the latter covering metabolic issues and cancer treatment.

Systemic Accountability, Fragmentation, and the Clinician in Charge

A 2023 Johns Hopkins study examined the medicine cabinets of people with obesity.[107] Half of the people diagnosed with both obesity and diabetes were taking one or more prescription drugs that had a side effect of reducing weight, which is good. Unfortunately, three-fourths of those with both conditions also responded that they were taking one or more medications that *increase* weight.

This dilemma is emblematic of what happens when people with multimorbidity are treated by multiple physicians, each trying to reduce symptoms associated with their area of expertise; however, none of the physicians involved has a holistic view of the person's treatment plan or responsibility for their overall outcome. In 2020, the Chief Medical Officers of England, Scotland, and Northern Ireland issued a statement singling out disease-specific approaches as a systemic problem in medical training and practice:[108]

> "Treating each disease in a patient as if it exists in isolation will lead to less good outcomes and complicate and duplicate interactions with the healthcare system. Training from medical school onwards, clinical teams, and clinical guidelines, however, all tend to be organized along single disease or single organ lines. As a result, a single patient may take multiple drugs recommended by different guidelines and see several specialists treating subcomponents of their overall health problem in isolation ... Good vertical integration exists from bench to bedside for a single condition or disease, but there is little or no horizontal integration between diseases that often coexist."

Dr. Ilana Yurkiewicz, an oncologist at Stanford University Hospital, spotlighted this problem in her book *Fragmented*. Although she had control over her patients' cancer treatments, she had little ability to understand or manage other aspects of her patients' care. Often, she would have to contact other specialists managing a patient's diabetes or kidney issues to coordinate treatment or to get context on the patient's situation absent from their electronic record. The time and energy required was exhausting and meant no one had a complete handle or authority over the patient's care. Fragmentation, Yurkiewicz concluded, is "the single greatest problem underlying American health care ... [the] fallout is an incalculable and compounding cascade of problems throughout the entire health care system."[109] She is not alone. There is growing consensus among physicians about the threat of fragmentation, although there is little agreement about what to do.

Service industries outside of health adapt their organizational design and performance indicators to resolve issues of shared responsibility. Some prefer functional organizations that group teams by expertise (like marketing or engineering) but require interdisciplinary teams drawing on representatives from each area. Others use a general management structure in which an interdisciplinary effort is overseen by a generalist, who is also responsible for the overall result. Either way, the common thread is that there is a shared bottom line and an executive who is ultimately responsible for the team's results.

Health care poses a few unique challenges. The recipient of health services are people, human beings, not a product or a piece of software. Human factors are at play in the clinician-participant dynamic, in terms of how well a recommended course of action is explained and received. Human factors are also at work in the interplay among clinicians. A tacit bargain among medical professions is to defer to each other's area of specialty, and to expect the same courtesy in return. Finally, no one on the clinical care team is tied to the aggregate long-term consequences of present-day treatment decisions. As a result, fragmentation defeats efforts to solve chronic disease.

Life for Health's solution is the Clinician in Charge role. It requires that a single physician—whatever their specialty—has ultimate authority and responsibility for a participant's treatment plan. That means they have the power to order changes in treatment (within clinical guidelines) even if that countermands the recommendation of a specialist with greater expertise. The goal is to root out duplication or offsetting treatments, and align clinicians around helping participants achieve health outcome goals. Clinicians in Charge hold everyone on the treatment team accountable for sharing information and context that others may need (now or in the future) and ensure there is a clear narrative about what decisions were made and why, even if the outcome is not as desired. The Clinician in Charge is also responsible for discussing progress with participants and adjusting treatment plans with them. The responsibility and authority vested in a Clinician in Charge is qualitatively different than that given to hospitalists or care coordinators. They are in charge in every sense of that term, backed up in Life for Health by institutional and financial frameworks that makes genuine ownership of results possible.

ENDNOTES

105 BMI is a problematic measure of metabolic health for many reasons. A very muscular person might have high BMI but still be healthy. Conversely, a person may have a low BMI and be metabolically unhealthy. BMI thresholds for obesity also vary by background and ethnicity. It also does not capture issues of fat composition or distribution. I include BMI here to describe Frank's situation since it is so widely used by insurers to qualify for metabolic syndrome treatments.

106 Companies that create ICHRAs could also deem that medical costs incurred through a Life for Health plan qualify for reimbursement as an out-of-pocket expense.

107 Almazan E, Schwartz JL, Gudzune KA. Use of medications associated with weight change among participants in the All of Us research programme. Clin Obes. 2023 Oct;13(5):e12609. doi: 10.1111/cob.12609. Epub 2023 Jul 16. PMID: 37455380; PMCID: PMC10528729.

108 Whitty C J M, MacEwen C, Goddard A, Alderson D, Marshall M, Calderwood C et al. Rising to the challenge of multimorbidity BMJ 2020; 368 :l6964

109 Yurkiewicz, Ilana, Fragmented: A Doctor's Quest to Piece Together American Health Care, 2023.

15. ENVISIONING SUCCESS

> "Done correctly the working backwards process is a huge amount of work but it saves you even more work later."
>
> –Jeff Bezos

Having described Life for Health structurally and in terms of the participant experience, let's connect these perspectives by exploring what it would mean for Life for Health to succeed as an enterprise.

Chapter 3 established that the best way to increase healthspan and cut spending is to end multimorbidity. We quantified the opportunity in terms of societal benefits in the $15 trillion range, with potential annual health savings of 25% to 50%. So how will we know if Life for Health enterprises, in aggregate, are on a path to having meaningful impact? How many people must join Life for Health entities? What must their outcomes look like and over what time frame to have confidence that it is working?

Working backwards is a process popularized by Amazon Founder Jeff Bezos and his management team to help product development teams test assumptions about how well new products or services meet customer needs.[110] A key step is to write a mock press release announcing the new offering. Product teams scrutinize this draft making multiple rounds of changes to develop the sharpest, most distilled set of features, differentiators, and value propositions. Then, the team works backwards to identify design, production, and service level requirements.

I decided to do a working backwards exercise for Life for Health but instead of writing a new product announcement, I wanted to focus on questions of impact listed above, and define the levels of growth and outcomes Life for Health enterprises would need to achieve to impact multimorbidity prevalence. Following is the draft press release:

Life for Health Surpasses Twelve Million Participants
90% regain metabolic health within two years;
75% maintain it a decade later, generating $300 billion in medical savings

Houston, TX and Atlanta, GA—Life for Health Inc., a pioneer in efforts to solve chronic disease, announced that it has surpassed twelve million participants, equivalent to the third-largest health insurer by enrollment in the US. Long-term outcomes data published this month in the New England Journal of Medicine by an independent team of researchers from leading research universities showed that 90% of participants with metabolic syndrome regain normal metabolic function within two years of joining. Three-fourths of individuals who have been Life for Health participants for a decade or more achieved diabetes and obesity remission within 30 months of beginning treatment and have continued to maintain metabolic health for a majority of the their time in Life for Health.

Metabolic health is defined by Life for Health as having met no more than one of the diagnostic criteria for metabolic syndrome, which includes abdominal obesity as measured by waist circumference, triglyceride levels greater than 150 mg/dl, low HDL cholesterol, blood pressure above 130/85 or taking high blood pressure medication, or fasting glucose above 100 mg/do or taking blood glucose medication.

Metabolic syndrome prevalence among individuals with a Life for Health tenure of at least five years decreased from 50% at the time of joining Life for Health to 15% at the end of the period. The median age of metabolic syndrome onset or relapse among participants with a Life for Health tenure greater than five years increased from 54.2 years to 62.2 years.

Life for Health participants and their employers have realized **$300 billion** in direct medical savings over the last decade compared to spending on a matched sample of comparable individuals. Life for Health participants have received **$30 billion** in outcomes-related payments from Life for Health plans as a result of their success in restoring and maintaining their metabolic health.

"It has been transformative for everyone in the energy industry," said Jane Doe, CEO of Big Energy Corporation, one of the largest integrated energy producers in the US. "Team members have seen dramatic improvements in their health situations, gains that have translated into higher take-home pay, much lower medical spending, and a healthier, more loyal workforce. The results have exceeded all of our expectations."

According to a companion study in the New England Journal of Medicine by leading insurer actuaries, Life for Health participants' improved health status should save $1.5 trillion in medical expenses between now and participants' entry into Medicare. Medicare's future savings are estimated to total between $1.5 and $2 trillion compared to what it would have spent had Life for Health participants entered Medicare with metabolic syndrome.

To date, Life for Health participants have contributed over 30 billion actionable health data points integrating voluntarily-provided information from personal health trackers and data from almost 350 million daily recordings, 100 million medical checkups, and 50 million genomic and blood panel tests.

"Life for Health data and participants helped us design the first long-acting continuous metabolic health device integrating continuous blood metabolite monitoring (including blood glucose and cholesterol levels) and infusion of long-acting medications to manage cardiovascular, insulin, and inflammatory factors," said Dr. John Doe, Chief Medical Officer of Evangelyx Corp. "We were able to validate efficacy three years faster by accessing data from Life for Health participants. Pre-qualifying Life for Health participants for late-stage clinical trials of new treatments has reduced total time to market by a year and saved 25% of trial costs."

About Life for Health

Life for Health is the leading provider of treatment and financial services to solve chronic disease. It partners with top life insurers to underwrite group and individual universal life policies, funding interventions to restore and maintain participants' health, increase healthspan, and reduce health costs. Life for Health participants receive ongoing predictive risk and preventive health treatments and have guaranteed access to cancer treatment at NCI Cancer Centers. Life for Health has established landmark outcomes-based pricing arrangements for key medications and treatments, including GLP-1 treatments, lowering the up-front cost to restore metabolic health by 50%.

Measuring Impact

So what would results like these mean in terms of multimorbidity, and why emphasize these metrics? The headline summarizes the key takeaways about impact and value, underscoring the importance of attracting and retaining a large number of participants, demonstrating success at reversing disease, and translating improved health trajectories into lower costs. This chapter focuses on the first two questions. We will return to cost savings in Chapter 17.

The first question is how many participants must Life for Health offerings attract to have real impact? There are about ninety-three million Americans between 35 and 64 years old who have private health coverage. If about 60% of these people have some stage of metabolic syndrome, Life for Health, with twelve million participants, would have a 20% market share of privately-insured working age Americans with metabolic syndrome. That would be roughly equivalent to the number of similarly situated Americans covered by each of the two largest private health insurers. That would be meaningful scale, and a strong indicator of product-market fit and value.

Switching to outcomes, Life for Health's initial success will depend on its ability to help a very high percentage of participants regain metabolic health, and to provide an increasingly predictable time frame for this to happen. A 90% success rate within two years sounds aggressive;

however, it is in line with long-term studies of metabolic surgery outcomes showing that three-fourths of surgery recipients achieve obesity and diabetes remission within a couple of years. Longer-term trials of GLP-1 drugs, in which participants receive intensive medical and non-medical supports, shows a similar trend. More than 90% of people in a tirzepatide clinical trial achieved normal blood sugar ranges in addition to significant weight loss.[111]

The next question is whether initial gains can be maintained long term. As mentioned earlier, this is the most uncertain part of Life for Health's mission as startups providing holistic weight, diabetes, and metabolic care begin to scale. However, here too, long-term remission data is a helpful guide. Helping 75% of participants maintain metabolic heath for at least half a decade is eminently possible, and the kind of consistency that Life for Health approaches will have to achieve to result in the multimorbidity reductions outlined in Chapter 3. A central proposition of Life for Health to be validated in practice is that the combination of financial, structural, and long-term incentives will drive better clinical practice and participant engagement.

The final set of outcomes—the percent of participants with multimorbidity, and the median age of multimorbidity onset or relapse—returns to the key big picture metrics described in Chapter 2 to assess overall progress against multimorbidity. Specifically, is Life for Health improving the composition of the chronic disease cascade, and if so, by how much? Thus, the release includes a statistic reporting a reduction in multimorbidity prevalence among participants of five or more years from 50% to 15%. This success is also captured by the eight-year increase in the age of metabolic syndrome onset or recurrence, from a median age of 54 for participants when they joined to 62 after five years. To achieve this, Life for Health would have had to keep a majority of people with metabolic syndrome upon joining from relapsing, along with a majority of people who did not yet have full-blown metabolic syndrome from progressing to having it. In other words, Life for Health would have to succeed in helping participants at both ends of the chronic disease cascade.

The press release also underscores the importance of changing the language and rigor with which the health care system's results are discussed. Real improvements require entities intent on ending chronic disease to provide transparent, audited data about participant outcomes. As discussed in Chapter 3, discussions about health care need to shift to focus on questions of disease prevalence, severity, and healthspan. These are the metrics that should be at the center of public discourse about Americans' health and our return on medical investments.

ENDNOTES

110 See Bryar, C. and Carr, B., Working Backwards: Insights, Stories and Secret from Inside Amazon, 2021.

111 See Jastreboff, Ania M et al. 2024. "Tirzepatide for Obesity Treatment and Diabetes Prevention." New England Journal of Medicine, November. https://doi.org/10.1056/nejmoa2410819. and Popovic, Djordje S., et. al. 2024. "Achievement of Normoglycemia With Tirzepatide in Type 2 Diabetes Mellitus: A Step Closer to Drug-induced Diabetes Remission?" *Journal of Diabetes and Its Complications* 38 (8): 108800. https://doi.org/10.1016/j.jdiacomp.2024.108800.

16. TWO SYSTEMS ARE BETTER THAN ONE

"They were too tethered to the ideas they already had. That's everybody's trouble. They just can't accept a new idea because the space is occupied by the old idea."

–Charlie Munger, Vice Chairman, Berkshire Hathaway, 2023 interview

The old idea in health care is that the system is *a* thing, unitary, monolithic. It was a logical view a century ago, defensible even a half century ago, but no more. Increasing healthspan requires two systems, each tailored to the essence of the medical challenges to be solved. Routine and Emergency/Elective Medicine can be covered by health insurance while Serious and Predictive/Preventive Medicine are covered by life insurance. Figure 16.1 shows key attributes of each system:

Figure 16.1: Envisioning Two Systems for Health Care

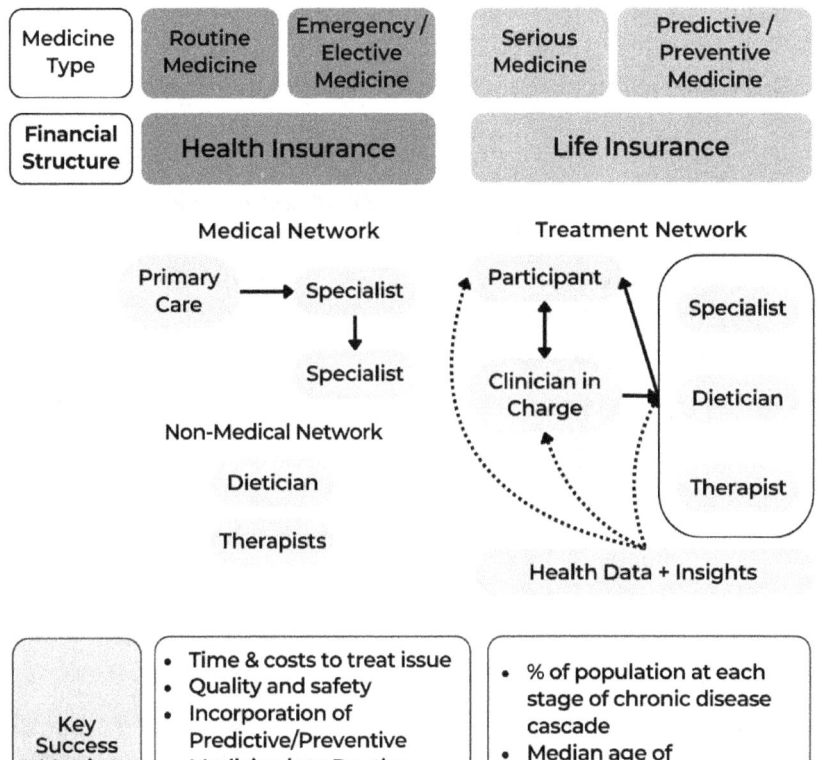

One of the challenges in describing a new system is to imagine how we get from the status quo to a new reality. Is it ever smooth? Or is it necessarily bumpy, with lots of fits and starts? Chapter 3 provided an illustration of success in a new normal, with multimorbidity prevalence declining by one-half to two-thirds from current levels (28% prevalence) to somewhere between 8% and 14%.

It's impossible to say with precision what the path from now until then looks like given unknowns relating to accelerants (e.g., technological breakthroughs) and points of friction (e.g., demographics, and regulatory forces). Figure 16.2 provides one lens, illustrating how total spending in status quo systems and Life for Health could play out over the next few decades. The dotted line in Figure 16.2 represents spending in health insurance while the solid line represents spending in Life for Health.

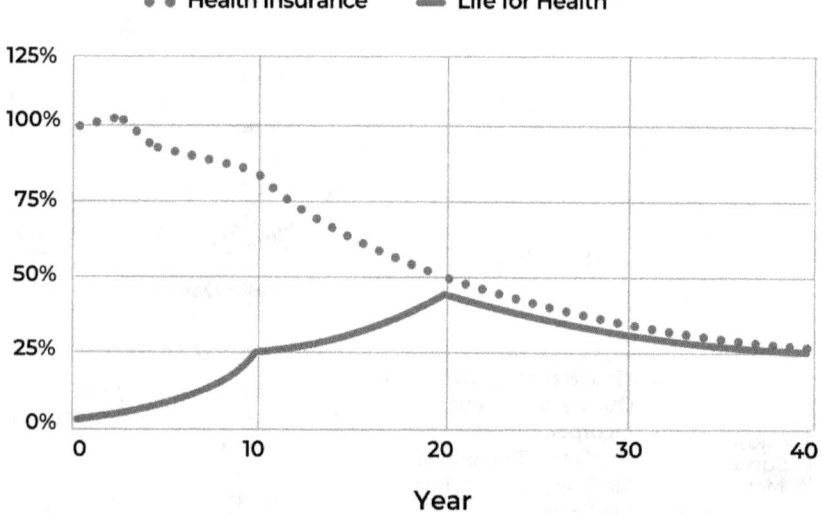

Figure 16.2: Two Systems Spending Over Time
(as a % of current spending)

The illustration highlights how quickly Life for Health spending could increase if large employers, life insurers, and investors cooperate to accelerate a transition, reaching 25% of current chronic disease-related spending in health insurance. That may not sound like a lot but this 25% is on a total current spend of about $4 trillion annually. Life for Health approaches could be generating about $1 trillion or more in annual revenue within a decade.

The second takeaway is that during the first decade, Life for Health spending will increase faster than health insurance spending will go down. Summing the two lines together, total spending across both systems would increase over the first decade to about 115% of current levels. Why is that? Because people joining Life for Health with multimorbidity will require additional investment, above current spending in many cases, for a year or two to restore metabolic health. Once participants regain metabolic health, annual savings accumulate quickly, as we will see in the next chapter. However, as Life for Health is growing rapidly, gaining participants, investments in new joiners (in their first and second years) will exceed savings for those in their third years or beyond. In addition, there will continue to be a very significant amount of continued spending to treat multimorbidity within status quo health insurance especially Medicare and Medicaid.

The transition of chronic disease care (and spending) accelerates in the second decade, at which point both multimorbidity prevalence and total spending across both systems also start to improve rapidly. By this point, Life for Health will have become the preferred approach to solve metabolic issues. Annual savings for Life for Health participants in the "maintain" stage of their journey will more than offset investments to help new participants reverse disease. By then, today's cutting edge GLP-1 therapies will have come down in price, with some losing patent protection, wider use of innovative outcomes-based pricing (such as that proposed in Part V), and greater competition. Longitudinal data from Life for Health participants and a growing clinician network organized around Life for Health approaches will make upfront and ongoing interventions more reliable.

Finally, Life for Health will increasingly be attracting new participants at the earlier end of the chronic disease cascade who require smaller upfront investments to reverse or prevent disease. Meanwhile, the number of Americans entering Medicare with multimorbidity will start to decline, delaying and reducing late in life hospitalization costs within health insurance. An added reality, distasteful though it is to say, is that by the second decade, older Americans who today have advanced multimorbidity and account for a disproportionate share of current spending are more likely to have died.

By the third and fourth decades, positive spillover effects will kick in as lower metabolic disease prevalence reduces the incidence of cancer and neurodegenerative disease. Here too, longitudinal data will prove decisive in advancing Predictive/Preventive Medicine across a range of conditions, along with improvements in food supply. Within a generation and a half, total medical spending across both systems could approach half of current levels.

Will it really take four decades to realize health improvements and savings? Probably, yes, if history is a guide. Large-scale health changes take three to four decades from inception through uptake before being generally adopted. This is about how long it took for vaccines to end fatal infectious diseases to be widely and routinely used. Similarly, the fight to stop premature heart-related deaths took about four decades. It's been four decades since the initial work on GLP-1 therapies began, and two decades since the first GLP-1 drug came to market. There are reasons for optimism, principally advances in biological understanding, big data, and artificial intelligence. Equally, there are reasons for pessimism created by the demographic and budgetary pressures in public health insurance programs which will play out in both federal and state politics. The reunification of science and finance within Life for Health could provide an additional boost, especially if food makers are able to reengineer (or de-engineer) food to improve nutritional value and eliminate harmful pollutants.

However long it takes, it is clear that *Life for Health* is orders of magnitude more likely to solve multimorbidity than the status quo. Absent *Life for Health*, total health spending over the next four decades would continue to grow inexorably upward, as shown in Figure 16.3. Against this backdrop, the near-term increase in health spending under Life for Health to reverse disease is very small compared to what chronic disease prevalence and spending would be absent it.

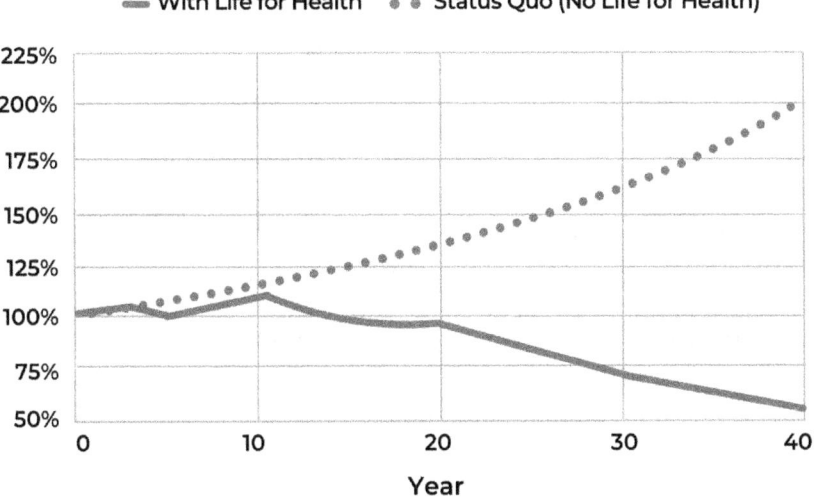

Figure 16.3: Total Health Care Spending With and Without Life for Health (as a % of current spending)

Even if obesity prevalence plateaus, as some data suggest may be happening, future chronic disease risk will continue to accumulate. Rising cancer and dementia rates will continue to drive spending upward in absolute terms and even faster as a percentage of GDP as healthspans continue to shrink. In this context then, the uptick in total health spending in Life for Health's first decade is a temporary blip, and the alternative of persisting with the status quo, far worse.

17. THE ECONOMICS OF LIFE FOR HEALTH

"There are only two ways to make money: one is to bundle; the other is to unbundle."

–Attributed to Jim Barksdale, Netscape CEO

Life for Health's economics hinges on two bets. The first is that investments in efforts to restore metabolic health can be recouped many times over in subsequent years in the form of lower health costs. The second bet, addressed in Part IV, is that collecting deep, longitudinal data about participant actions and outcomes will accelerate abilities to predict disease and preventive efforts, and tangibilize the value of preempting or delaying disease. This chapter focuses on the first bet.

In Chapter 14, we met Frank, a 42-year-old with advanced metabolic syndrome. Before joining Life for Health, annual costs to treat just his metabolic issues ran about $10,000. With standard approaches to manage symptoms, those costs could double in the ensuing decade as his multimorbidity worsens, progressing to liver disease, osteoarthritis, and more advanced heart disease. The difference between Frank's projected health expenses under the status quo and Life for Health is illustrated in Figure 17.1:

Figure 17.1: Annual Medical Expenses, status quo versus Life for Health

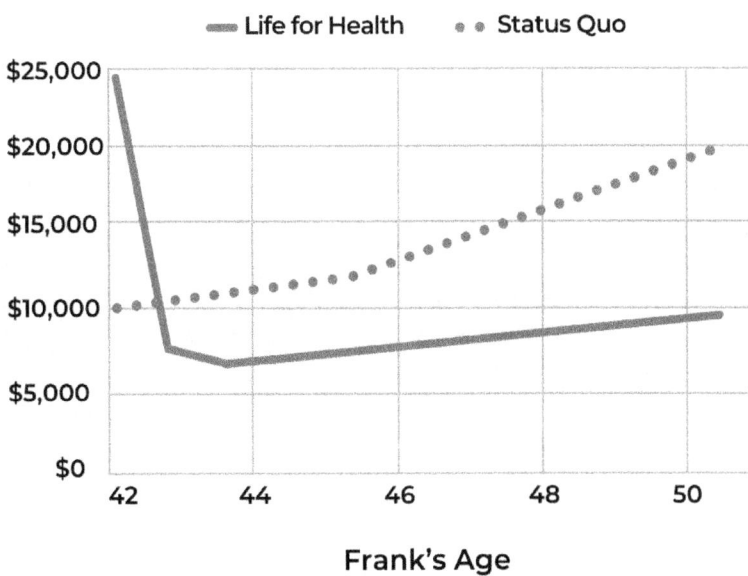

After joining Life for Health, Frank decides to undergo metabolic surgery, the most expensive one-year option to reverse disease, but also one of the most effective. First-year metabolic health costs total $25,000, twice the amount that would have been spent to manage his symptoms. However, Frank has an excellent response to surgery and regains metabolic health within a couple of years. His annual medical costs drop dramatically, well below the trajectory of spending he and his employer/insurer would have faced absent disease reversal. The gap between these two lines represents the first bet, that a higher up-front investment to reverse disease translates into massive savings over time. Life for Health monetizes this difference, sharing the risk and value among employers, participants, insurers, clinicians, and Life for Health entities. Here's how.

Shifting Health Insurance Premiums to Life for Health

Health insurance is where the money is, to co-opt Willie Sutton's explanation of why he robbed banks. It is where funds, sloshing around the RPS Vortex, go to waste. In 2023, health insurers earned about $1.1 trillion in premium revenue, about double what they earned a decade ago.[112]

Life insurers, by contrast, take in about $200 billion annually in individual and group life premiums, about 20% of health insurers' take. Life for Health is fueled by shifting premiums and therefore spending to Life for Health, decreasing the aggregate amount spent in both systems over time.

Transitioning health insurance dollars to Life for Health can happen in stages, with the first stage focusing on the approximately 30% of premiums associated with working age individuals employed by public and private-sector entities and self-employed individuals. The second wave can focus on Medicaid, which accounts for an additional 30% of annual premium dollars.[113] This work can start in parallel but shifts in the private insurance market are likely to move faster than in Medicaid. The final 40% of health insurance premiums are associated with Medicare, where costs will naturally come down over time, as lower multi-morbidity prevalence among working age Americans rolls forward into Medicare.[114] Likewise traditional Medicare and Medicare Advantage programs might incorporate Life for Health approaches to adopt Serious and Predictive/Preventive approaches among retirees.

The best place to start in the first group is with larger companies that self-insure. These companies, generally employing 200 or more workers, account for about two-thirds of private-sector jobs. Self-insured companies pay for workers' health costs directly using a mix of company funds, (i.e., a share of revenue) and worker contributions. Health insurers act as plan administrators, providing access to their network of clinician, hospital, and drug supply contracts. Insurers, acting on behalf of companies, establish coverage and reimbursement terms; manage enrollment; and make payments to clinicians, hospitals, and pharmacies using funds set aside by the company. Self-insured companies have the most to gain from improving workers' health since every dollar saved will add to company margins.

Why would a company take on the risk of paying for their employees' health care? Because, it turns out, it's often cheaper for larger companies to self-insure than to pay a health insurer to assume that risk. Reinsurers provide self-insured companies with an additional measure of protection, helping them cap exposure to extraordinarily large individual health claims, or limit total outlays in a year across the workforce.[115] Companies with fewer than 200 employees are more likely to purchase fully funded coverage in which health insurers take on actual medical costs in exchange for annually-set premiums.[116]

In both structures, rising multimorbidity and costs have either required greater direct spending or higher premiums, eating into revenue and wages faster than revenue growth. Companies' future cost outlays increasingly look like the red line in Figure 17.1, with symptom management costs escalating at an ever-faster rate, especially for workers 45 and above. Multimorbidity-related health costs are an even bigger problem for public sector employers like school systems, public safety departments, and state agencies where workers skew older, have longer tenures, and often qualify for retirement health benefits. In addition, private companies are shouldering more of the costs to treat multimorbidity in Medicaid since lower rates paid to doctors and hospitals through Medicaid leads insurers to shift costs onto private plans.

Life for Health gives self-insured companies a way to reduce total healthcare spending by shifting the fastest source of rising costs, metabolic multimorbidity, out of the status quo. CFOs or heads of human resources could simply tell health plan administrators, "We are going to take all the money we now spend on metabolic health issues with you and move it over to Life for Health; expect the amount of funds flowing through you to decrease accordingly." The amount shifted to Life for Health would be a pro rata share of current and projected costs (and associated company and worker contributions) associated with metabolic issues. This is essentially what Mark Cuban's Cost Plus Drug Company is doing now for prescription drugs, shifting funds spent through traditional pharmacy benefit arrangements into his direct purchase model. Life for Health replicates this idea on a larger scale, focusing initially on clinician and hospital spending on metabolic dysfunction.

To break down how this works, let's trace how premium dollars would flow into health insurance and Life for Health over time, once again using our exemplar participant, Frank. Assume his employer self-insures and requires workers to contribute 20% of expected health costs. To use round numbers, assume Frank's medical costs in a year total $15,000, of which two-thirds, or $10,000, was spent on metabolic issues. Once Frank joins Life for Health, this $10,000 will be redirected to be spent through Life for Health. (The $10,000 includes $8,000 of company funds and $2,000 of Frank's contributions). The remaining $5,000 of health spending not associated with metabolic issues would continue to be spent in existing health insurer administered arrangements for Routine and Emergency/Elective treatments. Figure 17.2 illustrates what happens in the existing arrangement and under Life for Health:

Figure 17.2: Reallocation of Health Insurance Premiums to Life for Health

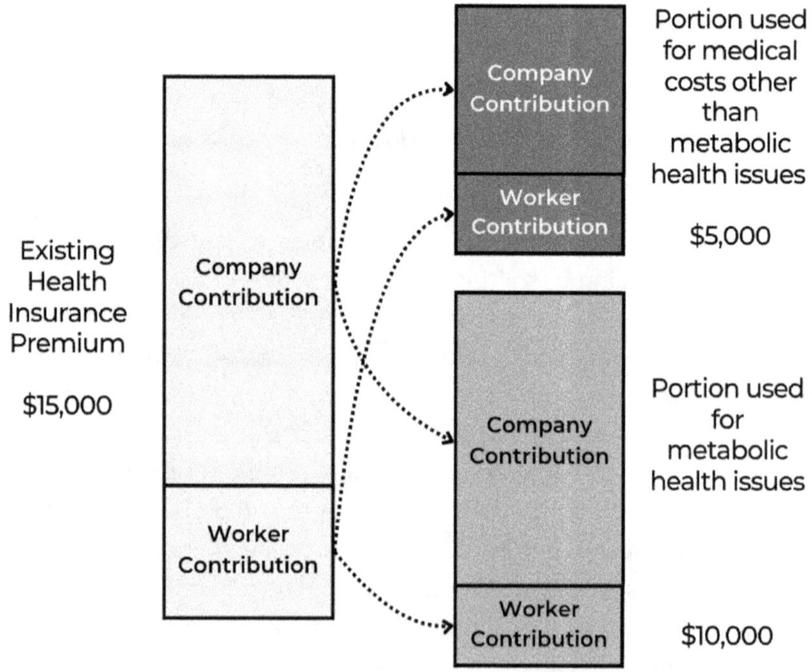

The Up-front Intervention and Beyond: Who Does What?

Once Frank joins Life for Health, he undergoes metabolic surgery to reverse disease. The surgery and immediate follow-up care costs $25,000. This cost is split 50/50 between Frank's employer and the Life for Health entity, $12,500 each, meaning Frank's employer spends about $2,500 more in the first year than they otherwise would have to manage Frank's symptoms. There is very little incremental risk for the employer in exchange for much greater long-term gain. Figure 17.3 illustrates how the cost of the upfront, or initial treatment plan, is split:

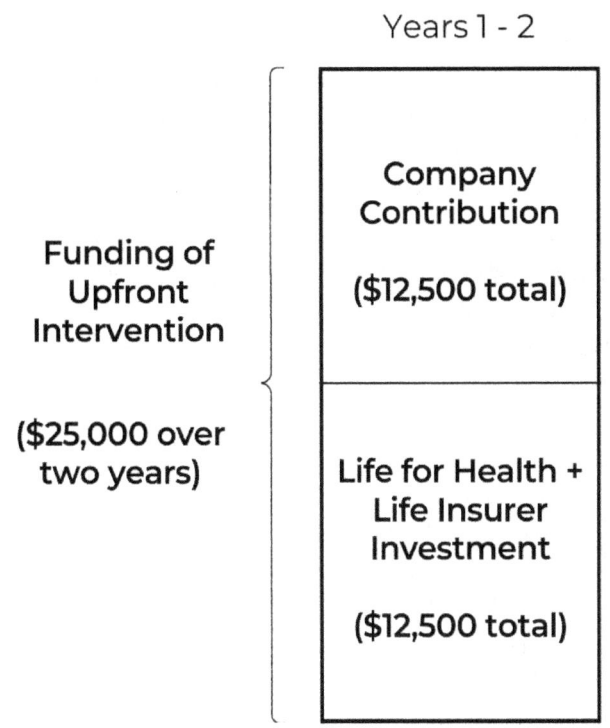

Figure 17.3: Financing of Upfront Intervention to Reverse Disease

It takes Frank a couple of years to regain normal metabolic function following surgery, so health savings compared to the expected trajectory take a couple of years to achieve a meaningful gap. Quickly, however, this value increases as Frank reduces use of blood pressure, statin, and diabetes medications, and the frequency of hospitalizations or other metabolic-related treatments decreases.

Once Frank's metabolic metrics are within normal ranges, treatment shifts into the "maintain" phase, focused on preserving health gains and preventing recurrence. Each of the entities involved in Life for Health, including participants, share in medical cost savings compared to an agreed-upon baseline or index of similarly situated individuals, as agreed by the company and Life For Health.[117] The difference between the actual costs and the reference cost is shared among the employer, Life for Health, and participants (in the form of Health Outcomes Payments). A portion of these savings may also be shared with clinicians depending on participants' outcomes.

The gap between metabolic costs under Life for Health and the status quo grows over time as Life for Health participants enter the maintain phase while peers in the status quo experience advancing disease and increasing costs. Life for Health participants could achieve ongoing metabolic health costs in the $5,000 to $6,000 a year range, translating into savings of about $7,000 in the first year after regaining metabolic health (i.e., the difference between $5,000 in annual metabolic health costs in Life for Health versus $12,000 for those in the status quo), as shown in Figure 17.4:

Figure 17.4: Realizing the Value of Efforts to Maintain Metabolic Health

	Annual Costs, Years 3/4		Annual Costs, Years 5+
Life for Health	$5,000	→	~ $6,000
Status Quo	$12,000	→	~ $20,000+
Annual savings	$7,000	→	~ $14,000+

Annual savings split among:	• Participants • Company • Clinicians • Life for Health / life insurers

The magnitude of annual savings increases over time, reaching as much as $14,000 within a few years as Life for Health participants' annual metabolic health costs stabilize in the $6,000 range, versus those treated in the status quo, who will see annual costs rise steadily to the $20,000 a year range. Over a decade, cumulative medical outlays for Life for Health participants *could be 30% to 50% less* than similarly situated individuals treated through health insurance. The magnitude of the gap will vary depending primarily on a participant's age, how advanced their metabolic syndrome is, and how well they can maintain a consistently better health trajectory. Those who are younger but have more advanced disease will realize larger comparative gains.

Now that we have quantified how much is at stake, over time, the next question is where does the money to "share" savings come from? In a structure with a self-insured employer, it is the company that realizes the savings compared to what they would otherwise spend on Life for Health participants, so they are the source of the funds to be shared. The employer makes payments to the Life for Health entity for clinical care costs plus an agreed-upon share of health savings. Life for Health then distributes funds to clinicians depending on their performance, and to participants' life insurance policies depending on their success in achieving health outcomes. Figure 17.5 illustrates contractual relationships (solid lines) and payment flows (dotted lines) in a Life for Health system that includes a self-insured employer.

Figure 17.5: Summary of Payment Flows in Life for Health

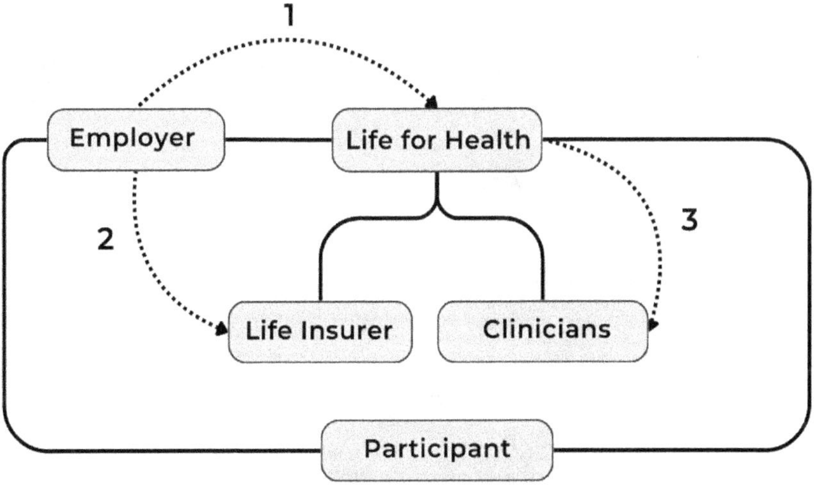

Payment key: 1 = Employer payments to Life for Health entity for clinical services plus a share of savings. 2 = Employer group life insurance premium payments to life insurer. 3 = Life for Health entity payments to contracted clinicians, including any savings share or other performance-based payments.

Employers make Life for Health available to employees as part of a group life offering, funding the incremental group life premium, and underwriting a portion of the up-front investment to restore participants' metabolic health. After the up-front period to "regain" health the employer continues paying for participants' actual medical expenditures, as would have been true absent Life for Health. However, payments for metabolic health treatments now flow to the Life for Health entity, which is responsible for managing participants' metabolic health. Employers share medical cost savings over time, as determined using an agreed benchmark.

Participants' health care finances change in two ways after joining Life for Health. First, a portion of their insurance premiums are used by the employer to help fund metabolic health treatments. Second, participants receive payments over time based on the degree to which they achieve agreed-upon health outcomes. Individuals who repeatedly fail to achieve health goals, for reasons other than a health situation or emergency, would face a predetermined increase in their premium in subsequent years.

Clinicians' contract with Life for Health entities to provide predictive, preventive, and treatment services. Their compensation is based on the type of services provided, with a portion tied to actual participant outcomes over time. Clinicians are paid by the Life for Health entity using funds provided by employers.

Life Insurers underwrite the group universal life product offered in tandem with Life for Health. Policy premiums would be paid by employers to the insurer, as happens now under any other group life arrangement. Life insurers that participate in funding up-front interventions with Life for Health entities will receive a pro rata share of Life for Health's share in annual health savings.

The Life for Health entity helps underwrite up-front interventions, establishes clinician relationships, and oversees participants' treatment plans, goals, and progress. Life for Health is compensated through a share of savings from participants' lower annual medical costs compared to a baseline or reference level of spending established with employers. Life for Health's incentives are closely aligned with those of participants and insurers since most of their return is realized after the two-year up-front window, as participants seek to maintain better health trajectories.

How Each Constituency Gains

Life for Health's economic structure demonstrates that it is possible to build a new system outside of existing arrangements, repurposing funds already spent.

Employers finally have a means to control health costs. For a relatively small incremental increase in spending they will realize years, even decades, of significantly lower medical costs. Employers will realize second-order benefits, too, in the form of lower absenteeism and increased worker retention.

Participants are much better off than in the status quo, gaining access to a system that co-invests with them to improve their current and future health. Life for Health ends the pernicious effect of the health insurance wage tax, replacing it with an opportunity to build up savings within life insurance policies tax-efficiently. Annual Health Outcomes Payments would add up quickly. A 42-year-old participant who hits key health goals for nine years, earning $1,500 each year, would have about $35,000 in additional savings by age 65. In exchange, participants take the risk that they might pay more under Life for Health than they do now, if they choose not to undertake therapies necessary to reset metabolic health or are unable to regain or maintain metabolic health despite recommendations of their clinicians and counselors.

Clinicians who have been seeking new ways to solve multimorbidity holistically (integrating medical and non-medical approaches), will have—in Life for Health—an alternative to the constraints of traditional health insurance. They will have more time and space to establish relationships with the people they treat, and opportunities to participate in the value created over time. Life for Health is an opportunity for clinician-entrepreneurs to differentiate themselves based on their ability to reverse or maintain participants' health and to help integrate technology and clinical practices that generate better outcomes.

The **Life for Health** entity and **life insurers** benefit financially from underwriting a new system to solve multimorbidity through their share of health savings and—in the case of life insurers—a larger, customer base with comparatively better, and continually improving mortality and morbidity risk profiles.

The biggest long-term winner is Medicare (not even shown on the diagram) since it is the entity that ultimately picks up the tab for later in life, advanced chronic disease treatment costs.[118] In addition, insights gained from Life for Health participants' longitudinal data will help postpone or mitigate the next greatest disease threats, in terms of disease burden, cancer and ADRD.

With this more complete picture of Life for Health's economics, we can return to the paragraph from the "working backwards" press release in Chapter 15 describing the economic benefits:

> *Life for Health participants and their employers have realized **$300 billion** in direct medical savings over the last decade compared to spending on a matched sample of demographically comparable individuals. Life for Health participants have received **$30 billion** in outcomes-related outcomes payments from Life for Health plans as a result of their success in restoring and maintaining their metabolic health.*

The $300 billion in medical savings represents the savings in metabolic health costs for Life for Health participants during the preceding decade compared to what those costs might have been in the status quo. Participants could expect to receive about 10% of the savings, with the remainder shared among employers, clinicians, Life for Health entities, and life insurers.

Life for Health as a Direct-to-Consumer Offering

Individuals employed by a company that does not offer a Life for Health can still participate through a direct-to-consumer (DTC) offering. The arrangements would be a bit more complex given the way health insurance now works. In an employer-sponsored version, Life for Health's clinical care costs are funded by reallocating premium dollars that a worker already pays. In a DTC offering, the worker's premiums for health care would need to be bifurcated between Life for Health and traditional coverage, ideally in a such a way that does not require the worker to pay more in aggregate. Is this possible?

In the best case, enterprising health insurers would partner with a Life for Health entity to offer a bundle of health insurance and Life for Health. The health insurer would cover Routine and Emergency/Elective Medicine while Life for Health would cover Serious and Predictive/Preventive Medicine. This would be the easiest option for an individual to buy coverage directly, although it would require bargaining between the two insurers over the boundaries of each other's risk.

Another possibility is to combine Life for Health with a high-deductible health insurance plan or an ICHRA (the new health insurance reimbursement account described in Chapter 11). A high-deductible plan would result in lower health insurance premiums, freeing up funds to purchase Life for Health coverage directly. ICHRAs would allow individuals to use funds provided by their employer to shop for coverage, cobbling together health insurance plus a Life for Health offering.

In either option, the Life for Health benefits would work the same way as in the self-insured model, with life insurers and Life for Health entities co-investing in treatments to help participants reverse metabolic disease followed by interventions to maintain a better health trajectory. Figure 17.6 outlines how contractual relationships and money flows would work in one of these arrangements:

Figure 17.6: Summary of Payment Flows in Direct-to-Consumer Arrangement

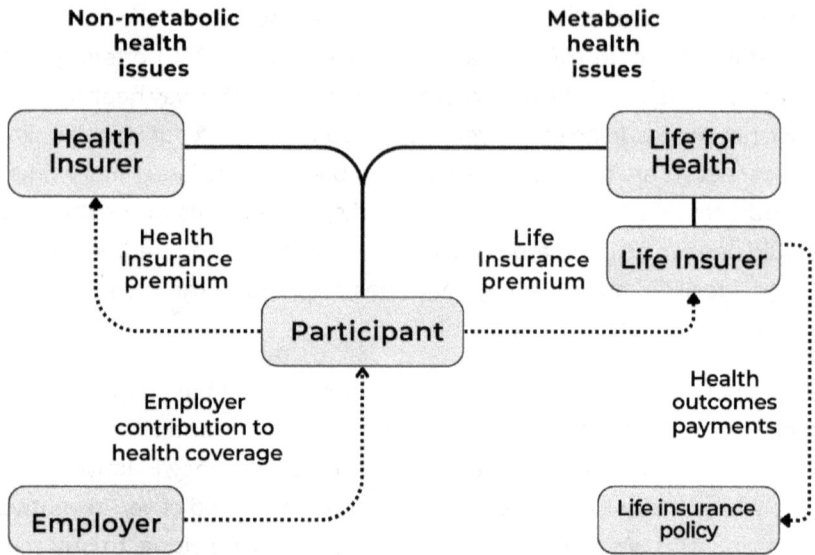

The viability of a Life for Health DTC offering would be improved by changing the ACA's requirement that a person receive all required health services from the same insurance plan. When the ACA was written, lawmakers naturally assumed health insurers would be the only source of medical coverage and wrote into law provisions requiring health plans to provide a minimum set of services. This makes it complicated (but not impossible) to unbundle some services like metabolic health from traditional insurance arrangements. Changing the law to ensure that individuals receive coverage for required services in aggregate, while giving them the freedom to buy coverage from multiple entities, would make it easier to unbundle chronic disease treatment.

What Happens When Participants Change Jobs?

A key aspect of Life for Health's value is its ability to sustain participant relationships for many years. So what happens when participants who join Life for Health through an employer-offered benefit change jobs?

The best scenario is if the participant's new employer also offers Life for Health, in which case the participant could roll over coverage from one company to the next without interruption, including to roll over any cash balance (as happens with retirement plans) if the companies use different insurance underwriters.[119] Participants who join a company that does not offer Life for Health could enter into a DTC Life for Health plan, as described above, converting their group life policy into an individual universal life contract. If neither of these options are available, or the participant cannot afford full Life for Health coverage on an individual basis, the universal life premium could be adjusted downwards for a period, providing for life insurance coverage only. In addition, the participant might continue to see Life for Health clinicians for periodic checkups and metabolic health assessments.

What About a Multiyear Health Insurance Plan?

Recognizing the mismatch between the long-term nature of chronic disease and the short-term nature of annual health contracts, some entrepreneurs and health policy experts have urged health insurers to start offering multiyear coverage, allowing companies or individuals to sign up for a few years, with coverage provided at a fixed rate. This, they argue, gives employers and individuals cost certainty and affords insurers longer time horizons to make health investments. What would it mean to Life for Health if insurers offered multiyear coverage?

As a general rule, anything that increases the alignment between long-term health threats and longer term coverage is a positive for Life for Health. Multiyear coverage would be especially helpful to cover Routine and Emergency/Elective Medicine, encouraging insurers to adopt Predictive/Preventive Medicine in routine care.

However, multiyear health policies, by themselves, will not solve the essential challenge of chronic disease and age-related disease since they require multidecade alignment and open-ended policy durations. Simply extending the health insurance term is insufficient to focus insurers on reversing or preventing disease that may not manifest for decades. As we have seen in all the studies about postponing chronic disease onset during middle age or reversing multimorbidity, the goal of interventions when someone is 40 or 45 is to change their health trajectory when they are 60 or 65. Establishing multiyear health plans will not change the mismatch in timing between an intervention and the full realization of value.

An additional problem is that the incentive for health insurers to invest in a person's health diminishes towards the end of a preset term. It kicks the one-year time horizon problem forward a few years, but inevitably in a four- or five-year policy structure, 20% to 25% of policyholders will be in the final year of a multiyear term.[120] The beauty of forestalling chronic disease with universal life insurance is that the policy's final duration is unknown at the start, encouraging Life for Health entities to do as much as possible to reverse disease and prevent recurrence since it's unknown how long a participant will remain in the arrangement.

Likewise, financial frameworks to solve long-lived risks must provide a means for policyholders to share in the value of their efforts over time. It's not clear how this could be done effectively through health insurance or health savings accounts, especially when a perfectly good savings vehicle with well established prudential and regulatory standards (i.e., life insurance), already exists. Finally, multi-year health insurance does not address the key flaw of the status quo, our continued use of a single system to solve fundamentally different acute and chronic issues. For these reasons, life insurance remains a better framework to deliver Serious and Predictive/Preventive Medicine than multiyear health insurance.

Summing Up

This chapter's goal is to demonstrate that *Life for Health* is economically viable and financially appealing. Massive sums trapped in the status quo can be freed and redirected to much more productive uses. The unit economics are sound and the necessary direction of travel in how we pay for health care is clear.

As we have seen, the RPS Vortex's dirty secret is that it already forces advanced chronic disease costs to be socialized. Insurers let multimorbidity-related liabilities build up for decades without reserving funds to cover eventual costs, only to dump the unfunded liabilities onto Medicare. *Life for Health* reverses this process, allowing participants to translate better health over the course of their working years into savings to defray the cost of less protracted late in life illnesses.

The problem is that to achieve this kind of long-term gain, we first have to wring existing multimorbidity out of the system. In this sense, costs to reverse disease which require more funds at first, are a kind of one-time transition payment to get unhealthy Americans back on track, health-wise. As built-in liability is worked down, and new liability prevented, the economic script will flip. Individuals can build assets to offset future costs instead of society continuing to accumulate a ballooning, unfunded liability.

Asking if it is worth it to invest more now to reverse future disease is, in effect, caving to the RPS Vortex's view that a decade and a half of late in life multimorbidity is, well, inevitable. It's not. Looking back four decades after building *Life for Health*, it will be clear that our current dilemma of rising multimorbidity liability is the real anomaly.

As much as stakeholders in today's system—individuals, clinicians, employers, and health entrepreneurs—have been ready for change, they have lacked an economically viable alternative. *Life for Health* calls insurers' bluff, betting that funds now pouring into sick care can be used much more productively in a system built around long-term outcomes. At this point, really, what have we got to lose?

ENDNOTES

112 National Association of Insurance Commissioner, 2024, "U.S. Health Insurance Industry, 2023 Annual Results," 1.
113 National Association of Insurance Commissioners, U.S. Health Insurance Industry, 2023 Annual Results, p. 13. Medicaid premiums include amounts paid by states to private entities to provide health care to Medicaid enrollees. Medicare premiums include payments to private health insurers under the Medicare Advantage program plus costs for individuals in traditional Medicare.
114 Note, however, that as spending in the first two categories will decline faster, Medicare's share of total health premiums will probably increase.
115 Self-insured employers enjoy some regulatory benefits as well since rules governing health plan funding are part of the law governing retirement benefits, called ERISA, rather than the ACA.

116 The Kaiser Family Foundation estimates that 80% of workers at larger companies are covered under self-insured plans but only 10% to 20% of workers at small companies. See Kaiser Family Foundation, "2023 Employer Health Benefits Survey," October 18, 2023. https://www.kff.org/report-section/ehbs-2023-section-10-plan-funding/

117 Similarly situated individuals could include a peer group of individuals of the same gender and age range with similar comorbidities and disease severity.

118 Interestingly, Medicare health actuaries may not see the program as a beneficiary and might even model Life for Health approaches as costing the program funds. This is because current cost estimates are a function of years in the program. Someone who lives longer, in this view, automatically costs more, and since the number of years that a person pays into Medicare is fixed, living longer post-retirement necessarily costs the system more. However, Medicare's own data about the exponential increase in cost as a function of multimorbidity, rather than age alone, and other modeling of increased healthspan, demonstrates that postponement of multimorbidity costs will more than offset additional years of coverage. Indeed, reduced multimorbidity during prime working years will also increase the amount of Medicare tax revenue received.

119 IRS rules governing rollover of cash balance amounts from one plan to another generally apply to individual policies. Ensuring similar treatment for group life offerings may require clarification from the IRS and/or state insurance regulators.

120 A related practical issue with multi-year health insurance is that the Medical Loss Ratio test, which is now performed annually to verify that insurers pay out at least 80% of premiums, would have to be done on a multiyear time frame commensurate with multiyear policies.

18. WHAT'S "IN IT" FOR LIFE INSURERS?

Having explored Life for Health's economics, we turn now to why life insurers should participate in Life for Health.

From World War II until 2010, life insurers enjoyed a tacit and mutually beneficial alliance with health insurers, protecting families against financial loss after a wage earner's early death while health insurers democratized access to life saving and life extending treatments. Life insurers had as close to a sure thing as possible in terms of betting on longer lifespans as anti-smoking campaigns took hold and clinicians and drugmakers revolutionized cardiac care and cancer treatment.[121] During the 1970s and 1980s, they could price policies using the previous decade's mortality rates knowing that the risk of early death would continue to go down as medical care improved. It was such a good bet, in fact, that life insurers built up a lucrative business selling annuities, to hedge the flip side of mortality risk, compensating Americans worried about outliving their savings. They succeeded so well that today, annuities are a larger source of life insurance revenue than traditional whole or universal life policies.

The macro picture for whole life policies, insurers' bread and butter, was buffeted in the 1980s by high inflation and interest rates followed by wave after wave of tax-advantaged savings products including IRAs and 401(k) plans. Wall Street added to the pressure in the 1990s and beyond, introducing cheaper investment options such as low-cost index and exchange traded funds. Life insurers adapted, picking up business managing pension assets and expanding annuities while the core business stagnated.

As life insurers adapted to stiffening competition for customers' savings, their alliance with health insurers fell apart. Lifespans continued to edge upwards especially for wealthier clients buying annuities, but healthspans for younger workers began to shrink. Health insurers profited more from managing symptoms than stopping disease, as had been the case in earlier years. Life insurers got a bitter taste of this reality when they began offering long-term care insurance, with the idea of helping protect aging Americans born in the interwar years against in-home or nursing home care. Unfortunately, the policies ran headlong into the rising tide of multimorbidity, with payouts for care vastly exceeding predicted levels. Policy buyers were both much sicker than they had seemed *and* they ended up living longer than underwriters had anticipated. It was a mess, sending some insurers into bankruptcy. Meanwhile, Americans entering their prime working years faced rising education and housing costs, and recoiled as they watched parents endure much longer, more painful declines than their grandparents. They bought lower value term policies to protect against early or accidental death but increasingly took a pass open-ended whole or universal life policies. Today, the two sides of mortality risk held by life insurers—whole life policies and annuities—are unbalanced. Insurance conferences are full of panels focused on longevity risk even as most Americans face shorter healthspans and lower lifetime savings potential.

Life for Health offers life insurers a chance to broaden their customer base and reclaim savings that are now misspent within health insurance to manage symptoms instead of forestalling disease. In other words, Life for Health allows life insurers to reclaim control of their demographic future from health insurers without having to become a health insurer. Already, some life insurers are seeing how health insurers' short-sighted thinking is adding to their risks, most immediately in early cancer detection. While health insurers restrict access to cutting-edge diagnostics like liquid biopsies, fearing they will only drive up treatment costs, some life insurers are stepping into the breach, promoting the tests to whole life policyholders, recognizing the benefit to reducing mortality risk.

Life for Health Helps Life Insurers Manage Key Risks

When life insurers issue whole or universal policies, they face three risks:

- Mortality risk—the chance that a policyholder will die prematurely.
- Lapse risk—the chance that a policyholder will terminate a policy earlier than desired.
- Adverse selection risk—the possibility that a person is predisposed to buying coverage because they know, or suspect, that they are more likely to incur a claim.

Miscalculating or mispricing these risks hurts insurers' profitability, as happened with long-term care coverage. Life for Health helps insurers mitigate all three.

By definition, Life for Health reduces mortality risk. Participants join Life for Health with significantly greater risk of an early death, given their metabolic health issues, but this can be priced into the initial premium. Quickly, however, Life for Health improves participants' mortality risk, creating actuarial cushion. Likewise Life for Health policyholders that life insurers want to keep long-term are less likely to lapse prematurely because they need savings to offset serious illness costs.

It's the third risk, adverse selection, where things get interesting. All insurers face the problem that people who apply for coverage have superior knowledge about their own health and behaviors and are unlikely to be forthcoming about ones that might increase premiums. The problem is especially acute in life insurance since policies can run for decades, and life insurers only get one shot to assess an applicant's risk profile before the policy is written. After that, the insurer is locked into coverage at rates specified in the policy. As a result, insurers try to solve for adverse selection by increasing prices on all policies by some amount, figuring that slightly higher premiums for everyone will offset the risk that a few—or maybe not so few—are deceptively bad apples.

Understandably, actuaries might look at prospective Life for Health participants with a jaundiced eye. Isn't it likely that people with poor or declining metabolic health, who want to join, also have a greater disposition to make improvident behavioral choices, given their "going in" metabolic syndrome? Well, perhaps in some cases, but this is unlikely to be true for the vast majority of participants. In a traditional life policy, a person has to die for their beneficiaries to get paid. Someone who likes to drive motorcycles 100 mph or do crazy stunts *is* more likely to die, and there is no way the life insurer can reduce their risk (provided they pay their premiums on time).

That's not the case in Life for Health. The greatest value under Life for Health from getting and staying healthy is realized by *the policy holder themself.* They garner the lion's share of the financial benefit while they are alive. Along the way, Life for Health clinicians, although walled off from life insurers, are working with the participant to manage those risks, with frequent data along the way to see how a person is doing. A second factor is that having poor metabolic health is not purely a function of a person's behavior. As we know, the food environment and life situation are powerful factors, along with genetics. That's what's so compelling about surgery and GLP-1 drugs, and likely to be even truer of future treatments. They directly attack food cravings, and potentially other risky appetites, mitigating negative environmental factors.

Still, as mentioned earlier, while reversing disease has little or no technology risk, maintaining better health trajectories long-term is less clear. So the Life for Health participant experience will stratify policyholders into two groups, those who have poor metabolic health *despite* their better instincts, versus those whose poor metabolic health is due, to some degree, to unhealthy choices. Life for Health then divides the latter group between those whose behavior can be changed in response to financial and non-financial incentives versus those who cannot.

This latter group, those whose behavior does not change after interventions to reverse disease or maintain health, represent the greatest potential risk to Life for Health entities and life insurers. Anticipating this possibility, Life for Health is designed to test participants' motivations during initial onboarding, in choosing which interventions to reverse disease, and thereafter during the ongoing process of setting, measuring and refining health outcome goals. Life for Health adds a strong human dimension through participant-clinician relationships along with mechanisms to involve participants in peer groups that create collective accountability. Still it's possible that a small group of individuals are unresponsive to all of the incentives along with the prospect of higher premiums. What incentive would such a person have to remain in Life for Health? Doing so would almost certainly cost more than health insurance alone with no incremental benefit. In short, individuals who are unwilling to do their part (having isolated any other medical explanations) are likely to terminate coverage voluntarily.

Over time it is reasonable to think that Life for Health participants who remain participants for many years or decades will come from the first two groups, those who actively want to improve their healthspan and those who are able to change behaviors within Life for Health. It's impossible to zero out adverse selection, but every part of Life for Health is built to minimize it.

The Life Insurance CEO's Dilemma

That all sounds great, but life insurer CEOs will still get internal pushback. Skeptics may point to the industry's historic bar against being involved in policyholders' medical decisions, or getting involved in the regulatory and operational challenges of providing health services. As discussed earlier, these issues are solved by Life for Health's organizational structure. Insurers would not have information about individual policyholders' medical situations or roles in developing the clinical network or managing clinician payments. Health care activities are managed by Life for Health entities, meaning life insurers do not have to get pulled into the machinations of coverage or health insurance rules.

The bigger question for life insurer CEOs is whether the potential gains of reversing and preventing multimorbidity are worth the risk? Right now, life insurers are doing reasonably well selling annuities and managing retirement assets, and although insurers are starting to see the benefit of acting earlier to improve cancer survival, chronic disease is a much tougher nut to crack. Some industry insiders will argue that instead of trying to reverse multimorbidity, life insurers should just increase prices to compensate for multimorbidity risk.

The Debate in the Executive Suite

How might this debate play out within life insurers' upper ranks? Let's imagine that the CEO of a top insurer convenes their executive team to debate Life for Health. Some of the team are energized about underwriting efforts to improve healthspan while others look very troubled.

"How do we make this work economically?" one of the skeptics asks. "People with obesity and diabetes are risky. People cannot afford the premiums our risk models suggest are necessary but if we under-price, we will get stuck with a pile of risk."

"Exactly," says the CEO. "We've got limited avenues to grow and the policyholders we'd like are stuck as well. Whole life policies will be too expensive and later on they will not have enough savings to buy a meaningfully sized annuity. This is how I see it." The CEO hits a button on the presentation control, displaying the following chart:

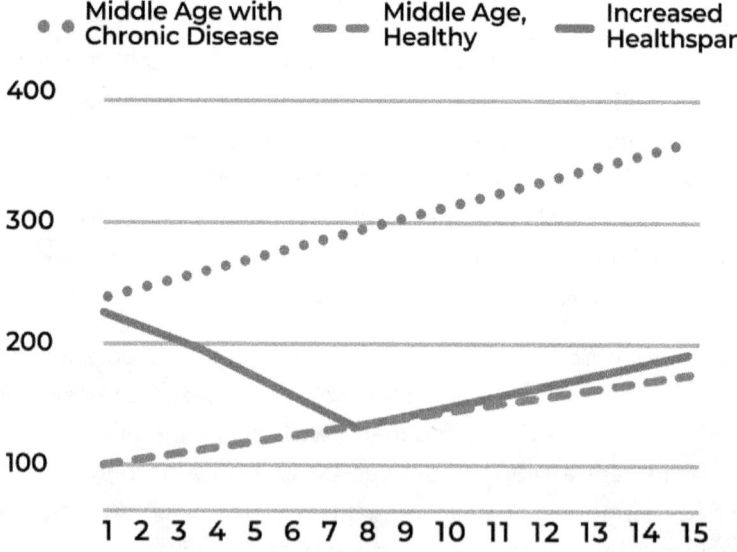

Figure 18.1 Life Insurance Rates With and Without Life for Health (Premium Charged a Middle Aged, Healthy Person = 100)

"The dashed line is where we would set premiums for healthy people with little or no chronic disease or history of smoking. The problem is they're becoming a much smaller part of the population overall, a third at most of people in their prime working age, and most of them will have less savings than their parents did. The dotted line is what our models say we need to charge people on the road to multimorbidity, which they'll never be able to afford. So the price line looks good in our risk models but the actual revenue is zero."

"Yes," says the head of sales, "but our front-end sales costs are going down now, with better tech, AI, cheaper ways to price. We can underwrite faster and cheaper, and make more over time on that limited slice with new products."

"Margin improvements are promising and," says the CEO, looking at the head of innovation, "your teams have done great work, but a company cannot live by margin alone. These capabilities will soon be table stakes. Customers will expect speed and convenience, voice AI and so on, by default. We can AI the heck out of everything but that only goes so far unless we can grow new policyholders by 20%, 25% over the next few decades. Improving margins won't increase the addressable market."

"What about annuities?" asks the sales head. "The number of people who are living longer is increasing in absolute terms. There's a lot of hay to be made there for while Gen Z and others start to accumulate wealth."

"Sure, there's value in annuities," responds the CEO, "but everyone is going after that group, and as multimorbidity starts to increase, the pool of people 55 plus who can afford an annuity is going to shrink. Gen X and Gen Z are going to sit on their housing assets longer, just like their parents, but unlike them they will have a lot less cash to buy an annuity. We can't put all our eggs in that basket."

The CEO pauses to let that sink in, then continues. "Our best way to grow is to help move people from the dotted line towards the dashed line. We can pray that the health insurers or Amazon Health or someone else is going to do it, but I doubt it. Those kinds of health services will focus on primary care and convenience, not reversing disease. And we all know the health insurers are a mess. Look how quickly they backed out of Medicare Advantage. Miracle weight loss drugs? They will help but who's going to ensure that people stay on them or actually stay healthier long-term? Big companies will just as soon wash their hands of health coverage than try to fix it. I hear it already: just give workers the money we would otherwise have spent on them, cap it, and let them figure out what insurance they need. We have to get ahead of that, and help companies make better choices for their people. If we want to increase policyholders and make sure we're not taking on bad risk, we have to invest to make it happen. So the solid line is where we need to get comfortable. We are the only industry that can realize the value of delaying disease. Everyone else makes money off treating it. Can we make good money and bring in millions of policyholders we will never otherwise have? Those are the questions."

It's the innovation head again: "But we've started with the early detection cancer tests, right? Helping people figure out if they have early cancer and getting preventive body scans will get cheaper. Why do we have to put our capital on the line when time could solve this?"

"True, yes," the CEO begins, "early cancer detection is getting better but it is taking too long to have the kind of broad impact we need to shift mortality. Early cancer detection or dementia tests still pick up issues too late making it more about managing illness instead of really postponing or ending it. We have a chance to capture much more of the value of preventing illness, just as we gained from anti-smoking." The CEO paused.

"Look at it this way: health insurers are getting a trillion a year in premiums or more to treat symptoms. We do very well serving people who are healthy, wealthy, and wise, but there aren't that many of them. We have to help change people's health trajectories much earlier and see if the big diseases can actually be pushed as far into the future as possible. The greatest and most valuable differentiator will be to help Americans live longer in better health *while* building up savings in a tax-efficient way. Is it risk-free? Of course not, but these are risks we understand and deal with every day. And it's a damn sight less risky than hunkering down and hoping for miracle drugs to save us or for our health insurer friends to figure this out. Time is not on our side, and hope is not a strategy."

The CEO stops and looks around the room. There are more faces that are lit up by what he's saying than those staring away into the middle distance. That's okay, not everyone is going to make the journey, but the journey is going to happen whether it's wanted or not.

ENDNOTES

121 Increasing auto safety measures, workplace safety, and building codes helped as well, lowering the risk of accidental deaths.

19. LIFE FOR HEALTH IN MEDICAID

As Life for Health gains traction with private enterprises, it will also need to be adapted for use in Medicaid. There are about fifteen to twenty million Medicaid-eligible adults nationwide between the ages of 35 and 64 who probably have some form of metabolic syndrome, qualifying them to join Life for Health.[122]

Unfortunately, integrating Life for Health into Medicaid requires more than just a cut and paste of the approach described in Chapters 13 through 17. Medicaid recipients move in and out of the program at a fairly high rate. About 9% of adult enrollees enter or leave Medicaid coverage in a year. Another 8% of adult enrollees disenroll only to re-enroll during the following year.[123] Sometimes enrollment cycling is due to short-term income fluctuations. More often it may be the result of an administrative change or documentation error that causes disenrollment. Whatever the reason, people moving into and out of Medicaid coverage experience breaks in care, impeding the kind of consistent treatment required to improve long-term health.

This means that the Medicaid version of Life for Health needs to provide continuous coverage for enrollees even after they leave Medicaid if their employer does not offer Life for Health. This would be a big change in the way Medicaid works, essentially voucherizing the Medicaid Life for Health benefit so that Medicare-enrolled participants can continue in the program even if they no longer receive any other Medicaid benefits.

From the outside, this might seem unfair. Why should a former Medicaid recipient who works for a company that does not offer Life for Health be able to maintain their Life for Health coverage when a work colleague who was not in Medicaid could not join through a company-sponsored benefit? The case for doing so is to equalize the opportunity for every American to regain their health, regardless of their past income. An adult in Medicaid is extremely unlikely to have built up the assets or wealth that would enable them to join Life for Health on a direct basis after leaving Medicaid. Likewise, people who start on GLP-1 therapy only to stop are very likely to regain weight especially if they have limited resources to buy healthier food.

Another way of looking at it is that someone who leaves Medicaid has roughly a one-in-ten chance of returning within a year, and probably higher in the first few years after leaving Medicaid, given the tenuousness of lower-income Americans' economic situations as they try to work their way into the middle class. It does neither the participant, Medicaid, nor private insurers any favors if someone who is able to reverse metabolic issues while enrolled in Life for Health through Medicaid goes on to reenter obesity or diabetes if they no longer have access to Life for Health clinicians or interventions. The eligibility window after someone departs Medicaid to participate in Life for Health need not be indefinite. It can be time-limited, or tied to achievement of an income threshold. However the benefit is bounded, it is vastly preferable for everyone, including taxpayers, to keep someone on track to maintain a better health trajectory.[124]

Life for Health Arrangements in Medicaid

So how practically would Life for Health work in Medicaid? Essentially, state Medicaid programs would be in the same position as a self-insuring company in the private sector version. As happens there, the state Medicaid plan would offer Life for Health as a combined group life and chronic disease plan for individuals with any stage of metabolic syndrome. The participant experience and benefits would be identical as in the corporate version. Medicaid-enrolled participants would receive treatment for metabolic health issues including interventions to reverse disease and maintain health, plus access to Predictive/Preventive Medicine and coverage for cancer diagnostics and treatment. All other health care including Routine and Emergency/Elective Medicine would be provided under regular Medicaid health plans.

Upon joining, Medicaid participants would receive a group life plan with premiums paid by Medicaid. As in the private offering, participants would undergo a comprehensive exam and agree to undertake interventions to restore health including nutritional and behavioral counseling. Medicaid participants would go through the same goal-setting processes with a Clinician in Charge, including virtual and in-person checkups to verify health progress. Health outcome payments for those who achieve health goals would be deposited into the cash balance of their life insurance plan. Likewise, as described in Part IV, Medicaid recipients could contribute data to longitudinal research and be compensated as is true for private plan participants. Similarly, funds and earnings would accumulate on a tax-deferred basis, with earnings excluded from Medicaid income tests.

From Medicaid's perspective, the Life for Health entity would serve a similar role as a Managed Care Organization (MCO) that contracts with state Medicaid programs to provide health services. The cost of upfront interventions to reverse disease would be shared between the state Medicaid agency and the Life for Health entity, with the latter compensated in future years based on reductions in medical spending for participants versus similarly situated Medicaid recipients not enrolled in Life for Health. The face value of the group life policy could be set formulaically based on an enrollee's age and family situation (i.e., less coverage for solo individuals and higher coverage for those with children).

The resulting system is illustrated in Figure 19.1:

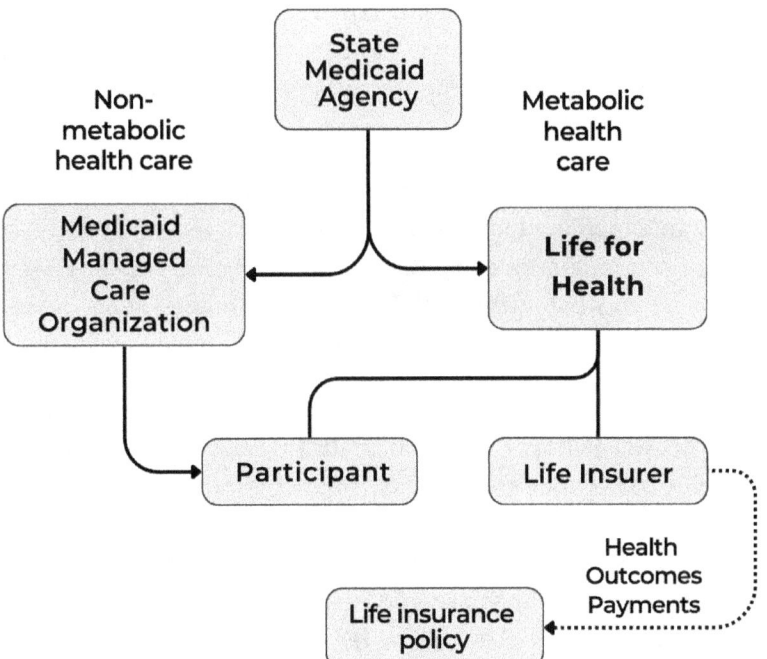

Figure 19.1: Entities and Payment Flows in Medicaid

How would the system work if a Medicaid-enrolled participant leaves Medicaid, assuming the portability approach described previously is in place? As in the private sector, there are a couple of possibilities.

One version is that the participant is employed by a company that offers Life for Health in which case their Medicaid arrangements could simply be rolled over into the private sector offering. They would continue to receive metabolic health treatments through a Life for Health entity.

The other possibility is that the ex-Medicaid beneficiary's new employer does not offer Life for Health. In this case, the individual would continue to receive metabolic health treatment from the Life for Health MCO entity. Medicaid would cover the difference between the former recipient's ability to pay premiums and Life for Health's outlays for the participant's metabolic health issues. The state Medicaid provider would seek reimbursement for these amounts, plus group life premiums, from the former recipient's employer or private sector health insurer.

Establishing Life for Health within Medicaid will require support from elected and appointed federal and state leaders, including issuance of waivers from federal rules by CMS (perhaps through CMMI's existing authorities) and potentially administrative or legislative action at the state level.

As in all governmental actions, solving a problem is as much a function of political will as policy or administrative finesse. In that respect, Life for Health is a winner for governors and legislative leaders in red and blue states. All governors face increasingly difficult health spending outlooks, including costs for state employees and retirees as well as Medicaid enrollees. This is especially true in southern and midwestern states which tend to have smaller income tax bases and, as shown in Chapter 2, high prevalence of metabolic syndrome.

For conservative governors, *Life for Health* offers a unique public-private framework to improve state employees' and poorer residents' health situations, reducing long-term public health spending. It is pro-business as well as fiscally conservative. For blue state governors, *Life for Health* is an opportunity to increase access to cutting edge medical services, tackling one of the greatest sources of socioeconomic disparities. State leaders from the right and the left will be working in concert, each from their preferred ideological perspective, toward the same goals: improving their citizens' health futures while reducing payouts to sick-care focused health conglomerates.

ENDNOTES

122 This is based on Medicaid-provided data on adult enrollment before COVID (2017) and post-COVID (2021 and 2024) and the estimated prevalence of obesity among adult Medicaid recipients (40%). See, e.g. KFF Reports on Medicaid enrollees, CMS Medicaid and CHIP Enrollment Trends Snapshot.

123 Medicaid and CHIP Payment and Access Commission, "An Updated Look at Rates of Churn and Continuous Coverage in Medicaid and CHIP", October 2021

124 A smaller problem in Medicaid's current structure relates to the cash balance in Life for Health associated policies and eligibility rules for senior citizens seeking Medicaid long-term care benefits. Most states require older Americans to exhaust virtually all their liquid assets to qualify for long-term care coverage, with liquid assets defined in almost all states to include the cash balance on life insurance policies above $5,000 to $10,000 (depending on the state). Obviously, this will be an issue for a Life for Health participant over 65 who has accrued tens of thousands of dollars of savings in their policies over the prior years in anticipation of post-retirement medical costs. Making Life for Health participants over 65 spend down their cash balances to qualify for long-term care coverage would be self-defeating since anyone who needs Medicaid's support for long-term care is almost certainly also incurring, or soon to incur, material health costs. This problem could be solved by allowing life insurance policies associated with Life for Health arrangements to have a higher asset exclusion threshold, with the proviso that use of cash balances would be limited to covering medical costs.

PART IV

REALIZING PREDICTIVE/PREVENTIVE MEDICINE

20. PREVENTION, PREDICTION, TRUST, AND TRANSPARENCY

> "So the one thing that was missing across the board was trust. And the second thing that was missing was transparency. And that was really straightforward and simple to get to. And so I was like, okay, let's do this, but let's be transparent and let's do it on a cost plus [pricing] basis so people saw our costs so they would trust it."
>
> –Mark Cuban, Co-founder of Cost Plus Drug Company

Reversing disease and achieving better health trajectories is the first half of *Life for Health's* mission. The second half is to establish Predictive/Preventive Medicine as a coequal branch of medicine. If Serious Medicine is the muscle and bone of stopping chronic disease, Predictive/Preventive Medicine is the brain.

As we have seen, preventing disease is a long-standing dream of political leaders, clinicians, and health economists. But it very stubbornly remains just that, a dream—and one that, like a distant desert mirage, keeps receding from view. Why? Chapter 5 offered part of the answer, that we continue to hold to a misguided notion that one system can serve short-term *and* long-term medical challenges. But, even after solving that conceptual gap, a number of practical issues remain.

The biggest barriers relate to valuing prevention. Although health economists are adept at calculating the potential value of forestalling disease, it is much more complicated with preventive measures to assign a value to specific measures than it is for a drug or treatment. If a person has high cholesterol and takes a statin, it's easy to measure how much their lipid levels change. It's much harder to identify the role of diet, exercise, or sleep or assign a preventive value to each. This is a fatal problem in the RPS Vortex, where everything is priced based on inputs or activities.

A second barrier is the Prevention Paradox, the tendency to prioritize use of newer and more expensive therapies in individuals with more severe disease. That's what's happening now with GLP-1 drugs. Demand for the drugs is increasing sharply as evidence of their efficacy accumulates. Insurers are responding by changing reimbursement rules to cover only those with higher BMIs.

Ironically, prioritizing better therapies based on severity seems to be supported in chronic disease by clinical trial data, where those with more advanced metabolic or autoimmune conditions tend to show the greatest benefit from using a newer therapy (versus existing therapies or a placebo). The greatest weight loss in GLP-1 trials occurs among recipients who have the highest pre-trial weights or BMIs. However, multi-year outcomes data for metabolic surgery suggests that the less time that someone has had obesity and diabetes, the greater the chance of achieving long-term remission.[125] The statistical conundrum is that people who have obesity or diabetes for fewer years tend to have lower BMIs or less severe blood sugar levels, lowering the absolute and relative magnitude of using cutting edge drugs. Thus, the paradox. We measure value and efficacy over short periods, prioritize access to those who have the greatest response (within those timeframes) and withhold access to those earlier in the disease process until they, too, progress to advanced disease.

Why should we have to choose? Yes, of course, drugs can be expensive and funds to pay for them are not unlimited. Well, actually, that's not quite correct. *Current* funds are very limited but the present value of long-term disease remission and longer healthspans would unlock a lot more funds, especially if a person with less advanced disease is more likely to achieve a great *long-term* outcome. Likewise, the current drug pricing paradigm is not carved in stone. It can be changed, as discussed in Chapter 29.

The best answer to the Prevention Paradox is suggested in Chapter 3, to create a system that attacks metabolic syndrome at both ends of the chronic disease cascade at once. Reverse or blunt illness among those with the advanced situations but work equally hard to prevent onset or progression among those in the earliest stages.

Another challenge is tailoring preventive measures to people's unique situations and capturing which interventions, alone or in combination work for people, when, and why. Many medical measures like vaccines can be used universally among a target population without modifying doses; however, non-medical preventive measures must be customized and adjusted frequently. Wellness and longevity experts offer general advice about what we *should* do: eat nutritious food; don't overeat; don't smoke or drink alcohol; move and exercise; get eight hours of sleep; minimize stress; eliminate harmful pollutants. However, "eat nutritiously" can entail different diets depending on a person's situation, metabolism, and environment. The devil is in the details to select the best measures and mix them up periodically to keep participants motivated and yield consistent results. The toolbox of preventive *approaches* is broadly usable but the *measures* and dosages used at any point varies from person to person, and changes over time with changes in their life situations.

A final challenge is changing the way predictive and preventive research is conducted. The gold standard approach to test drug efficacy is a double-blind randomized control trial, in which people are randomly split between treatment and placebo arms (with representative populations in each arm), with neither participants nor clinicians able to tell easily if the person is getting the novel treatment, an existing treatment, or a placebo. Dr. Kevin Hall, a longtime NIH researcher (who recently resigned from the NIH), is one of the few nutrition scientists who has even come close to recreating drug-like trials for dietary questions, running weeks-long studies that isolate study participants on NIH grounds and control food intake. It's impossible to double-blind treatment so he and his team rotate people between different diets to replicate the effect. Even then, protocols like these are impossible to execute at scale or for long periods. As a result, studies of preventive measures like diet and exercise rely on self-reported data, which is unreliable. As the misanthropic TV character, Dr. Gregory House, puts it, "people lie."

So if we have to rely on observational trials, comparing outcomes using real-world behavior, we need different and richer kinds of data, and contemporaneous collection of biosamples. Participants might have to share grocery purchases, do daily weigh-ins, or connect apps and devices like CGMs to upload data automatically. Perhaps even a daily or weekly blood sample. This is not crazy. Insulin-dependent diabetics sometimes test their blood multiple times a day. The threshold of data used to form conclusions will have to go up, along with the rigor and transparency of data analytics. It's hard, but in a system like Life for Health it is achievable, especially with compensation on offer.

Longitudinal Data in Life for Health

Life for Health provides a rare opportunity to rethink these challenges and solve them in new ways. The following chapters provide an initial roadmap, highlighting the criticality of collecting longitudinal data to understand disease risks, and building trust with data contributors—giving them control over how their data is used and compensating them financially and intangibly through guaranteed access to relevant insights or interventions.

Chapter 21 provides historical perspective on two disease areas, HIV/AIDS and cystic fibrosis (CF), in which coalitions of trust among people with a disease, clinicians, researchers, drugmakers, and regulators greatly accelerated breakthrough treatments. These examples provide the foundation for what can be built systematically in Life for Health.

Chapter 22 illustrates how longitudinal data can be used to create virtual time machines, applying new technologies to biosamples collected decades earlier to reconstruct pathology and inform predictive disease models. Chapter 23 extends these ideas, explaining why we need to build health narratives, not just collect medical data, to understand the interplay of factors in complex disease, and build less biased AI models.

Efforts to build Predictive/Preventive Medicine must also address public skepticism about data collection. Big tech and social media firms have brilliantly spun the strands of online activity into corporate gold through algorithmic content feeds and targeted ads. This cannot happen with health data, even stripped of personally identifying information. Chapter 24 describes how data collection works in Life for Health, going beyond existing paradigms of either-or privacy to give participants greater control over how their data is used, and how participants can be compensated for sharing data.

Chapter 25 brings the preceding arguments together to explain how Life for Health addresses the biggest barrier in realizing preventive medicine—what's it worth? Essentially, how do we assess and share value from preventing disease over time?

Building Trust and Being Transparent

The possibility of Predictive/Preventive Medicine will remain just that, unrealized potential, unless Life for Health and the clinicians who work within it earn participants' trust. It's the first thing that billionaire entrepreneur Mark Cuban talks about when he describes the Cost Plus Drug Company, his insurgent effort to remake drug pricing, supply, and distribution. Americans are right, he says, to mistrust the opaque, convoluted ways of the status quo. Everything about the system's complexity invites suspicion—inexplicable bills and obtuse reimbursement rules. Patients and caregivers are forced to devote time and energy to battle claim denials and coverage changes even as they fight serious illness. Frustration and feelings of impotence in hard moments understandably calcify into deep and abiding mistrust.

Medical research, too, has had its share of ethical abuses and missteps. The expropriation of Henrietta Lacks's cancer cells without her permission and the Tuskegee experiments that left syphilitic men untreated, along with the harm done to infected female partners, were among the most horrific in American history. Ethical norms governing human research have greatly improved but transparency about research priorities, goals and findings (good or bad) remain opaque. Even when the

NIH and FDA required all clinical trials data to disclose results (including failures), many trial sponsors failed to comply. As a result, valuable insights are lost, and provocative research findings are hard to replicate, calling into question the validity of claimed advances.

The most recent crisis of trust arose during and after COVID. Amid a fast-evolving situation, public health leaders were loath to signal uncertainty about the nature of the virus and how it spread. Directives about hand washing and masking were reversed and insights about airborne spread were delayed. It was understandable in the initial confusion and fear of the first few months, but these missteps were followed by messaging about vaccines' benefits that conflated their value in reducing the risk of death with the ability to prevent spread. Debates over public school closures, masking, and vaccine mandates became politicized, with opinions on each issue hardening into opposing, absolutist views. Collection and reporting of public health data became an object of political pressure. The ability to make reasoned arguments or compromises disappeared. Then, once the threat receded, government scientists suffered an additional credibility hit, offering confusing explanations about whether public funds had been used to fund research that may have led to COVID, including work at the Chinese lab where the virus may have originated.

Thus, Life for Health's mission to build trust begins at an inopportune moment, with much public skepticism. As with Cuban's approach, the process of earning trust requires Life for Health to be authentic and consistent in what it promises and delivers. Participants must have real agency in health decisions, transparency about how data is used, and control over their data's use. The nomenclature of "participants" rather "patients" must be realized in tangible ways. Layers of insurer micromanagement like prior authorization must be removed and replaced with transparency about clinical practices, pricing, and participant outcomes.

Building trust ultimately depends on the strength of participant-clinician relationships. Life for Health shifts these discussions from a transactional, diagnostic focus to create an ongoing dialogue about participants' health trajectory, near and long-term goals, and quality of life priorities. This opens space for clinicians to reframe the predictive aspects of early detection as an ongoing process, one often characterized by shades of grey rather than a binary choice. Diagnosis may seem definitive, but it often comes too late in the disease process, and as a result, is also subject to error and nuance. Data gathering, diagnostics, and preventive measures are meant to reduce risk and give participants more time to take control over their health trajectory. Insights from all three activities help participants and clinicians understand their current situation and where things are headed.

The participant-clinician rapport is vital to make informed choices and set reasonable health goals, balancing risk and uncertainty. If people are not rational maximizers, and they are not, the process of dialogue at least puts instinctual tendencies to the test. Some clinicians argue that measures to improve early detection are fraught with danger, either overpromising resilience or evoking anxiety through false positives. These concerns are well-founded in the RPS Vortex, since information is invariably used to boost near-term financial returns.

However, in Life for Health, discussions about early detection do not begin with an observation like, "Oh, we should see if *you might have* X," where X is something quite fearsome. Rather, the conversation happens regularly and more naturally in the course of developing plans to achieve health outcomes, informed by continuous data gathering and participants' preferences about how aggressive they want to be in undertaking treatment.

This approach connects to the larger goal of enlisting participants to provide deidentified data for use by external researchers and product makers. However, this option is not discussed at length until a participant has made progress towards reversing disease, or other initial goals. In Life for Health, consenting to contribute data is not a one-way decision. Participants can stop sharing at any time if they change their mind. They can see how their data is being used including the names of research groups that license datasets with their information, information about study goals, and actual results, once available. To close the loop between research and practice, Life for Health clinicians and participants are notified about research findings relevant to their situations, including eligibility for clinical trials or new treatments.

The Participant Experience

Before going deeper into *Life for Health's* approach to data sharing, it is useful to walk through a concrete example, returning to the exemplar participant, Frank, introduced in Chapter 14. There, we focused on how Frank benefits from Serious Medicine. Here, we extend the narrative to describe how he, and all participants, would contribute to and realize benefits from, Predictive/Preventive Medicine.

When Frank joined Life for Health, he underwent a comprehensive health assessment including a full genome sequencing. This revealed that he has Lynch Syndrome, a heritable genetic disorder that confers higher colorectal cancer risk. As a result, Frank's Clinician in Charge added annual non-invasive colorectal cancer screenings to his treatment plan supplemented by multi-cancer early detection ("MCED") liquid biopsies every few years. MCED tests sift blood plasma for genetic matter cast off by tumor cells, indicating the presence of a malignancy. Frank's baseline colonoscopy was clear, but a liquid biopsy test three years later indicated the presence of colorectal cancer, subsequently confirmed with a colonoscopy. Frank's malignancy was found at an earlier stage thanks to discovery of his genetic predisposition and frequent but risk-informed use of non-invasive detection.

In keeping with Life for Health's commitment to provide access to top cancer diagnosticians and clinicians, Frank is referred to a Lynch Syndrome specialist at an NCI Comprehensive Center. Luckily, Frank's tumor has a genetic signature making him a good candidate for neoadjuvant immunotherapy. He receives a drug to help his immune cells detect and attack tumor cells before undergoing surgery to remove the tumor. After surgery, Frank has a complete recovery, with no detectable signs of malignancy, increasing his odds of long-term survival.[126] This illustrates how participants benefit from Predictive/Preventive

Medicine, with genetic screening and early detection tests providing the prognostic basis to apply Serious Medicine.

In the months following his metabolic surgery, Frank opts to make de-identified data available outside of Life for Health for research and product development. He decides to include his full health narrative since joining Life for Health, including genetic results, plus non-medical data including grocery purchases and outputs from sleep and exercise apps. Life for Health software provides AI-drafted summaries weekly to Frank (a cadence he selected), which he can review and revise. The software prompts him to do a monthly reflection on how he thinks he is doing and add any learnings from the prior month.

Apart from cancer risk, Frank's gene sequencing also reveals the presence of variants affecting his Alzheimer's risk. One mutation in a gene called APOE is actually protective, reducing Frank's likelihood of developing dementia. However, Frank also has gene variants that boost inflammatory response and production of harmful blood lipids, neither of which is surprising given how advanced his metabolic syndrome became at a relatively young age.

These gene variants make Frank a highly desirable candidate for Alzheimer's research. Through Life for Health, he pre-qualifies to join current or future studies analyzing protective APOE variants and others investigating lipid metabolism and inflammation. Blood draws taken every six months to verify Frank's progress towards metabolic health goals are included in a study tracing plasma proteins, helping inform research explaining associations between key protein levels and ADRD risk. This finding, along with a summary of other plasma protein studies, is provided to Frank and his clinician to inform future decisions about preventive measures and predictive testing.

At an annual check-in, Frank's Clinician in Charge speaks with him about enrolling in a long-term Alzheimer's risk study requiring periodic neuroimaging, cognitive testing, and CSF draws, which Frank agrees to do. He does not have to be requalified for the trial given his pre-qualification through Life for Health and automatic analysis of his medical and demographic situations. Frank enrolls after speaking with a nurse about study requirements and completing a study-specific consent.

Over the years, Frank provides 20,000 data points in addition to health narrative and electronic medical record treatment data, all collected in the regular course of his Life for Health relationship. Portions of his data are licensed by researchers in over a hundred observational and retrospective studies assessing metabolic surgery, colon cancer, durability of weight loss, inflammation, and Alzheimer's risk. A key aspect of Life for Health's participatory approach is to compensate individuals for data they contribute, as detailed in Chapter 24. Frank's share of licensing revenue during his first decade as a participant totals $20,000, a sum added to his insurance policy's cash balance that grows, thereafter, tax-free.

Frank's experience illustrates how much everyone stands to gain by establishing Predictive/Preventive Medicine on an equivalent plane with Serious Medicine. Frank lives longer than would have happened if his Lynch Syndrome had gone undetected or had the tumor only been found at an advanced stage. Insurers and product makers benefit from the evidence around predictive test accuracy and neoadjuvant treatment. Researchers benefit from being able to access and use his de-identified data, and multiple clinical trial sponsors can enroll Frank faster and more cheaply given Life for Health's approach to pre-qualify participants for future research.

This is how we realize the promise of connecting Serious and Predictive/Preventive Medicine, reinvesting data from those undergoing treatment for a particular set of issues to inform broader efforts to understand and detect other diseases that shorten healthspan and lifespan

ENDNOTES

125 See Purnell, Jonathan Q, Elizabeth N Dewey, Blandine Laferrère, Faith Selzer, David R Flum, James E Mitchell, Alfons Pomp, et al. 2020. "Diabetes Remission Status During Seven-year Follow-up of the Longitudinal Assessment of Bariatric Surgery Study." The Journal of Clinical Endocrinology & Metabolism 106 (3): 774–88. https://doi.org/10.1210/

clinem/dgaa849, and Jans, Anders, Ingmar Näslund, et. al. 2019. "Duration of Type 2 Diabetes and Remission Rates After Bariatric Surgery in Sweden 2007–2015: A Registry-based Cohort Study." PLoS Medicine 16 (11): e1002985. https://doi.org/10.1371/journal.pmed.1002985.

126 A 2024 study of Dutch patients showed this approach avoided the need for chemotherapy post-surgery, while improving long-term survival, a dual benefit of better outcomes and reduced toxicity for the individual with cancer. See: Chalabi, M., et. al. (2024). Neoadjuvant Immunotherapy in Locally Advanced Mismatch Repair-Deficient Colon Cancer. The New England journal of medicine, 390(21), 1949–1958. The potential value of immunotherapies to life insurers through lifespan improvements was analyzed by two economists, Ralph Koijen and Stijn Van Nieuwerburgh, in a 2020 paper. See Koijen, RS, Van Nieuwerburgh, S, "Combining Life and Health Insurance," The Quarterly Journal of Economics (2020), 913–958.

21. HOW PARTICIPATION AND TRUST ACCELERATES CURES

Looking back on his life and his battle against pancreatic cancer, Steve Jobs told biographer Walter Isaacson that he hoped "the biggest innovations of the twenty-first century" would come at "the intersection of biology and technology." Jobs was alive years after being diagnosed thanks to intense medical technology and, as a billionaire, he had the resources to buy time. He was one of the first in the world to have his tumor DNA fully sequenced, helping his doctors select or exclude treatments based on genetic features.

Jobs died as he lived, an irrepressible optimist, telling Isaacson: "I'm either going to be one of the first to be able to outrun a cancer like this or I'm going to be one of the last to die from it." If only. A dozen years on, more than a half million Americans have succumbed to pancreatic cancer. Today it is still the most lethal malignancy as measured by the ratio of annual deaths to new cases. His vision remains a distant hope. Why?

Jobs' premature death illustrates a hard reality of medical progress. Being a billionaire gives you access to the best that is currently available, but as John D. Rockefeller learned a century earlier, money goes only so far. Data is the real currency in ending disease not money, and knowledge based on validation at scale is the only lasting wealth.

Amassing the full context of the events that precede disease onset is impossible in a system that gathers data person by person, often not even starting until after diagnosis. It's much too little, far too late. Stopping disease has to begin earlier, enabling work to identify reliable risk predictors, and a program of ongoing vigilance to detect if a person is heading towards disease.

A real system to prevent disease begins with continuous data gathering, creating a deep and rich library to isolate risk factors, predict vulnerability and resilience, and prevent onset. Instead of only starting to gather information when something is amiss, the system encourages and rewards people to provide data on an ongoing basis. It's harder than it sounds, especially in a medical system that views patients as passive recipients of knowledge rather than contributors to it, and within a larger tech and media world that leverages behavior for profit. The health care system instills subservience while the media ecosystem engenders mistrust. Still, the foundations of a participatory and symbiotic approach exist, exemplified by efforts in HIV/AIDS and CF to organize individuals, clinicians, researchers, and drugmakers into durable coalitions to develop functional cures.

HIV/AIDS Sets the Template of Patient Activism

The mid-1980s were a dismal time in the fight against HIV/AIDS. Researchers were struggling to understand how the virus worked. US health agencies were dragging their feet in funding surveillance and treatment research, reflecting long-standing bias against gay men. In the Spring of 1987, activists changed the game, forming the AIDS Coalition to Unleash Power, better known as ACT-UP. Fusing disobedience and demonstrative public acts, its leaders disrupted politicians' speeches, blockaded NIH and FDA buildings and shamed politicians, bureaucrats, and drug companies over their inaction. In October 1987, during the National March on Washington for Lesbian and Gay Rights, activists unveiled the first AIDS Quilt on the Washington Mall. It pierced the public consciousness, illustrating the epidemic's extent and impact in the most tangible way. Luminaries in entertainment and the arts lent their names and voices to amplify ACT-UP's sense of urgency.

But attitudes in official Washington and federal research dollars did not begin to shift in a big way until the national media spotlighted the ordeal of an Indiana teenager, Ryan White, a hemophiliac who contracted HIV from an infusion of contaminated clotting factor. His school district barred him from attending school, fearing he might spread the virus. He and his mother went to court to reverse the decision, a battle they ultimately won. White died in 1990, but his profile in courage along with his mother's, decisively changed the political dynamic around HIV/AIDS.

About the same time, as scientists identified compounds that could extend life, ACT-UP and others pressed the FDA and the NIH to allow HIV positive people to take experimental therapies in parallel with clinical trials. Activists understood that some treatments would not work and might even be toxic. Still, they argued, broader access would accelerate trials and bolster results. Worst case, it would be a compassionate use. ACT-UP leaders focused on Dr. Anthony Fauci, a central figure in efforts to speed up drug development, who headed up the NIH branch responsible for HIV. Despite initial misgivings, Fauci relented in June 1989 to allowing "a parallel path" to give HIV-infected individuals access to experimental drugs still in trials, a move confirmed shortly afterwards by the FDA commissioner.

HIV/AIDS clinicians responded to activists' calls to build treatment networks; they built registries tracking who had taken what drugs, and shared progress and setbacks at frequent scientific conferences. The sense of mission spread word about which drugs seemed to help slow the virus down, and in which patients. Drug companies racing to develop combination therapies loosened intellectual property strictures, allowing proprietary compounds to be tested along with competitors' products. This synthesis of HIV positive individuals, researchers, clinicians, drugmakers, and regulators led to a remarkable string of scientific breakthroughs. The decade and a half from 1992 to 2007 brought five generations of HIV therapies to market, an unprecedented track record of innovation, including thirty plus FDA-approved drugs. Time ran out on millions of HIV positive individuals in the US and around the world, but tens of millions more are alive today thanks to those who lent their bodies and lives to accelerate science.

As antivirals became more effective, advocates shifted to quality of life issues. The original combination therapies meant taking lots of drugs, twelve or more pills a day at specific times, and many had wicked side effects. They wanted drugmakers to make treatments less toxic, cheaper, and easier to take. Pharma companies responded enthusiastically since winning all-in-one combination therapies could gain market share and improve treatment adherence.

Meanwhile, infectious disease clinicians had established aggressive HIV surveillance protocols, going back to the age of paper and pencils, including frequent testing and longitudinal tracking of viral loads. Researchers and clinicians noticed that a very small group of people were somehow able to resist infection, even after repeated exposure. These individuals, called "elite controllers," had a mutated form of a key gene, called CCR5, which coded for the main gateway HIV used to invade immune cells. Drugmakers scrambled to develop a drug to mimic the effects of mutant CCR5, hoping to block viral replication. The resulting drug bought critical years for HIV positive people during the mid-2000s until being replaced by superior antivirals.

The discovery of elite controllers underscores the importance of data gathering. The odds of finding people with unusual resilience increases dramatically with the number of people from whom data is gathered. In the legal profession it is said that hard cases make bad law but in biology rare variants can be diamonds in the rough. Another lesson is that the existence of outliers is context dependent. Until HIV came along, the CCR5 mutation had been unknown, having no practical value to carriers or noticeable impact on their survival.[127] However, once HIV emerged, the mutation took on immense value. Anomalies that are benign, even harmful, in one context become lifesavers in another.

Finally, HIV demonstrates how Serious Medicine breakthroughs can be reused in Predictive/Preventive Medicine. The four-in-one pill that is now the standard of care to stop HIV post-infection is also one of the best medical approaches to *prevent* HIV transmission, using a daily pill or a monthly injection. This is especially valuable for younger heterosexual women, who are now at greatest risk globally of HIV infection. Repurposing treatment to prevent infection may have already saved as many lives as the treatment itself, buying time while scientists design a long-acting vaccine.[128]

Cystic Fibrosis: Organizing Data and De-risking Clinical Trials

While HIV drug research accelerated in the late 1990s, progress against cystic fibrosis (CF), a heritable, inevitably fatal condition, stalled. Scientists knew that CF was caused by mutations in a gene to transport fluids out of cells. The dysfunction led to a life-threatening buildup of mucus, most dangerously in the lungs and digestive tract. In the 1960s, most people with CF died before they turned fifteen. By 2000, therapies helped people with CF live to forty, but they required hours-long daily regimens to clear fluids, suffering through life-threatening infections and frequent hospitalizations.

As fearsome as the disease was, it was quite rare. Only 35,000 Americans had CF. This made the economics of drug development very challenging. Why invest hundreds of millions to make a drug that might only benefit tens of thousands? Robert Beall, the head of the Cystic Fibrosis Foundation (CFF), the main patient advocacy group, heard this from one drug company after another. So he set out to change the risk-reward calculus to develop a treatment. Beall and his team set out to reduce drug R&D risks by, in effect, gift wrapping access to the CFF community, patients and clinicians, to accelerate research and clinical trials.

The CFF started by compiling data about every person with CF, their genetics, treatments, and clinicians. Beall hoped that every person with CF could qualify for *some* kind of future clinical trial, even though he did not yet know which disease pathways would prove to be "druggable." That was for a drugmaker to figure out, but it would be a much easier problem to solve, Beall wagered, with CFF's data. Once a lab-tested treatment was ready, CFF could mobilize eligible patients speeding up human trials.[129] Beall also created a clinician network, linking experts at CF treatment centers within a unified patient registry. He brought clinician and patient representatives into deliberations about how the data would be used, anticipating that drug development would require hard trade-offs, anticipating that when these arose, he would need community backing.

CF poses a thorny scientific problem. Although all disease forms are caused by mutations in the CFTR gene, some disease forms are much more severe than others. Sifting through the genomic data, researchers grouped mutations into three categories. One related to how cells collect fluid, the second to how fluids are transported to the cell surface, and the third to problems at the cell surface in getting fluid packages out. Most CF sufferers had some combination of the first or second issues while a small group, less than 5%, had the cell surface problem only.

Having aggregated patient demand, Beall went in search of supply—a hungry drug developer willing to tackle CF. He struck pay dirt with Aurora Biosciences, a small San Diego-based company commercializing a Nobel Prize-winning approach called high-throughput screening to speed up the laborious process of matching potential drugs to potential targets. Beall figured Aurora could de-risk the first stage of drug design, narrowing the range of targets and potential drug designs. Then, Beall hoped, he would be able to get a bigger drugmaker to finish the job.

Then fate intervened. A year after striking the CFF deal, Aurora was acquired by Vertex, just the kind of drugmaker that Beall hoped to attract. Vertex shared Aurora's mission of rationalizing drug design, but at first, its leaders focused on antivirals to treat HIV and Hepatitis-C. Work on CF seemed like a distraction. A year later, with little progress on antivirals, the tide shifted, and Vertex's leaders returned to Beall seeking to expand the CFF relationship. Beall drove a hard bargain, agreeing to co-fund research and expedite clinical trials, but insisted on a share of future drug revenue, and a seat at the table with Vertex scientists in making key development decisions.[130]

Almost immediately, the relationship was put to the test. Vertex scientists wanted to focus on the 5% of CF patients who only had dysfunctions in the cell membrane. Vertex and CFF knew that a functional cure for CF would have to solve more common and severe mutations affecting intracellular dysfunction but the Vertex team thought they would be able to move faster by focusing on the cell surface issue. It was simpler to solve and breakthroughs on that issue could be reused as part of a future combination therapy. Plus, they argued, clinical trials for a drug to help a few thousand CF patients would be smaller and could be completed relatively quickly. Vertex and CFF would either fail fast, in Silicon Valley parlance, or have the basis of something much bigger to solve more widespread issues. CFF's leaders agreed with the logic but it put them in a difficult position with the CF community, having to argue in favor of prioritizing work on a drug that, at least initially, would not benefit most patients. The years of trust equity built up by CFF's leaders paid off. Heartened by CFF's openness in explaining the near-term and longer-term plan and the tradeoffs, the patient and clinician community rallied behind the decision.

Sure enough, the strategy worked. The FDA agreed to a small clinical trial for the initial drug, which CFF helped to fill quickly. Once that drug was approved in 2012, work to solve the harder mutations accelerated. Again, Vertex tapped the patient registry and treatment network to speed clinical trials, winning FDA approval for a two-drug combination in 2014 that helped about half of the people with CF. Four years later, the FDA approved a three-drug combination, Trikafta®, which fixed most intracellular and cell surface issues. For the first time, Vertex and the CFF had proved that the core dysfunctions of a lethal genetic illness could be repaired using a small-molecule drug. From its original $40 million investment in Aurora, CFF received rights to approximately $4 billion in future sales. Later, CFF sold its rights to future royalties, plowing the windfall into new CF research and drug affordability programs.

The CFF relationship also saved Vertex. A dozen years after its first drug approval, almost all of Vertex's $10 billion in annual revenue comes from Trikafta® and a successor CF drug. This revenue stream enabled the company to acquire another, equally ambitious program, in this case to solve type 1 diabetes by restoring insulet cell function. Fittingly, the drug company that Vertex acquired began their work in 2017 in a partnership with Breakthrough T1D, the leading type 1 diabetes advocacy group, using an agreement modelled on the Vertex-CFF alliance.

Applying the Lessons of HIV & CF

The history of HIV and CF treatments underscore the value of collecting data ahead of when it might be needed, making it possible to stratify individuals by risk and malfunction and identify unique subgroups like elite controllers.

Second, both examples illustrate how critical it is to organize people to participate in research and pre-qualify them for future trials. Understand the clinician networks and the strength of the clinician-patient relationship. After trust and data, time is the most critical element to solving disease. Building networks of trust reduces the time to validate ideas and get treatments to market.

Third, building trust and transparency is a two-way street. Just as individuals contribute data to advance research, so too, they earn and rightfully expect a voice in shaping priorities and getting accelerated access to novel therapies. Experiences in HIV and CF demonstrate that in a climate of trust and aligned interests, people facing serious medical issues can handle ambiguity and hard choices.

Ironically, given so much political rancor over COVID, one of the first areas where these lessons have been applied is in efforts to understand Long COVID, a highly variable condition characterized by persistent neurological, circulatory, autoimmune, respiratory, energy, and mood dysfunctions. For some, the manifestations are profoundly disabling, while for others, they abate with time. In the pandemic's first year, a group called the Patient-Led Research Collaborative organized individuals to solicit, collect, and analyze longitudinal data about Long COVID symptoms and treatments that people were trying. Previously efforts like these had been run through an academic center or advocacy group, but in the face of a novel threat, there was space for a grassroots approach. Fortunately, too, some of the initiative's leaders had scientific experience which boosted the rigor and credibility of work to catalogue insights. Their work culminated in one of the most cited scientific papers of 2023, coauthored with cardiologist and COVID expert, Dr. Eric Topol.[131]

Their data and advocacy also helped redirect an NIH-run Long COVID effort that was floundering. Long COVID activists persuaded administrators to refocus grants on issues identified by collaborative members. In parallel, two Yale University researchers, Harlan Krumholz and Akiko Iwasaki, created an initiative called LISTEN to share research progress with advocates and solicit their input and feedback in identifying hypotheses to explore. All of this is progress, creating connective tissue among participants, advocates, and researchers. Grassroots energy, paired with respectful dialogue and data can be discordant, even messy, but builds durable coalitions supporting science.

Steve Jobs faced pancreatic cancer in many ways as an "n of 1." He had unique access to cutting-edge science and fought illness with bravery and determination. Yet, solitary crusades to defeat complex diseases seldom work. Victory requires the wisdom of the crowd, meaning much broader data and biosamples, and analysis of rich longitudinal data to identify disease mechanisms and therapeutic targets.

It may be true, as Shakespeare mused in *Julius Caesar*, that our faults are not in the stars but in ourselves, but so too, are our saviors. Preventing multimorbidity and other complex chronic and age-related diseases is an impossible mission without participatory research. Over time, data and experiences speak much louder than bullhorns and viral fundraising. Both are necessary, but data, trust, and organizing is decisive.

ENDNOTES

127 Research in the 2010s showed that the mutation might confer a small evolutionary disadvantage, making carriers' slightly more likely to die from some flu viruses.

128 Encouragingly, in 2024, a twice-a-year vaccine tested in over 2,100 women had 100% efficacy in preventing HIV infection. Bekker, Linda-Gail, Moupali Das, Quarraisha Abdool Karim, Khatija Ahmed, Joanne Batting, William Brumskine, Katherine Gill, et al. 2024. "Twice-Yearly Lenacapavir or Daily F/TAF for HIV Prevention in Cisgender Women." New England Journal of Medicine 391 (13): 1179–92. https://doi.org/10.1056/nejmoa2407001.

129 Goss, Christopher H., Nicole Mayer-Hamblett, Judy Williams, and Bonnie W. Ramsey. 2008. "The Cystic Fibrosis Foundation Therapeutics Development Network: A National Effort by the Cystic Fibrosis Foundation to Build a Clinical Trials Network." Children S Health Care 37 (1): 5–20. https://doi.org/10.1080/02739610701766859.

130 The story of Vertex and their work with CFF is chronicled in the book The Antidote by Barry Welsh.

131 Davis, H.E., McCorkell, L., Vogel, J.M. et al. Long COVID: major findings, mechanisms and recommendations. Nat Rev Microbiol 21, 133–146 (2023).

22. GETTING LONGITUDINAL

> "A record, if it is to be useful to science, must be continuously extended, it must be stored, and above all it must be consulted."
>
> –"As We May Think," Vannevar Bush, 1945

In school we are taught the scientific method: develop a hypothesis, gather data, analyze the data, draw conclusions, and revise the hypothesis. This framework works when the experimental question is well defined, the variables can be well controlled, and the underlying science is well understood. You might say these kinds of studies are "routine" science in the same sense of the word as in Routine Medicine, building on settled methods of inquiry.

Chronic disease confounds the standard approach, involving many many more variables and interdependencies. Research tells us *what* happens biologically as disease progresses, but it often fails to clarify *why* a chain of events occurred or differentiate between associations and causes. One study says one factor was decisive; another says the opposite or offers an alternative. Reconstructing the arrows of causation with so much heterogeneity is hard.

So we default to working iteratively, relying on long validation cycles to sort out conflicting data, muddling towards an answer. Animal models inform understanding of core biological mechanisms but are poor predictors of how these processes play out in more complex human biology. Predictive tests and chronic disease treatments require years before they are widely used (in large part because of friction in the RPS Vortex), adding years until real-world efficacy can be confirmed.

If only we had a time machine! Then, we could go back in time and rerun history, testing scenarios, and predict the future. It sounds far-fetched but in reality, the early versions of time machines are now possible.

In the early 2000s, in the afterglow of the Human Genome Project, there was a rush to get volunteers to allow their DNA to be sequenced. It was thought that aberrations in protein-coding regions, called the exome, would reveal key drivers of serious disease, paving the way for curative therapies. One of the first efforts began in the UK, as a public-private venture called the UK Biobank. It set out to sequence the genes of hundreds of thousands of Britons.[132]

Unfortunately, as pioneering neuroscientist Santiago Ramon y Cajal observed in his 1906 Nobel Prize lecture, "Nature seems unaware of our intellectual need for convenience and unity, and very often takes delight in complication and diversity." Decoding exomes proved to be vastly inadequate to decipher complex disease. If anything, it awakened a new appreciation for all the other parts of DNA that control gene expression, the role of single-stranded RNAs, and the complexity of cell-to-cell interactions.

UK Biobank leaders realized that their initial vision had to expand, and the databank had to deliver practical value. They pivoted to refocus on chronic disease, increasingly recognized by UK scientific leaders to be the country's greatest health threat. After 2015, Biobank researchers completed full genome sequencing and blood samples from 500,000 registrants, surveying each about health behaviors. They did body scans of 100,000 Britons, adding brain, heart and abdominal images to their library, along with data on bone density and body fat composition.[133] Participants agreed to let the Biobank import electronic health record data, allowing researchers to trace future health events.

England was not alone in building data compendiums. The US government launched a similar effort in 2018, called All of US, aiming to enroll a million Americans. European and Asian countries followed suit including China, South Korea, Japan, Taiwan, Finland, the Netherlands, and Israel among others.

However, the UK Biobank is the global leader, and today provides the substrate to build a time machine, connecting snapshots of Britons' genetics and health to future medical events. That's a start, but as every aspiring time traveler knows, time machines must enable travel backwards in time as well as forwards. Doing this requires ongoing collection of biosamples like blood plasma as well as medical data, plus non-medical information about diet, activity, and behavior. To work, the machines require data from a broad and diverse set of contributors, increasing the odds of finding outliers and determining which findings hold true for most of the population versus those that only apply to small groups.

Biosamples are critical because once arranged chronologically, researchers can go back in time, in effect, decades after samples were obtained, retesting them using technologies that did not exist years earlier. Scientists, now aided by AI-powered computing, can rewind history and replay it from multiple angles, looking for new clues about how disease develops, and why it may happen more rapidly in some people than others. It is like the movie "Groundhog Day," enabling history to be unspooled and stopped, with the system iteratively learning what might come next until it can accurately forecast "future" events accurately. At that point, researchers have, in effect, a time machine that can run backwards and forwards, not only capturing what is known to have happened, but also informing scenarios about what might happen and why. Initial efforts will be less reliable, but over time, with consistent data, the gap between predicted events and what actually comes to pass in the real world will converge, transporting us, biologically speaking, backwards and forwards in time.

Using Decades of Blood Plasma to Replay ADRD and Aging

That sounds like science fiction, except *it's already happening.* In 2022 a National Institute of Aging team led by Dr. Keenan Walker retested decades-old blood plasma collected from an offshoot of the Framingham Study, called the Atherosclerosis Risk in Communities (ARIC) Study. Over three decades of samples had been gathered from 16,000 people mostly living in rural Mississippi, North Carolina, and Maryland. ARIC's goal had been to see if there were disparities in cardiac care between bigger cities and less-resourced rural communities.[134] Critically, they decided to collect blood samples at regular intervals along with health data and causes of death.

Years later the plasma samples got a new lease on life. By the mid-2010s, scientists had developed a new kind of "omics" called proteomics, sifting through blood plasma and tissue samples to find differences in protein expression. This was impossible to do in the 1990s when the first ARIC blood samples were drawn. Decades later, the specimens could be reexamined in a new light (as they might be, again, decades from now!)

Walker's team focused on dementia risk, asking two questions: is it possible to see if changes in protein levels outside the brain correlate with dementia onset, and if so, which of the bodily processes experiencing abnormal protein fluctuations might affect cognition?[135] Focusing on protein levels outside the brain was daring, part of a long overdue rethink about the causes of ADRD.

Sure enough, the Walker team's time machine yielded valuable clues. Differences in blood plasma protein levels during midlife *did* correlate with future Alzheimer's onset. Processes experiencing significant deviations were not directly involved in cognition but had important roles inside and outside the brain in metabolism, immune and vascular function, and stress response. Follow-on studies found associations between Alzheimer's onset and proteomic markers for cardiovascular and kidney disease.[136]

Coincidentally, another team of brain researchers was following a similar path looking at functional breakdowns within the brain to create a taxonomy of ADRD subtypes. Here, too, researchers wanted to see if protein expression patterns in post-mortem brain tissue are associated with different forms of cognitive dysfunction. In essence, when does an anomaly cross the line into a pathology, and are patterns in protein changes characteristic to different forms of ADRD? As in the Walker studies, the brain researchers found useful associations, with many of the abnormally expressed proteins having key roles in the brain's immune system, and in maintaining healthy vasculature and synaptic function.[137]

Another time machine to understand patterns of aging is being developed by a University of California San Francisco team headed by Dr. Tony Wyss-Coray. Although we normally measure a person's age in years since birth, various parts of our bodies age at different rates. Wyss-Coray and his team wondered if protein level changes over time could provide a reliable measure of organ aging, and if so, if it these might also be helpful in predicting chronic disease risk.[138] Their initial answer to both questions is a cautiously optimistic yes. It is possible to identify if an organ, or tissue within it, is aging more rapidly using blood plasma protein, and even more encouragingly, accelerated organ aging seems to correspond with future disease onset. In the brain, for example, aberrant protein expression associated with decaying vasculature or synaptic health is associated with greater ADRD risk, paralleling findings in the studies categorizing different kinds of cognitive decline.

Does this mean that we can now predict ADRD or other chronic diseases using blood plasma alone? No, not yet, but efforts to do so will be greatly accelerated if researchers have access to a large longitudinal library of blood and tissue samples—such as might be provided by twelve million or so Life for Health participants!

These findings also underscore the value of building predictive models of disease risk. The initial objective is not to create something infallibly clairvoyant, but to understand the sequence of events that drive, or are driven by, mechanisms of risk and resilience. Time machine studies, and the models they inform, will help us understand heterogeneity in onset and progression and how pathology in one area spills over into another. Just as AI researchers have been able to create models that let us peer inside the black box of their algorithmic reasoning, so too, time machine models open the door to detecting future dysfunction before it happens, forestalling it through medical or non-medical means.

Finally, these studies reinforce the likelihood that different chains of causation beginning in different tissues or systems may culminate in similar kinds of dysfunction. Just as our phones' mapping applications provide alternate routes to get from one place to another, so too, our organs and tissues will travel different paths only to arrive at the same disease destination. Being able to predict these pathways reliably will transform preventive medicine into something akin to treatment, something that can be quantified, prescribed, and evaluated with rigor. Only time will tell, or rather, our time machines will.

A Real Women's Health Initiative

Amid this happy futurizing, it is a good moment to add a caveat. Longitudinal studies, while necessary to make time machines, also require transparency about goals and methods. Results must be scrutinized and replicated before being universally adopted. One of the clearest examples where these principles were not followed, to the detriment of tens of millions of women, occurred in the early 2000s in the Women's Health Initiative (WHI). Championed by Dr. Bernadine Healy, the NIH's first female director, the WHI was intended to redress profound gaps in understanding women's health issues during midlife and beyond. Preeclampsia expert Dr. Michal Elovitz summarizes the problem of chronic underinvestment in women's health issues, observing:

> "We have not been able to improve health for women from so many adverse outcomes and conditions because there has just been a tremendous lack of focus and investment in women's health and in the science needed to advance health. We remain not just in the dark about pregnancy but truly about women's health across the lifespan."[139]

The WHI was designed to be a longitudinal study, with parallel research on the safety and efficacy of menopause symptom treatments, and long-term cardiovascular health and cancer outcomes. Findings in the latter areas provided valuable data about differences in women's heart and stroke risk (versus men) as they aged. However, the finding that had the most immediate clinical impact, leading to a drastic reduction in the use of hormone replacement therapy (HRT) to counteract menopause symptoms, was also deeply flawed. Researchers wanted to assess if women receiving HRT had a greater risk of developing breast cancer. After just a few years of collecting data, leaders of the HRT arm halted the study claiming they had enough evidence to conclude that HRT's benefits were outweighed by greater cancer risk.

The problem was that the study was poorly designed, using a particular combination of estrogen and progesterone in the treatment arm that was soon replaced by safer versions. In addition, study data did not show that HRT increased risk in all women. Rather, as future studies confirmed, breast cancer risk was not elevated among women under 60 or those who were less than a decade into menopause. HRT only posed a significantly higher cancer risk among women over 60 or those who more than a decade post-menopause. This distinction was lost in translation, or a rush to judgment, and within a few years HRT use had dropped by 50%. It was not until 2017, when WHI researchers published long-term mortality results for study participants showing equivalent deaths between women receiving HRT and controls, that guidelines were revised to recommend HRT for women younger than 60 or within ten years of starting menopause.[140]

Missteps in the WHI are especially relevant to future chronic disease research and understanding risk and treatment response differences between women and men. Interestingly, although metabolic syndrome is equally prevalent in women and men, women are two to three times more likely than men to choose treatments like surgery or GLP-1 therapy, especially midlife women approaching or entering menopause. Likewise, it will be important to assess how obesity treatments impact women's skeletal muscle mass, bone density, and cardiovascular function—key aspects in which women's aging differs from that of men. Similarly, women have a greater risk of developing autoimmune conditions like multiple sclerosis, myalgic encephalomyelitis (also called chronic fatigue syndrome), and severe or chronic migraines. In each of these areas, assessments of treatment outcomes and side-effects will need to be designed to understand meaningful differences among subgroups of women, and between women and men.

Advancing Longitudinal Data Acquisition and Value

So how do the learnings from HIV, CF, Framingham, ARIC, and the WHI inform *Life for Health's* approach to longitudinal data collection?

Life for Health builds in data collection by design, embedding it in the regular treatment process instead of requiring separate, research-specific data collection. This reduces friction and the risk of data gaps or biases. The same data and biosamples used to inform treatment are reused to advance research into treatments and Predictive/Preventive Medicine. Longitudinal data becomes, quite literally, the system's lifeblood, enabling systems to trace participant outcomes, differences in clinical decision-making or practices, and informing research to prevent disease.

A second learning is to make research priorities and results transparent to clinicians and participants, involving both constituencies in the process of defining and ranking questions to explore. In 2024 the UK Biobank reported that over 30,000 researchers had access to its data, yielding over 10,000 scientific papers using its data. That's impressive, yet it's impossible to tell how study topics were selected, the degree to which they answered important questions, how many key findings have been replicated, and if and to what degree validated results have been translated into clinical practice. This is, in part, a function of the schism between science and finance (i.e., between R&D and clinical practice) as well as the absence of a system to value long-term outcomes.

Visibility into researchers' goals and study designs will help to highlight potential gaps in research priorities. This is true even today in terms of GLP-1 drugs, among the most heavily resourced areas of current research. It remains unclear, for example, why people with obesity and diabetes lose less weight than those with obesity alone. Perhaps most important for those taking and paying for GLP-1 drugs, why do people who stop taking the treatments experience significant weight rebound?[141] One intriguing possibility is that the fat cells of people with obesity undergo epigenetic reprogramming making the cells more susceptible to weight regain when excess energy intake resumes. We should ensure, then, that current or future clinical trials of drugs gather fat tissue samples (or other relevant data less invasively) to validate if this is true. Transparency about research priorities opens the door to dialogues like LISTEN, helping participants understand which issues researchers are focusing on and why, while giving researchers comparable insight into participants' highest value needs.

ENDNOTES

132 An earlier effort, called DeCode Genetics, began in Iceland in 1996 with the goal of compiling genetic data and medical records from much of Iceland's population, using the results to speed drug discovery.
133 Caleyachetty, Rishi, Thomas Littlejohns, Ben Lacey, Jelena Bešević, Megan Conroy, Rory Collins, and Naomi Allen. 2021. "United Kingdom Biobank (UK Biobank)." Journal of the American College of Cardiology 78 (1): 56–65. https://doi.org/10.1016/j.jacc.2021.03.342.
134 The primary driver of lower heart attack deaths until 1990 was improved acute treatment in hospitals, followed by greater use of stents and statins. However, ARIC found, death rates for lower-income Americans living in poorer rural and urban neighborhoods was disproportionately higher than those living in better-resourced areas in larger cities.
135 Keenan A. Walker et al., "Proteomics analysis of plasma from middle-aged adults identifies protein markers of dementia risk in later life.Sci. Transl. Med.15, (2023).
136 Dark, H.E., Paterson, C., et. al. (2024), Proteomic Indicators of Health Predict Alzheimer's Disease Biomarker Levels and Dementia Risk. Ann Neurol, 95: 260-273.
137 Tijms, B.M., Vromen, E.M., Mjaavatten, O. et al. Cerebrospinal fluid proteomics in patients with Alzheimer's disease reveals five molecular subtypes with distinct genetic risk profiles. Nat Aging 4, 33–47 (2024). https://doi.org/10.1038/s43587-023-00550-7
138 Oh, H.SH., Rutledge, J., Nachun, D. et al. Organ aging signatures in the plasma proteome track health and disease. Nature 624, 164–172 (2023). https://doi.org/10.1038/s41586-023-06802-1
139 "Mount Sinai Appoints Michal A. Elovitz, MD, as Inaugural Dean for Women's Health," Icahn School of Medicine at Mt. Sinai, February 21, 2023
140 The North American Menopause Society. The 2017 hormone therapy position statement of The North American Menopause Society. Menopause. 2017;24:728–753. doi: 10.1097/GME.0000000000000921.
141 Hinte, Laura C., Daniel Castellano-Castillo, et al. 2024. "Adipose Tissue Retains an Epigenetic Memory of Obesity After Weight Loss." Nature, November. https://doi.org/10.1038/s41586-024-08165-7.

23. FROM HEALTH DATA TO HEALTH NARRATIVES

"That new experience must build on data. Not data the way the old healthcare industry thinks about it. But rather data from what we might call a real-time, always-on, perpetual digital physical. The annual physical used to be the foundation of a doctor–patient relationship. Consider how flawed that is in this era, when we check jet engines, cars and factories with measurement systems that can spot a breakdown before it becomes serious—but can't tell if someone has a life-threatening virus until symptoms appear."

–Hemant Taneja, Stephen Klasko, and Kevin Maney, *UnHealthcare: A Manifesto for Health Assurance*

The word "data" gets used a lot in discussions of health care. In fact, it's the fifth most common noun in this book. Most data used in health care is clinical in nature, derived from electronic medical records. Clinical events are critical to understand symptoms, diagnoses, and treatments but they are insufficient to understand a participant's total situation. Time with clinicians accounts for at most two percent of a person's life. The other 98% of lived experience is just as relevant and valuable, what legendary radio commentator Paul Harvey used to call, "the *rest* of the story." Filling in the gaps between clinical events is critical to realize Predictive/Preventive Medicine.

A full health narrative includes and integrates four layers of information:

- First layer—medical record and clinical data. This is everything that happens within the health care system. In Life for Health, this also includes genomic data and biosamples collected during treatment.
- Second layer—non-medical and situational data. This includes demographic, job, and geographic information plus data from daily life such as meals, activity level, sleep, mood, and social interactions. In time, more of this data can be captured passively from quick voice notes, apps, and sensors.
- Third layer—the participant's narrative. This is the participant's ongoing commentary about their situation before, during, and after a medical situation. It captures their view of symptoms and actions as they happen, and their understanding of their treatment plan and progress.
- Fourth layer—reflective learning. This includes reflections by clinicians and participants (and, perhaps, caregivers) about their learnings and takeaways during key parts of their health journey. These insights are especially useful to help others like them in similar situations along with clinicians.

There is no question about the first category and little doubt about the potential value of the second, even though non-medical data is seldom integrated into the larger health narrative, as the authors of *UnHealthcare* point out in the quote at the start of the chapter. Some clinicians have a practice of reflective learning and add notes that equate to the fourth layer, but this practice is neither systematic nor consistently accessible to identify patterns in clinical decision-making.

The biggest gap is in the third layer, the participant's view of their situation over time. Their perspective adds important depth to understand what is happening during the many years of the "maintain health" phase, when motivation and consistency is key. Even the content and tone of recorded or written notes can be analyzed for insight, including to assess a person's voice and syntax for potential neurological issues.

The goal of gathering participant-generated date in both the second and third layers does not require obsessive self-monitoring but is intended to create a consistent practice of understanding a person's routine as well as unusual deviations. Important shifts may go unnoticed at first, only becoming apparent in hindsight when a pattern or phase shift can be seen. It's also important to capture participants' rationale about treatment decisions and later, how outcomes compare to their expectations. What did they learn that they wish they had known earlier? These insights provide powerful guidance for others facing similar situations, both contemporaneously and years later.

Most data collection can happen in the background using sensors in our phones, homes, or on our person, with participants controlling which data can be included. Software can do the work of bringing events together into a first-draft narrative, summarizing trends. AI can prompt quick question and answer interactions to clarify something or have the participant add context. Current capabilities are clunky and intrusive (or cloying), but their situational awareness will improve. The more data processed, the better software will become at identifying important deviations, and prompting time capture of contextual input from participants.

Even with a full narrative before a participant visit, clinicians may still begin by asking, "What is concerning you today," or "How have you been feeling over the last X weeks?" Participants' initial responses always give clinicians clues about a person's state of mind, however, soon neither participant nor clinician will have to rely on the participant's faulty memory of events to get an accurate sense of what actually has been happening.

Is this deep of a narrative *really* necessary to solve chronic disease? Yes, if we are to build reliable models that recapitulate and represent biological, environmental, and behavioral elements with fidelity. Much of the existing AI, trained on electronic medical records, is inherently biased or incomplete. Diagnostic codes and treatments are engineered to optimize for the RPS Vortex's financial rules. As clinician and health data entrepreneur Dr. Mitesh Rao has observed:

> "The tech stacks are not designed to truly collect deep, comprehensive data; they're designed for billing and so you're basically taking platforms that are built for billing and billing collection and trying to use that to now create data that's going to be viable for research or viable for AI. And that's very challenging."[142]

Life for Health's broader aperture provides a fuller, more unbiased chronology of participants' health experiences. Our health narratives contain multitudes, as do each of us. Ensuring that we capture and pay heed to the full humanity of health issues is not only right but critical, if we are to solve chronic disease in its many forms.

ENDNOTES

142 See Fierce Healthcare, "HLTH 2024 Recap: Five notable trends spotted by reporters and key takeaways from executives," October 28, 2024.

24. DATA PRIVACY, OWNERSHIP, CONTROL, AND COMPENSATION

> "[D]ata collection is best justified as a kind of 'bargain' struck between data sources and data users — provide us your data, recognizing this may encroach in some ways on your privacy, because it will permit us to provide advances in health care that will improve your life."[143]
>
> –Nicholson Price and Glenn Cohen, ethics scholars

> "Top-down ethical and privacy standards ... have not persuaded enough people to contribute their data to enable development of the vast data resources that twenty-first-century science ultimately will need. Those standards were, after all, *minimal* regulatory standards, not designed for the purpose of pleasing the public, and they have not done so."[144]
>
> –Barbara Evans, Professor of Law, University of Florida

Do you own your health data? Do you control how it is used? Are you compensated for its value?

These questions go to the heart of creating an economic framework to realize Predictive/Preventive Medicine and built participant trust. Currently, the answer to the first and third questions is unambiguously no. You don't own your data and you don't get compensated for it. As for the second question, control is a decidedly mixed bag.

That's because our current approach to health data confuses privacy and control, protecting identities but limiting contributors' ability to determine how and when data stripped of personally identifiable information (PII) can be used for research. Contributors face a binary choice whether to share, but once permission is granted, they receive no ongoing compensation for doing so. Nor is there a mechanism to inform contributors about findings relevant to their situations. These shortcomings are conscious policy choices that inhibit broader and more effective use of data to advance Predictive/Preventive Medicine.

Privacy and Control

Privacy rules governing medical data generally work well in terms of protecting identity. Access to know who a person is or to access their medical record directly is limited to treatment team members and other health providers like pharmacists. For any other entity or use, health records are stripped of PII including a person's name, Social Security or insurance member ID number, address, email, or phone number. Absent a cyberhack or theft, a person's identity should not be violated.

Control over de-identified data is an entirely different matter. Entities in the health care system have wide leeway to use it internally and externally once consent for use is granted. Data contributors lose control over their de-identified data either to limit or encourage its use. That decision is held by the health system or medical practice that collects the data and the rights granted to it under a consent form. This often means that medical data gets siloed, with access to researchers outside of the collecting system subject to that entity's arrangements with external researchers or participation in multi-entity data libraries. This puts the onus on the participant, if they join research conducted by one health system, to go through a new set of consents, when joining another institution's study, to make their data available, reentering information or health events that already exist elsewhere. It's monumentally inefficient.

A second problem is that privacy rules wall off medical data from non-medical information such as diet, activity, or behavioral information, making it difficult to establish a full picture of a person's situation. This separation is especially problematic for Predictive/Preventive Medicine since so many chronic disease questions involve overlapping biological, environmental, and behavioral factors. Medical researchers work in one world awash in clinical data, while social scientists labor away in another sifting through demographic, survey, or economic data. Each may be trying to answer the same fundamental question but neither has a full picture. Absent a change in the status quo, never the twain shall meet!

So should we relax privacy rules? No, there is no reason that participants cannot have *both* privacy and control. No one outside of a person's clinical team should know their true identity unless the individual gives explicit permission for PII to be shared. However, in a world where data is currency and insights are wealth, participants must have the ability to allow medical and non-medical data to be integrated, to know how their data is used, and to be compensated or receive other benefits for its use.

Life for Health advances these goals in three ways. First, it creates bidirectional transparency between researchers and participants. Participants can see how their data is being used and get informed (along with their clinicians) about findings relevant to their situations. Second, participants are compensated for data made available to researchers and product developers. Finally, Life for Health gives participants a voice in prioritizing research.

Bidirectional Transparency

A good rule of transparency is that a customer should never be surprised about how their data is gathered or used. In Life for Health that begins with a clear process to opt in to share data and an equally clear process to stop, later, if a participant changes their mind.

The operative word is "clear." Lawyers craft consents to provide maximum wriggle room for data recipients, often using phrasing that is inscrutable and one-sided. Participants have an all or nothing binary choice: share everything under the proposed terms or share nothing. The good news is that consents can be written in easier-to-understand, plain language. In 2024 a Brown University team of clinicians and academics began a fascinating effort to translate complex legalese into plain language comprehensible to people with varying levels of reading proficiency.[145] They had seen how complex documents peppered by "whereas" and "to the extent of" clauses confused surgery candidates and turned off potential research participants. Using AI plus human review, they rewrote surgery consent forms in plain language, improving patient understanding while also satisfying hospital lawyers. The same can be done for data consents and other documents relating to health data.

In Life for Health, participants receive information upon joining, and over time, about their rights and options relating to their health data, and have opportunities to speak with individuals to discuss specific scenarios. Participants are informed about the differences between how health data is used by their clinicians versus how it is used elsewhere within Life for Health on a de-identified basis to benchmark progress and verify that clinicians are using best practices. Participants get assistance to ensure data from third-party applications and services flow into their health narratives. Participants also learn how their data can be used to pre-qualify them for current or future clinical trials.

Once a participant is making progress in their initial intervention plan, Life for Health clinicians or personnel introduce the idea of making de-identified data available for use by vetted third parties. Participants can decide whether to opt-in, and if so which data to make available, in addition to the minimum set of clinical and demographic data points. They would be able to add or subtract data sources at any point or halt future data sharing altogether. As a general rule, participants would not be able to erase data previously provided since this could invalidate or disrupt past or ongoing studies.

Participants who share de-identified data externally can see which researchers license datasets that include their information, the researcher's purpose, and any interim or final results. Researchers accessing Life for Health data will be required to provide descriptions of their research, study goals, how data will be used, and relevant findings or publications once these become available. As with consent forms, human-directed AI can translate research descriptions into explanations appropriate for different levels of scientific background and multiple languages. Likewise, software can be used to screen or prioritize notifications to participants and clinicians about relevant findings.

Ensuring that participants understand how their data is used and the relevance of study results is a key part of building trust. It is a qualitatively different approach from clinical trial registries, which list studies but leave it up to clinicians or intrepid participant-researchers to decipher what they mean or hunt down relevant findings years later. Participants may engage infrequently with information from researchers unless they are actively managing a health situation. However, the information is there when they or their clinician needs it, and the mere fact of its availability tangibilizes Life for Health's commitment to transparency.

Compensation and the Blockchain

Life for Health participants who opt to share their data with researchers are compensated in three ways:

- Participants receive a base amount for contributing data regardless of how much their data is included in a licensed dataset. Payment amounts increase based on the types of data provided and the duration of contributions.
- Participants receive a share of licensing fees paid by researchers or product makers to access and use a Life for Health dataset that includes their information.
- Participants earn a share of revenue generated by products developed or validated using their data.

The base amount ensures that all participants receive some value for their data regardless of how often it is accessed. The second payment stream recognizes the incremental value of data as and when it is used by third parties. The third payment is a share in royalties from future product sales. While each participant's revenue share from an individual arrangement would be small, cumulative amounts could add up over time to thousands or tens of thousands of dollars.

A decade ago, the idea of providing potentially millions of micropayments to data contributors would have been prohibitively complex and expensive. Fortunately, computational capabilities have improved by orders of magnitude. AI agents and blockchain technologies could be used to preserve anonymity for contributors and researchers while creating a mechanism to authorize and track data access. Better known for their role in powering cryptocurrencies like Bitcoin, blockchains were originally designed to be used for all kinds of transactions. Blockchains to track health data access and licensing would run separately from systems used for cryptocurrency trading, even though they would use similar underlying code.

The key benefit of blockchain technology is that it allows data access and use to occur without storing any participant or researcher information, or underlying health data—even de-identified—on the list of transactions, called the ledger. All the health data is housed elsewhere, securely, in encrypted form. The blockchain serves as a combination gatekeeper, electronic padlock, digital contracting mechanism, and toll transponder—tracking each time a participant's data is used, the data elements licensed, the licensing entity, and key licensure terms. Only vetted and approved researchers would have access to licensed data. In 2021 a team of Harvard University and Baylor College of Medicine health data experts summarized the benefits of using blockchain technologies to manage data access:

> "[D]ata requesters could benefit from easy verification of the authenticity and provenance of health data, as well as automated and streamlined data procurement. Each user, for instance a prespecified set of research institutes, would be granted a particular access level according to the smart contract terms, and requests for data access could be made transparent." [146]

Their approach is just one of the many proposals to use blockchains for health data. In 2024, a team at Osaka University proposed a similar approach for electronic medical records. Other groups have suggested using blockchains to manage access to clinical trial data, to track the supply chain of prescription drug ingredients, and even to manage the chain of custody for organ donations.[147]

Life for Health could follow the Harvard/Baylor team's approach. Vetted researchers specify the profiles of individuals and data elements they want for a study, submit a request, agree to standard contract terms, and then get authorized to access their dataset using an encrypted key wherever the underlying data is housed. For example, a diabetes researcher might want data on individuals between 35 and 55 who have metabolic health metrics within a certain range, have taken certain medications but not others, and live in a mix of wealthier and impoverished areas. Once these parameters are finalized, the researcher would enter into a contract (or contracts) on the blockchain, and once confirmed, would receive approval and instructions to access data. A similar process, working backwards, could be used to calculate amounts owed to Life for Health entities and participants. The latter's share would be remitted to the cash balance of participants' insurance policies.

Participants' Voice in Governance

The final component of Life for Health's approach to health data is to give participants a greater voice in identifying and prioritizing research areas including often overlooked questions about quality of life. Participant representatives would also have access to periodic, independent audits of Life for Health data practices, with opportunities to confirm that data is being used in accordance with stated policies. Giving participants a role in identifying and prioritizing chronic disease research topics is not without risk or potential for controversy. People have strong opinions, especially when they or a loved one is facing a serious illness, and navigating conflicting views can be difficult. However, health is different. The risks of controversy or misunderstanding are worth it to ensure participant trust and engagement in accelerating knowledge and outcomes. This is especially true since capabilities that were once unimaginable or impractical are eminently feasible today, and this will be true again in the future. Building in norms and mechanisms for participant input will reduce surprise over new and potentially ethically contentious avenues of research and capabilities to predict disease risk. As Robert Beall and the CFF leadership surmised, and later found to be true, trust must be established long before hard choices arise.

ENDNOTES

143 Price WN 2nd, Cohen IG. Privacy in the age of medical big data. Nat Med. 2019 Jan;25(1):37-43. doi: 10.1038/s41591-018-0272-7.
144 Evans, Barbara J. n.d. "Power to the People: Data Citizens in the Age of Precision Medicine." https://pmc.ncbi.nlm.nih.gov/articles/PMC5673282/
145 See Ali, R., Connolly, I.D., Tang, O.Y. et al. Bridging the literacy gap for surgical consents: an AI-human expert collaborative approach. npj Digit. Med. 7, 63 (2024) and Mirza, Fatima N. et al.., The literacy barrier in clinical trial consents: a retrospective analysis, eClinicalMedicine, Volume 75, 102814, and interview of Drs. Fatima Mirza and Rohaid Ali on NEJM AI podcast, July 17, 2024.
146 Kostick-Quenet, Kristin, et al. "How NFTs could transform health information exchange." Science 375.6580 (2022): 500-502: See also, e.g.: N. Miyanishi et al., "Development of Trust Data Distribution Platform for Healthcare & Medical Data," 2023 IEEE EMBS Special Topic Conference on Data Science and Engineering in Healthcare, Medicine and Biology, Malta, 2023, pp. 103-104.
147 Igboanusi, I.S., Nnadiekwe, C.A., Ogbede, J.U. et al. BOMS: blockchain-enabled organ matching system. Sci Rep 14, 16069 (2024).

25. REALIZING PREDICTIVE/PREVENTIVE MEDICINE

Part IV began by listing key challenges to realize Predictive/Preventive Medicine, in particular the current problem of assessing and valuing preventive measures. In this chapter, we explore how Life for Health solves this problem using the ongoing cycle of health outcome goals, longitudinal data, and the long-term life insurance relationship to quantify value over time.

The first issue—determining *which measures* actually prove to be effective—is a red herring, a ghost of the RPS Vortex's fixation on valuing inputs over outcomes. Systems built around inputs assess value in volumetric terms, as a function of activities or resources used. As we have seen, the nature of prediction and prevention, like detection, is a continual process, rather than a one-time prescription. The nature of activities that a participant undertakes from one period to the next is less important than the direction and consistency of results. In one period, a participant may focus on reducing consumption of ultra-processed food or sleeping more than five hours a night. Depending on their results, in the next period, they may change the activities to test new approaches or make progress on adjacent health goals. Sometimes, changing methods is necessary simply to create variety and stay motivated.

Either way, the quantification of value is in the direction, rate, and magnitude of change in the participant's health trajectory, not the degree to which progress can be assigned to individual activities. Quantifying preventive value is, like calculus, an understanding of realized rate of change, in absolute terms and versus expectations. The nature of aging, for the time being, is about avoiding or managing decline. The goal is to keep the most recent period of results and longer-term trends above expectations. If that happens, great. Less so if they fall short, suggesting a need to try new interventions, increase effort, or both. If results repeatedly fall below expectations, it's time to rewrite the plan or go deeper (using longitudinal and narrative data) to identify why results are unsatisfactory.

Determining interventions with participants, objectively assessing results, and adjusting as needed *is* the hard work of clinicians in Predictive/Preventive Medicine, just as maintaining effort and engagement *is* the hard work of participants. Neither succeeds without the other. Increasingly, preventive medicine combines hard biology with motivation, helping clinicians and participants choose interventions appropriate to goals, and then rewarding outcomes monetarily and by reinforcing feelings of self-efficacy and mastery.

Life for Health's financial structure connects these micro decisions to the big picture, aligning clinicians, participants, and insurers, and linking the compensation of each to outcomes over time. Upfront investments to reverse disease create the longer-term opportunity to realize value, but actualizing this potential accrues over many years. Breaking value assessments into smaller chunks of time sidesteps the misguided instinct to make high stakes predictions about the value of individual activities.

Solving the Prevention Paradox

The other big barrier to Predictive/Preventive Medicine is the Prevention Paradox, our tendency to prioritize use of newer and more expensive treatments in people with more advanced disease. Chapter 3 demonstrated that extending healthspan to lower health spending requires work at both ends of the chronic disease cascade, reversing mid-stage and advanced disease while also preventing onset. It is suboptimal to concentrate on those who may see the greatest near-term change or among those with little or no pathology. We must do both.

Life for Health's answer to the Prevention Paradox is to increase health outcome payments by age to balance between disease severity and time to retirement. Generally, health outcome payments are lower for younger participants than older ones. That's because younger people have more years (i.e., chances) to hit health goals and therefore more time to earn outcome payments and realize capital appreciation on prior awards. Conversely, the value of reversing multimorbidity, or stopping a person's progression into it, increases as a person approaches retirement, since the likelihood of health expenses rapidly increasing in a foreseeable timeframe is much greater. Call this the urgency factor. Balancing these two factors equalizes the present value of intervening simultaneously at both ends of the chronic disease cascade.

To be concrete, a 35-year-old with only one metabolic condition has three decades to earn health outcome payments. They have a strong incentive to prevent multimorbidity, and the incentive to do so increases as the prospect of future outcome payments increases, on top of earnings accruing on past payments. Conversely, a 55-year-old with multimorbidity has a much greater chance of incurring a series of very costly hospitalizations in the coming decade or two. The value of reversing their multimorbidity is high even if they have fewer years to accumulate savings. Accordingly, health outcome payments that increase with age equalize the incentive for insurers *and* participants to reverse or prevent multimorbidity, reflecting the increasing risk-adjusted benefit of forestalling multimorbidity as someone ages.

The trick is to get the relationship between the payment and the underlying risks roughly correct, taking into account age, innate factors like genetics, the person's life situation and environment, and the future cost to treat advanced disease. Predictive models (i.e., the time machines described in Chapter 22), once they are validated with real-world data, will prove valuable to designing payment amounts. These cannot be too favorable to either younger participants or those who are older, or who have advanced disease. Fortunately, solving for these factors is a perfect challenge for life insurance actuaries, who have deep experience pricing complicated risks.

Figure 25.1 illustrates what a Health Outcomes Payment curve might look like, using age 45 as the midpoint of expected working years. The magnitude of age-adjusted payments is shown on the vertical axis, expressed as the percent that would be paid to a 45-year-old. The health improvement payment for a 35-year-old is 75% of a 45 year old's amount; whereas, the payment is 135% for a 55-year-old and 150% for a 60-year-old.

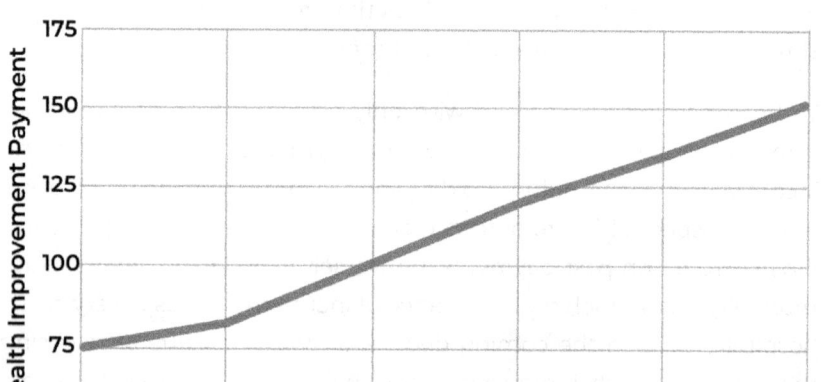

Figure 25.1: Relationship Between Age and Payment
(Payment to 45 year old = 100)

Being able to provide participants with curves like this, translating them into scenarios of potential value over time, will help them see in concrete terms what they stand to gain over time, and establish clear expectations about their role in realizing better health.

Longitudinal Data and Participatory Research Increases ROI Certainty

A key challenge in solving chronic disease is reducing the variability in outcomes. The degree to which clinicians and insurers can increase the predictive accuracy of interventions reduces the risk of investing in them, or at least increasing certainty about the time frame to earn returns. In some sense this is true for all medical discoveries. Treatments succeed to the extent that they pinpoint a crucial place of dysfunction or cellular process and are able to intercept or reverse pathology. Chronic disease adds the challenge of time dimensionality. There is seldom a single critical point, it is a cumulation of multiple factors over time.

Longitudinal data from a broad and diverse group of participants provides the quantitative basis to reduce variability in outcomes, either by better matching interventions to situations over time, or by refining the durability of an intervention's effect. There will always be groups of people who respond unusually well or unusually poorly, outliers who have unique risk or resilience. Currently, chronic disease treatment is massively fat-tailed until advanced multimorbidity sets in, at which point the cascade of accumulating dysfunctions becomes all too predictable. So the goal of longitudinal data gathering is to shrink the width of the outcomes distribution, to reshape it into something more like a normal distribution with the center of the curve as tall as possible. This, too, is why we need to work both ends of the chronic disease distribution with equal intensity, to reverse multimorbidity and prevent people from starting down the road towards it.

Longitudinal data from millions of participants can be integrated with data from other biobanks or collectives, improving the accuracy of forecasted health trajectories and the likely efficacy of treatments and preventive measures. We can build a reliable understanding of how improving one aspect of chronic disease has positive spillovers on other disease risks, especially, for example, how inflammation caused by metabolic dysfunction might also lower cancer or ADRD risk. Understanding interdependencies and intervention effects will reduce the risk premium to use novel therapies more broadly, faster, and enable better pricing of interventions like gene therapies that may only need to be administered once to work for decades. Life for Health greatly improves the system's ability to quantify value over time and apportion benefits as outcomes are realized.

Ensuring Equity

So what ensures that Predictive/Preventive Medicine will be broadly accessible? Given deeply entrenched health disparities, might all of this new knowledge and predictive capability just benefit the wealthiest and most educated? Might advances in Predictive/Preventive Medicine actually drive life insurers to price out people based on their genetics, or combinations of biological and environmental factors?

The short answer in the current system is definitely yes. If we continue to do as we are doing now, poorer and less educated Americans would benefit less. But that's also because the current system is about *avoiding* risk. *Life for Health* flips the dynamic by embracing it. That's not marketing bravado, it is the essence of the system's design. There is no value in getting a bunch of information about future disease risk from a broad swathe of Americans only to sell it to a wealthy niche. The economics do not work. The value of Predictive/Preventive Medicine can only be realized by applying the findings as broadly as possible.

People who have already entered multimorbidity in their forties and fifties—individuals who right now are the *least attractive* to health insurers—are actually the *most valuable* potential Life for Health participants—even if they have relatively modest incomes. That's because most of Life for Health's value comes from redirecting extraordinary sums that health insurers spend on symptom management, reallocating these to change the risk of future disease timing and severity. In financial parlance, it's like buying a high-yield junk bond issued by a company that everyone worries will go bankrupt, and reengineering their product offerings to be much more certain over time that they will make good on interest and principle. A junk-rated entity can reliably be turned into, if not an AAA credit, at least one that is investment-grade.

That only works by focusing on people who are at greater risk, which inevitably given today's socioeconomic disparities, includes individuals with less wealth. No doubt this will require a lot of innovative thinking and some political activism in state capitals to enlist governors, state legislators, and administrators. Grafting Life for Health into Medicaid and in effect voucherizing it to follow poorer people as they reenter the workforce. This sends the strongest possible signal that Predictive/Preventive Medicine is for everyone, regardless of their socio-economic circumstance.

This is where Life for Health's commitment to transparency matters as well. Whether or not insurance regulators require it, Life for Health entities and life insurers should publish data about the range and long-term value of health outcome payments, and methodologies used to calculate them. *Life for Health's* success as a concept and as a series of enterprises depends on the quality of execution and the predictability of results. The broader the access, the more everyone benefits practically and financially.

PART V

LOOKING FORWARD

26. THE BIG UNLOCKS

Life for Health is designed to solve chronic disease, but its approach also provides a framework to solve seemingly intractable problems in cancer and ADRD and drug pricing. In addition, Life for Health's existence will have spillover benefits in keeping Medicare solvent and improving food quality.

Chapter 4 discussed two studies quantifying the value of ending disease, both of which emphasized the importance of solving multiple chronic and age-related diseases in tandem. Life for Health does this insofar as participants who reverse metabolic disease and maintain health will also have lower risk of developing cancer and ADRD. However, *Life for Health* goes farther, providing longitudinal data to supercharge research like that discussed in Chapter 22 to understand disease processes and predict or prevent onset. In addition, *Life for Health's* use of life insurance as a financial framework opens the door for participants to access qualitatively better diagnostics and treatments, wherever they live, increasing their survival and accelerating validation of novel therapies.

Related to this, *Life for Health* provides a framework to change the way breakthrough drugs for chronic and life-threatening conditions are priced. Instead of paying drugmakers full value when a drug is taken, Life for Health enables a portion of the drug's value to be tied to recipient outcomes, measured and paid out over time, potentially even beyond a drug's patent expiration. This allows upfront prices to be reduced, increasing access, while preserving the ability of generic drugmakers to produce cheaper copies once a drug patent expires. Drugs to treat a particular symptom or that have short-term effects could continue to be priced as drugs now are, with innovators earning their return during a fixed patent window and consumers realizing most of the benefits thereafter. However, just as we should not get locked into a one-size-fits-all approach to health care, so too, we can have two systems to price drugs, with the second system designed to share value over time based on actual outcomes. Life for Health increases the attractiveness of this model for drugmakers since it offers the potential to prequalify participants for future drug trials, reducing drugmakers costs and risks to bring a novel treatment to market.

Life for Health's existence will also have spillover benefits in the political realm. Reducing multimorbidity will directly benefit Medicare, and indirectly Social Security as well, by delaying and reducing post-retirement health costs and helping Americans save more for retirement. No one will be more pleased than politicians of all ideological flavors who are now locked into a fight over diametrically-opposed approaches, neither of which—partisans of both sides acknowledge off-the-record—actually reduces multimorbidity. Left-leaning politicians push to de-privatize insurance, expanding publicly financed care, even as they know this is fiscally and politically impossible. Meanwhile conservative politicians advocating benefit cuts to shore up Medicare finances know that this too is a political landmine, especially as the electorate ages. *Life for Health* provides a path out of this impasse, recentering the debate around efforts to prevent illness before people enter Medicare and maintain healthspan into retirement.

Finally, *Life for Health's* success in reducing metabolic disease will provide incontrovertible evidence for the harmful role of unhealthy food products and packaging in fostering obesity, diabetes, heart disease, allergies, and inflammation. Life for Health data will help force a reckoning, bringing into focus the magnitude of nutrition-related illness and the ways in which the RPS Vortex benefits, as a result, by continuing to deliver sick care. Even as some healthy food advocates argue for a rerun of the class action lawsuits strategy deployed against Big Tobacco, a faster result will be achieved by compelling food companies to fix ingredients and make healthier produce more accessible, or fund future health costs associated with metabolic syndrome. In other words, create bigger sticks and tastier carrots.

27. ENDING CANCER AS WE KNOW IT

> "Why are we not doing more to detect the earliest sign of cancer instead of chasing the last cell with draconian treatment options? ... Cancer must be prevented at a precancer level. I am not the only one saying this."
>
> Dr. Azra Raza, *The First Cell*

It is increasingly common to hear health policy experts question how many research dollars go into cancer treatment. Why spend so much on cancer when doing so only extends life a few years? It's one of the least thoughtful things that some of the smartest people say.

The nub of the idea goes back to an observation by Professor Jay Olshansky, a coauthor of the 2013 study cited in Chapter 4 about the need to solve multiple chronic and age-related diseases at once to increase longevity and healthspan. Solving cancer *alone*, Olshansky argued, will not meaningfully increase lifespan since people would succumb to other age-related conditions. His point was not that cancer research per se is fruitless, but that solving cancer had to be just one arm of a multi-pronged assault.

It is true that the amount of survival benefit provided by many cancer drugs seem unimpressive when first approved, providing only a few weeks or months of life extension compared to existing therapies. The reason for this is that new drugs are usually tested on advanced malignancies which have developed ways to resist existing treatments and adapt quickly to block new ones. Malignancies are devious and have remarkable survival instincts, co-opting and hijacking nearby cells to protect against attacking immune cells or drugs.

Once a drug is approved, clinicians start to see bigger survival gains as the drug is used off-label or in earlier rounds of treatment. Occasionally a breakthrough like immunotherapy yields significant gains from the outset. However, even immunotherapies only work some of the time against some tumors, and some of the better results have come when they are used at the very earliest stages, even before surgery.

So, progress in cancer over the last couple of decades is very much a *Tale of Two Cities*. Clinicians have steadily increased survival rates for many breast, colorectal, thyroid, and prostate cancers, and blood and immune cell cancers that are susceptible to targeted treatments or immunotherapies. However, five year survival rates are still under 50% for lung, pancreatic, ovarian, bladder, and brain cancers.

The best way to improve outcomes in these harder to treat cancers is to find them earlier or, even better, to predict cancer risk, increase targeted surveillance, and preempt nascent tumors before they are able to start growing.

To date, this preventive ideal has only been achieved in the small minority of cancers that have clear genetic drivers such as ovarian and breast cancers caused by mutations in the BRCA gene. There genetic tests can alert BRCA carriers to risk, allowing women to undergo prophylactic surgery to remove ovaries, fallopian tubes, or breasts and greatly reduce their cancer risk.[148] Still, disease-causing BRCA mutations occur in only about 4% of women. Cancer, like chronic disease, is more likely to result from a series of gradual breakdowns, hastened by unrepaired DNA copying errors or erosion in immune cells' ability to detect or stop malignant stem cells.

This is why the question posed at the start of this chapter by Dr. Azra Raza about stopping cancer before it starts is so urgent. Dr. Raza knows much of what she writes, with decades of experience treating complex blood cancers, and as the partner to an accomplished cancer researcher who battled and ultimately succumbed to a fatal leukemia.

If fighting tumors after they are established is such a struggle, she asks, why not invest more resources and effort to find tumors at their earliest stages? How might we, in other words, *predict* cancer risk and *prevent* onset, and if we could do that, how then could we intervene earlier and decisively? As with multimorbidity, solving cancer means working both ends of the disease cascade at once, stopping advanced disease from progressing or recurring while preventing onset among those at risk. This is why the Life for Health playbook holds lessons for cancer as well as chronic disease.

Screening and Early Detection

Today, most cancer detection relies on broad screening based on age and family history. It can be effective but it's far from efficient, producing many false positives that require follow-up tests and biopsies. Even in breast cancer screening, where new MRIs improve imaging, predictive accuracy is low for the substantial minority of women with dense breast tissue. Malignancies in the pancreas or ovaries are routinely undetected until they are advanced. Lung cancer is detectable on low-dose CT scans, but the fastest growing segment of lung cancer cases involve non-smokers who are unlikely to have a chest x-ray or scan until they become symptomatic. Digestive and breast cancers are becoming more common among younger adults, but lowering age thresholds to start broad screening would catch comparatively few cases relative to the large increase in screening costs.

Fortunately, the prospects for accurate and less invasive screening got much better in the early 2010s when a Franco-German team demonstrated a blood test that could detect breakaway tumor cells, a process they called "liquid biopsy."[149] Parallel work under legendary cancer geneticist Bert Vogelstein and longtime collaborator Ken Kinzler went one step better, able to detect microscopic tumor DNA fragments rather than an entire cell. These discoveries led to a slew of Multiple Cancer Early Detection (MCED) tests, which promise to assess the presence of multiple cancers at once using a single blood draw, costing just a few hundred dollars a time. It sounds amazing, and it is, except like all new technologies, MCEDs will need to be refined.

Currently, the tests are most useful to predict whether and how quickly someone already undergoing cancer treatment might have a recurrence. This is tremendously valuable since most people do not die during their initial bout, but months or (more often) years later when a tumor recurs or spreads. Use of liquid biopsies to detect even a miniscule number of cancer cells in blood after treatment, called residual disease, helps clinicians and patient calibrate the frequency of future surveillance and determine how aggressive to be with adjuvant therapies to suppress a recurrence.

For detecting new cancer, MCEDs work as well as other screening approaches for the most common solid tumors such as breast and colorectal cancer. Unfortunately, most current MCEDs do not outperform existing measures in terms of detecting low-survival pancreatic and ovarian cancers earlier, although this capability is likely to improve soon. However, MCEDs are vastly more accessible than conventional screening requiring just a blood draw, and are cheaper than having to get separate mammograms and colonoscopies.

Unsurprisingly, health insurers and some clinicians are reluctant to pay for MCEDs, arguing that until they are extremely reliable, their very ease of access is a detriment, increasing use among the worried well, heightening diagnostic anxiety, and leading to unnecessary biopsies. A contrary view is that MCED tests will improve more quickly with broader use. Dana Goldman of USC, lead author of the 2013 study cited in Chapter 4 on the value of solving multiple diseases of aging, points out that only 15% of the 1.3 million cancers diagnosed each year among 50–79-year-olds are found in early stages. "If multi-cancer early detection tests were used to complement existing screening," he wrote, "the net benefits to society – even after accounting for screening costs – would be substantial."[150] Interestingly, among the advocates for wider MCED use are some forward-thinking life insurers, which, seeing the world Goldman's way, now subsidize policyholders who want to be tested.

Finding the First Cells

Life for Health's first big unlock in cancer is to help drive greater MCED use and accelerate work to improve accuracy, especially in combination with other prognostic factors within participants' health narratives. This will improve clinicians' abilities to target MCED use, mitigating concerns about overdiagnosis, and improve MCED's power to detect harder to treat cancers earlier.

Just as scientists are building time machines to understand ADRD, so too, in cancer. An Oxford University team used UK Biobank blood samples to identify proteomic signatures of future cancer onset. They reported that it is possible to identify cancer-associated protein signatures as much as seven years before cancers were diagnosed, concluding that "the combination of observational and genetic approaches can improve our ability to identify proteins most likely to have a causal role in cancer development and progression."[151] This is the essence of Dr. Raza's argument about finding the "first cell," trying to understand risk and timing while a person is still *precancerous*, and then tracing what happens in and around and in cells that become part of the tumor or adjacent tissue.

Wider use of MCEDs and proteomics within people fighting metabolic syndrome or who have family histories of cancer also will expand libraries of specimens and data that can be reassessed in the future as new analytical capabilities are developed. Access to Life for Health participants will enable researchers to identify new predictive biomarkers and validate their utility in clinical practice.

As predictive value improves, MCEDs can be used more confidently and intentionally. People at greater risk because of genetic vulnerabilities or aberrant protein expression would have a basis to undergo prophylactic measures (as BRCA risk gene carriers now have) or more intensive ongoing surveillance (as is done with early-stage prostate cancer). Once again, as in metabolic health, work to detect earlier improves predictive accuracy which improves the accuracy *and* efficiency of detection and prevention.

Increasing Access to Best-in-class Treatment

Life for Health's second big unlock in cancer is to equalize access to cutting-edge diagnostics and treatment as soon as a malignancy is detected. As discussed in Chapters 13 and 14, Life for Health insurance policies cover and guarantee access to diagnostics and treatment at one of the approximately 75 National Cancer Institute Comprehensive Cancer Centers ("NCI-CCCs").

This is because people who go to NCI-CCCs live longer post-diagnosis than people who do not.[152]

Why might this be? Diagnostic and treatment protocols change faster in cancer than any other medical specialty. NCC-CCCs have more clinicians with experience treating complex tumors, and established protocols to integrate surgery, medical oncology, and radiation therapy within a single center. Clinicians at top cancer centers also run or participate in clinical trials testing novel treatments, giving participants with relevant situations a head start on trial access.

Tens of thousands of cancer patients each year get treated at NCI-CCCs but unless they live near one or have a rare malignancy that requires specialized care from the outset, many patients only get referred to a top center after a tumor stops responding to treatment, recurs, or spreads, at which point it is harder to stop. This is unsurprising. As we have seen with chronic disease, geography and income are often barriers to access elite care. In cancer, righting this wrong is not just a question of equity, it's one of advancing science. Those who would benefit from greater expertise earlier do not receive it, depriving clinicians of a case and data that could validate or disprove the value of using a newer therapy earlier in treatment. The individual is worse off, but so is everyone else.

Life for Health's first promise is that any participant can get diagnostics at a top center. This is the key to increasing survival odds, including access to tumor genome analyses like the one Steve Jobs had. These and other tests to classify tumors and identify unique features are critical to determining if the malignancy is more or less likely to respond to a particular treatment. Equally important is to ensure that test results are actually used in selecting treatments. That may sound bizarre but it's a real issue. A 2022 study exploring the use of tumor genomics in a form of lung cancer particularly susceptible to targeted therapies found—shockingly—that only half the people who took a genomic test *even received their results*. Of the half who did, *almost a third* did not receive the correct targeted therapy.[153] At NCI-CCCs, doing the right tests and making sure they are used in treatment planning is a standard protocol.

It may be that a participant's tumor does not require treatment at an NCI-CCC. Well-established or highly effective treatment protocols can be provided at an oncology center or hospital near the participant's home, in what's referred to as "the community setting." Getting treated locally is not inherently better or worse, medically-speaking. The problem is that the process to determine if a person should be treated there or at an NCI-CCC is haphazard. As a result, people who really need a top center's capabilities may not get access until much later in the treatment process while others who have straightforward malignancies who go to an NCI-CCC because they have the means or live close by could be treated just as effectively in the community setting.

In effect, Life for Health's guarantee of upfront access to an NCI-CCC flips the status quo approach to triaging cancers. Diagnostics at the NCI-CCC determine the best place to be treated and should expedite clinical trial enrollment for people who qualify.[154]

This may strike you as logical, even uncontroversial, except—as with everything in the status quo—operating norms are subject to financial concerns. Oncologists working in smaller or rural markets might rightfully worry that NCI-CCCs will "steal" potential patients, impressed by the prospect of treatment at a top center, especially if Life for Health covers travel and treatment costs. In actuality, the Life for Health approach might improve the financials of community setting oncologists, helping NCI-CCCs build regional or multistate affiliations with local practices improving the efficiency of how and where people are treated, and qualifying community setting practices to serve as clinical trials sites.

Life for Health's goal is to ensure that cost and distance never bar a participant from getting a full understanding of their tumor's characteristics and the most appropriate treatment options, along with the ability to choose the clinical team in whom they have the most confidence. From there, so long as the participant's interests and outcomes are paramount, anything else to rationalize economics between top centers and community practices should be possible.

Would NCI-CCCs be able to handle increased patient flow, if only for diagnostic workups? The short answer is yes, based on a 2021 study by a University of Pennsylvania team, looking at NCI-CCC capacity. They found that between 2011 and 2016, patient flow at top centers jumped 40% (starting from a relatively low base), whereas patient volumes in community hospitals grew only 10% at community hospitals (starting from a much higher base).[155] However, patients going to top centers did not experience delays in treatment initiation, despite increased patient volume, suggesting NCI-CCCs have sufficient capacity to do more. The only group that experienced a delay in starting treatment were individuals first seen at a local hospital who were then referred to an NCI-CCC—exactly the situation Life for Health is seeking to preempt.

Health economists might worry that Life for Health's grant of easier access to top centers will increase costs, especially if this "NCI-CCC first" approach is adopted by other health systems. Yes, treatment at a top center is likely to cost more than treatment in a rural hospital or one located in a lower cost city. Focusing only on the initial treatment cost, however, misses the point. The idea is to delay, perhaps indefinitely, any need for second or third-line treatments down the road. Paying more for a single round of treatment that keeps cancer at bay for many years is better than paying less for a first round of care, only to be followed in short order by a second or third round of treatment, often at a top center.

These kinds of financial tradeoffs will go away as well, if—as Dr. Raza argues—we focus more resources on reliably predicting and preventing cancer. The long-term goal, as in multimorbidity, is to reduce incidence or increase age of initial diagnosis. Solving cancer is less about *treating* everyone better and more about reducing the need for treatment in the first place. Life for Health increases the odds of both.

ENDNOTES

148 Interestingly, in another sign of how the status quo is stacked against preventive medicine, people who undergo these procedures due to a disease-causing mutation are not included in counts of cancer survival, even on a probability adjusted basis.

149 Pantel, Klaus, and Catherine Alix-Panabières. "Circulating tumour cells in cancer patients: challenges and perspectives." Trends in molecular medicine 16.9 (2010): 398-406.

150 Nadauld, Lincoln, and Dana P Goldman. 2022. "Considerations in the Implementation of Multicancer Early Detection Tests." Future Oncology 18 (28): 3119–24. https://doi.org/10.2217/fon-2022-0120.

151 Papier, K., Atkins, J.R., Tong, T.Y.N. et al. Identifying proteomic risk factors for cancer using prospective and exome analyses of 1463 circulating proteins and risk of 19 cancers in the UK Biobank. Nat Commun 15, 4010 (2024).

152 See, e.g. Wolfson JA, Sun CL, Wyatt LP, Hurria A, Bhatia S. Impact of care at comprehensive cancer centers on outcome: Results from a population-based study. Cancer. 2015 Nov 1;121(21):3885-93 and Taylor, A. O., Doucette, K., Ma, X., Chan, B., Ahn, J., & Lai, C. (2023). Facility type and volume impact outcomes in acute myeloid leukemia—a National Cancer Database Study. Annals of Cancer Epidemiology, 7; and Desjardins MR, Kanarek NF, Nelson WG, Bachman J, Curriero FC. Disparities in Cancer Stage Outcomes by Catchment Areas for a Comprehensive Cancer Center. JAMA Netw Open. 2024 May 1;7(5):e249474

153 Some percent of individuals, unspecified in this study, may not have received their results because they passed away or declined further treatment. See: Sadik, H., Pritchard, D., et. al. "Impact of Clinical Practice Gaps on the Implementation of Personalized Medicine in Advanced Non–Small-Cell Lung Cancer," JCO Precision Oncology, October 31, 2022.

154 A much less direct version of this idea is being developed by AccessHope, an affiliate of an NCI-CCC in Los Angeles called City of Hope. AccessHope sells a benefit to employers/insurers enabling policyholders to have their cancer treatment plan reviewed by a top center's specialist. That clinician then contacts the employee's oncologist of record to provide treatment recommendations. The challenge with this approach is that it relies on workers knowing that the benefit exists and then ensuring that their local oncologist listens to or discusses their case with the center specialist.

155 Frosch, Zachary, Nicholas Illenberger, Nandita Mitra, et. al. 2021. "Trends in Patient Volume by Hospital Type and the Association of These Trends With Time to Cancer Treatment Initiation." JAMA Network Open 4 (7): e2115675. doi.org/10.1001/jamanetworkopen.2021.15675.

28. UNDERSTANDING AND PREVENTING ADRD

If you have ever wondered about the political impact of chronic disease, consider that *Roe v. Wade* might still be the law of the land if not for ADRD. In 1992, Justice Sandra Day O'Connor wrote a decisive opinion preserving abortion rights. Fourteen years later she resigned from the court prematurely to care for her husband, then battling the later stages of ADRD. Her successor, Justice Samuel Alito, proved to be an implacable foe of abortion, authoring the 2023 *Dobbs v. Jackson Women's Health Organization* opinion overturning *Roe v. Wade*. Had she been able to stay on the Court into President Obama's term, she might have been replaced with a more like-minded jurist.[156]

ADRD afflicts the mighty and the humble with equal terror, little by little erasing everything that defines us as individuals—first memory, then cognition and autonomy, and finally, any sense of self. ADRD has taken a former president (Reagan), a former prime minister (Thatcher), and two of the greatest college basketball coaches in history, Pat Summitt and Dean Smith. Yet, for all of its awfulness, neuroscientists are still at a loss to define disease variants in terms of early pathology and progression. The lack of treatments mean that medical spending is relatively low even if long-term care costs are increasing rapidly. Once effective treatments emerge, medical spending will also skyrocket.

As with cancer, Life for Health's greatest initial contribution will be to reduce overall risk since metabolic issues, inflammation, and vascular degeneration are all strongly associated with ADRD risk. However, Life for Health's larger contribution will be in providing much richer data to supercharge the kinds of research described in Chapter 22, accelerating efforts to understand what causes different ADRD variants and how they can be prevented. Brain imaging and tests using blood plasma and cerebrospinal fluid (CSF) reliably detect pathology once it is well advanced. It's known that certain genetic variants, especially in combination, increase disease risk, but these are a small minority of all cases.

Why ADRD remains such a mystery is beyond the scope of this book but how we came to be in this position underscores the importance and value of building longitudinal health narratives (including biosamples) to demystify ADRD. Briefly, efforts to understand the disease got sidetracked for almost two decades by a near religious belief among neuroscience leaders that one of the potential hypotheses about what causes ADRD was, in fact, definitively correct. Research studies seeking to amass data in support of that hypothesis received grant dollars and high-profile coverage in top science journals. Advocates for this view downplayed the importance of metabolic syndrome as a contributing factor despite data linking vascular degeneration and diabetes to ADRD. Critics of the hypothesis and those interested in broadening the search to explore alternatives were attacked and defunded.[157]

One reason why is that for many years the only human tissue that brain researchers could study came from the brains of people who died with, or from, advanced ADRD. Looking at post-mortem brains, researchers noted an extraordinary buildup of toxic protein clusters within and between neurons. These clumps primarily consisted of aberrant forms of a protein called amyloid which build up in ADRD, creating plaques between neurons, eventually disrupting communication between neurons across synapses. Another protein, called tau, aggregated within neurons, hastening their death.

Three decades ago, a group of brain researchers hypothesized that amyloid buildup was both the primary sign of ADRD as well as the primary cause. Whether this happened because the brain overproduced toxic variants or lost its ability to clear them remained an open question, but the prime directive of ADRD research became to figure out how to dissolve or erase aberrant amyloid. Advocates of the amyloid hypothesis minimized tau's role, although some tau researchers believed tau tangles within neurons were as important as amyloid. While the two camps disagreed on which toxic protein came first or mattered more, everyone—among research leaders, that is—agreed that protein buildup was at the root of ADRD.

The amyloid hypothesis gained momentum when rodent studies showed that animals programmed to overproduce mutant amyloid developed progressive ADRD-like issues. Furthermore, when the process was reversed, and amyloid erased, the symptoms disappeared. These findings were bolstered by studies among a small group of people who had a rare genetic predisposition to overproduce toxic amyloid. The consensus became unstoppable when multiple drug companies signed on to develop drugs to penetrate the brain (no easy task) and clear aberrant amyloid.

Then the waiting began. One by one, amyloid clearing drugs failed or produced potentially life-threatening side effects that outweighed any potential benefit. Early losses were chalked up to difficulties with designing drugs to get to the right places in the brain and attack toxic amyloid without disrupting blood flow or healthy cells. Many drug companies called it quits but three soldiered on, pouring billions more into R&D. After forty failed drug trials, three drugs won FDA approval, although the first of these was withdrawn, leaving two others still on the market.

Ironically, it was the *success* of the latter two drugs in clinical trials that doomed the amyloid hypothesis. That's because the drugs were so effective at clearing toxic amyloid. Some trial participants had 100% clearance, a remarkable feat of medicinal chemistry. Yet, ADRD continued to advance in every trial participant.[158] The amyloid clearance goal line had been crossed but cognitive decline continued apace.

Undoubtedly, toxic amyloid and tau buildups play *some* role in ADRD but it's clear that other pathology, upstream of amyloid, is at the root of disease risk and onset. Today, a new generation of ADRD scientists is revisiting ideas previously spurned, focusing on the interplay among brain cells other than neurons including astrocytes (which support neuronal and synaptic function), oligodendrocytes (which insulate nerve fibers) and microglia (which comprise the brain's immune system).

One iconoclastic neuroscientist, Dr. Karl Herrup, characterizes ADRD within the brain as a "disease of the [synaptic] neighborhood." The failure of multiple cells that support synapses or metabolic processes within them, perhaps caused by factors outside the brain, leads to a cascade of dysfunction an eventually, an unrecoverable breakdown in neuronal circuitry.[159] Overactivation of the brain's immune cells may spur inflammation, disrupting neuronal, astrocytic, and microglial function. Another possibility is that dysfunction in mitochondria—the energy generators in all cells—degrades brain metabolism, spurring inflammation. Probably, as Herrup suggests, multiple pathways to dysfunction lead to a similar end state, ADRD. However it plays out, Herrup argues, "the interconnected natures of the neighborhood interactions [drive] a region-specific feed-forward destruction of specific functions."[160] In other words, it's a cascade, a confluence of breakdowns that may at first be disconnected, but which coalesce, causing spillovers akin to metabolic syndrome and aging.

Today, most ADRD researchers acknowledge that ADRD probably results from years of incremental breakdowns in brain metabolism, immune regulation and inflammation, vasculature, and is influenced by events outside the brain. Studies like those discussed in Chapter 22, tracing protein expression anomalies inside and outside of the brain lend credence to these ideas. And, interestingly, through all the years that drug companies chased amyloid clearance, the only intervention that seemed to consistently help postpone ADRD was regular vigorous exercise, an intervention that is most readily associated with metabolic rather than cognitive health.

This brings us back to *Life for Health*. Longitudinal health narratives will provide the critical substrate to understand the relationship among genetic, proteomic, environmental, and behavioral factors, and connect hypotheses with real-world human data quickly. With so much data and much better analytic tools, we are much less likely to get stuck in another ideological cul-de-sac, as happened with amyloid. It will be too easy to find confounding or contradictory data.

Life for Health-generated libraries will accelerate validation of time machine-like predictive models and potential preventive measures. Life for Health also will provide regular access to a diverse participant pool, enabling more frequent non-invasive testing such as blood draws or (for those who consent) head MRIs. Finally, Life for Health creates a much wider universe of non-medical data to draw upon to improve early detection, including activity, voice, and environmental data, and to reliably associate metrics of cognitive function with metabolic function and behavioral patterns.

Finally, *Life for Health's* deep clinician-participant relationship will provide a cultural benefit, slowly changing attitudes about the possibility to prevent or delay even normal cognitive decline. Many Americans approach ADRD now as many viewed a cancer diagnosis in the 1950s or early 1960s, as a veritable death sentence. Life for Health clinicians' relentless emphasis on extending healthspan and preventing disease will change the conversation about cognitive decline and ADRD, moving the focus from fearing a dreaded disease to preserving function, with those at risk more closely tracking relevant metrics along the way. Ultimately, most Life for Health participants will come to believe, as happened in cancer, that fatalism is no way to live.

ENDNOTES

156 In a sad postscript, ADRD also claimed Justice O'Connor's life in 2021.
157 ADRD research joins a number of other recent diseases where leading researchers disregarded outside-the-box ideas that ultimately turned out to be both correct and life-saving. Proponents of mRNA therapies, ultimately used in the most successful COVID vaccines struggled for years to get funding or validation. One of the Nobel Prize winning co-discoverers of the technique to use mRNA therapeutically was denied tenure and lost her academic post. The possibility of using GLP-1s to induce weight loss was a many decades effort, as well, including some very near misses where top

drug executives might have stopped the work. However, ADRD stands alone in terms of how the field was misdirected by, in one case, questionable data and decades of unwillingness to consider research avenues that are beginning to be validated.

158 The drugmakers argue that their treatments slow disease progression, although this is the subject of much debate, or would work better if given earlier -- a refrain frequently heard from amyloid advocates over the years as various treatments failed to halt the disease.

159 Herrup, Karl, How Not To Study a Disease, 2021, MIT Press, 191-2

160 Herrup, pp. 199, 204.

29. PRICING DRUGS FOR ACCESS AND OUTCOMES

> "We try never to forget that medicine is for the people. It is not for the profits. The profits follow, and if we have remembered that, they have never failed to appear. The better we have remembered it, the larger they have been."
>
> –George Merck

Drug prices are too high! It's one of the few health care refrains on which most politicians agree. The villains in this narrative are drugmakers, who are tarred as profiteers exploiting patent rules to pad their bottom lines. Are the critics right? Sometimes yes, sometimes no. Drug company CEOs argue in their defense that innovation is risky and expensive. Their discoveries save lives and livelihoods but the cost of developing a new drug has skyrocketed. Are they right? Again, sometimes yes, sometimes no.

The heart of the problem is that we rely on a single approach to price drugs, echoing the larger conceptual belief that a unitary health care system can solve everything from short-term and routine issues to decades-long and complex ones.

Breakthrough drugs that have extraordinary *potential* value or ones that can be given once but work for years confound the current drug pricing paradigm. Today's prices are volumetrically based, paying drugmakers a fixed price when the drug is taken or administered. Makers of branded drugs have a limited timeframe to recoup as much revenue as they can before the drug loses patent protection and can be made and sold as a generic. The system works for short-acting medications or those that target a single biological mechanism, like blood thinners or insulin. It breaks down, however, if the drug has multi-system effects that add up to a very large future value, has a durable long-term effect, or can be taken infrequently, perhaps even once.

GLP-1s meet two of the three criteria, providing multisystem effects and tremendous potential long-term value. Given timebound patent protections, Novo Nordisk and Lilly (and others that follow) understandably maximize price during early years on the market, a policy that often makes them too expensive to be covered by health insurers. This limits access and reduces near-term and long-term societal benefit. People who seek access have to settle for cheaper, symptom management medications until prices come down or the drug goes generic. Meanwhile, a person's chronic conditions advance, increasing the odds that they will progress to multimorbidity, and earlier than they otherwise might have. Years later when a drug goes generic, it becomes in a sense, too cheap, with pricing based mostly on manufacturing costs. The original drugmaker gets no ongoing benefit from the clinical value of their innovation, nor do they have much incentive to ensure that people take medication consistently to keep multimorbidity at bay. Both the depressed access early on and the depressed value later undermines efforts to solve chronic disease since most of the drug's value lies in its ability to forestall more serious disease in the future.

Drug pricing debates often start with a statistic about the magnitude of prescription drug spending, now estimated to be thirteen to eighteen percent of total health spending.[161] The essential drug spending statistic to anchor around, however, is this: 90% of prescriptions are for generic drugs, and these scripts account for just 18% of total spending. That means (flipping the ratios) that just 10% of drugs—all branded, and mostly to treat advanced chronic disease or cancer—account for 82% of spending. This ratio may shift slightly in favor of branded drug spending if expected demand for GLP-1 drugs materializes, but the overall point remains. The overwhelming majority of drugs consumed will be generic while the overwhelming majority of spend will be for branded drugs.

Opponents of drug price controls cite the ongoing dominance of generic prescriptions as proof that the current system works. Yes, they admit, drug prices are higher when a new product enters the market but look at how much prices go down as other competitors enter that disease category and then plummet once a drug goes generic. Supporters of price controls make the opposite case, that drug companies earn far too much during patent exclusivity periods, and drive consumers and physicians to overuse/overprescribe new products even if they do little to improve outcomes. Further, they argue, drug companies abuse patent laws by getting slightly reformulated versions approved as new entities, delaying or thwarting generic competition.

Unfortunately, when it comes to breakthrough treatments for multi-morbidity like GLP-1s, both perspectives miss the point. Denying broad access to new drugs allows future chronic disease burdens to accumulate while increasing the time required to assess if a new multi-system or long-acting drug really works as promised in clinical trials. However, simply pushing down drug prices during the patent window will inevitably reduce the capital available to develop new drugs.

A better answer is to do both, increase access in early years and increase drugmakers' returns for treatments that yield strong outcomes. In this approach, drugmakers agree to set early-year prices much lower than current practice in exchange for the right to receive ongoing payments based on actual patient results even after a drug goes generic. This kind of outcomes-based annuity pricing (OBAP) aligns drugmakers with recipients, clinicians and insurers, increasing the drugmakers' interest in making sure their drug reaches everyone who stands to benefit, and that drug recipients are getting ongoing clinical guidance and reinforcement to take medication, for as long as it continues benefitting them.

The good news is that Life for Health's long-term framework provides a ready-made infrastructure including ongoing outcomes monitoring to make OBAP arrangements operationally feasible. In addition, Life for Health's prequalification of participants for future clinical trials offers a new approach to lower their risk and costs to bring new drugs to market.

How Drug Pricing Became One Size Fits All

Before going deeper on the economics of OBAP, it's useful to understand how the current drug pricing paradigm developed and why, like the RPS Vortex, it's better suited for acute treatments or symptom management.

Today's pricing approach was codified in 1984 in the Hatch-Waxman Act, a landmark statute hammered out by Republican Senator Orrin Hatch, chair of the Senate Health Committee, and his House Democrat counterpart, Henry Waxman. The two were opposites in every way, physically, ideologically, and temperamentally—Hatch the tall and taciturn, stiff-collared Reaganite, while Waxman was shorter, more voluble, and passionately liberal. Yet this political odd couple joined forces to solve long-simmering questions about drug patents, clarifying how and when generic drugs could enter the market. Waxman wanted a short patent exclusivity period and measures to speed up generic drug approvals. Hatch, more sympathetic to branded drugmakers, wanted to ensure they could earn a sufficient return to develop new drugs.

The Hatch-Waxman Act balanced these interests. Drugmakers could continue to set and negotiate prices with insurers without government regulation during the patent protection period. New drugs would have a 20 year patent life, although the exclusivity period would vary depending on how quickly the drugmaker could win FDA approval. Once patents expired, generic drugmakers could sell chemically identical versions at lower prices and would have a streamlined process to show the FDA that their products worked as well as branded versions. Practically speaking, the lawmakers figured, disease areas that needed new drugs like heart disease and cancer, would invite multiple drugs, keeping a lid on prices even during patent exclusivity periods, reducing the risk that any company would have a monopoly.

It's important to see this agreement in the context of the time. Premature cardiac death rates in 1984 were still high, statin drugs still almost a decade from winning FDA approval. Almost thirteen years on from Nixon's war on cancer declaration, chemotherapy drugs had improved but were also very toxic. Most new drugs took the form of small-molecule pills that needed to be taken regularly, or intravenous medications delivered in doctors' offices or hospitals. The pharmaceutical industry was different then, too, with tens of equally sized US and European competitors. Biotechs like Genentech were starting to grow but were still very young.

In the early 2000s, it seemed that Hatch-Waxman was delivering on its promise. A wave of new statin drugs came to market, followed by anti-clotting medication Plavix, transforming heart disease treatment and establishing cholesterol levels as a closely watched metric of cardiovascular health. When the first statins went generic in the mid-aughts, prescribing rates jumped as unit costs plummeted. Cancer, too, had early wins with the first therapies targeted to specific genetic or molecular tumor features.

Then the pendulum swung. A series of missteps by Big Pharma companies resulted in less investment to design the "next statin" (i.e., transformational drug classes). Merck withdrew a now-infamous anti-inflammatory drug, Vioxx, that caused more serious bleeding incidents than disclosed during FDA review. The swarm of class action lawsuits that followed empowered the big companies' legal arms encouraging growth through acquisition and less investment in internal R&D. The wisdom of this path was validated by the failure of drugs to treat ADRD, obesity, menopause symptoms, and nicotine addiction. Unlike in Silicon Valley where the mantra was to "fail fast," new drugs seemed to fail slowly and very expensively—often only after drugs entered late-stage clinical trials and drugmakers had sunk hundreds of millions of dollars. The pharmaceutical business underwent a series of mergers, seeking a kind of safety in building a portfolio of products targeting a mix of conditions. Larger drugmakers kept in-house R&D expertise in larger disease areas like diabetes, heart disease, or behavioral drugs, but increasingly, cutting-edge medications were acquired from startups or biotechs who had taken on the risky phase of drug design.

Big Pharma and biotechs increased resources going into targeted cancer drugs and biologic drugs using monoclonal antibodies to combat autoimmune conditions like multiple sclerosis and psoriasis and undertreated issues like migraine. These drugs tended to have a higher hit rate and were longer acting than pills, and therefore more lucrative. New anti-autoimmune drug classes achieved increasingly long disease suppression, requiring less switching if a drug stopped working, and longer periods between injections. Biologics manufacturers also pushed patent boundaries, seeking to extend protection by developing self-injectable and longer-acting versions, while arguing that generic versions of biologic drugs, called biosimilars, were less effective.

Targeted cancer therapies evolved, too. First approved to treat advanced malignancy in one type of cancer, drugmakers and clinicians worked quickly to try drugs in earlier treatment rounds, in different combinations, and in other organs or tissues. Increasingly, they believed, the genetic drivers of tumor growth were as important to fighting cancer as where in the body the tumor originated. The mid-2010s added immunotherapy drugs to the cancer arsenal, a long-hoped but hard to realize approach to awakening immune cells to attack tumors. The most successful drug designs were increasingly seen to be platforms, as in software development, rather than standalone products. Immunotherapy blockbusters from Merck and Bristol Myers, when used before surgery, could even preempt the need for chemotherapy.

Late in the decade the pharma landscape was upended by GLP-1 drugs, long-used to combat diabetes, now reformulated to last longer and reach the brain's appetite circuitry. As in cancer, drugmakers sought new combination therapies, with Lilly becoming the first to introduce or test GLP-1s targeting two or three hormone receptors. Outside of metabolic issues, a few biotechs finally succeeded in developing gene therapies that promised to solve disease by permanently repairing or circumventing broken genetic code. Given once, the drug companies hoped, they might last decades, even forever.

The basis of many drugs' value changed, as the nature of breakthrough drugs shifted from short-acting pills to control symptoms to long-acting drugs that induced remission or prevented more expensive, future treatment. The number of times a drug was taken became less important than how broadly a drug worked, how well and for how long. GLP-1s still had to be injected weekly, potentially forever, but their systemic effects went beyond obesity or diabetes. Likewise, one-time gene therapies saved hundreds of thousands of dollars of treatment for rare but debilitating heritable blood conditions. The logic of basing drug pricing on pills or shots crumbled.

Changes in drug technology and the bifurcation between smaller drug startups and large pharma companies coincided, after 2010, with an equally profound shift in how drug prices were set among drugmakers, insurers, and pharmacies. Policymakers operated in the belief that branded drug prices within a disease category were roughly the same, and that pricing aligned with disease severity and drug efficacy.

In practice, a drug's true price became detached from fundamental value, driven instead by a convoluted maze of pricing schemes and payment flows to accommodate different private and public insurer drug coverage rules. In the middle were entities called pharmacy benefit managers (PBMs), companies tasked to act as honest brokers in negotiating prices paid to manufacturers and paid (in turn) by pharmacies and insurers. Quickly, PBMs became gatekeepers of drug access, and equally quickly, many ceased to be honest, or at least independent, brokers. The three largest PBMs, controlling almost two-thirds of drug coverage decisions, were acquired by health care conglomerates that also owned insurers or pharmacy chains. By 2020, CVS owned an insurer (Aetna), a PBM (Caremark), and the largest pharmacy chain (CVS). UnitedHealth owned a top insurer, a top PBM, and the leading benefit consultant, Optum Health, which advised companies about how to structure health and drug benefits. The integration of PBMs as affiliates of insurers was especially problematic given the MLR, the ACA formula that required insurers to pay 80% of premiums received in claims. Now under the same holding company roof, it invited insurers to overpay PBM affiliates, inflating those units' profits at the expense of insurance units' regulated margins.

No longer did drug companies negotiate over the price or coverage terms of individual drugs. Rather they had to optimize coverage across their entire product line-up, strong-armed by PBMs who could pocket the difference between high list prices and the amounts paid by pharmacies. Meanwhile, the drug companies tried to get competitors' products shunted onto costlier drug pricing tiers. Continuous price negotiations among PBMs, drugmakers, insurers, and pharmacy chains became a floating craps game as first one manufacturer and then another jockeyed for price and access advantages. The net result of these machinations is that the actual price paid for a specific drug was hard, if not impossible, to identify. The link between price and value dissolved.

Generic drugs hardly fared better. A few drugmakers gained dominant positions in supplying insulin injectables and epinephrine pens to reverse severe allergic reactions, driving list prices far above production costs. In other areas, PBMs pushed prices so low that generic manufacturers ceased production, causing supply chains to fray or rely on single factories or suppliers for critical ingredients. Drug stockpiles dwindled rapidly if a critical supplier went offline, as happened in 2023, when many US hospitals had to ration access to a couple of key chemotherapy drugs.

The final element undermining the Hatch-Waxman regime is the (by now) familiar specter of rising multimorbidity prevalence. Statins, anti-clotting, and blood sugar drugs that entered the market in the 1990s and early 2000s succeeded in slowing the advance of individual conditions, delaying life-threatening or costly heart attacks and hospitalizations. However, as multimorbidity advanced, people started taking four, five, even more medications. Treating cholesterol or blood sugar alone was at best a stopgap, a goal likely stymied by the offsetting effects of drugs prescribed by different specialists. Advanced disease could not be stopped by drugs alone. Where new metabolic syndrome drugs once replaced costly hospitalizations, most newer ones became supplements to inpatient care. When the 2021 Inflation Reduction Act gave Medicare the power to bargain directly with drugmakers, it was little surprise that seven of the first ten drugs selected managed symptoms of advanced metabolic syndrome.[162]

Reducing Clinical Trial Cost and Risk

Drugmakers are unhappy as well, continually buffeted by investor demands for new and better blockbusters while having to pay increasingly large amounts to PBMs to ensure patient access to their products. It was a game that they learned to play and profit from even as their leaders knew that the game was increasingly corrupt.

Fortunately, there *is* something that drugmakers desperately want that could induce them to adopt outcomes-based pricing for breakthrough drugs. That is to lower clinical trial costs, the single greatest risk to bring a drug to market. It's estimated that the cost to develop a new drug from start to FDA approval requires between $1 and $3 billion in capital depending on the disease area and the drug's complexity. About a third to half of that cost goes to design the drug's chemistry and method of delivery. These front end R&D costs are now dropping thanks to AI, open-access protein libraries, and visualization tools that allow drugs to be designed with computers, reducing the risk of synthesizing a dud. However, development budgets for the clinical phase continue to increase, already accounting for 50% to 70% of total R&D costs.[163]

The economic math of clinical trials is formidable. There are only so many clinicians and offices or hospitals qualified to treat people in a trial. Drugmakers try to minimize the number of sites, but that goal clashes with the reality that qualified participants may be widely dispersed, meaning only a handful of people are treated at a particular location. The more targeted a drug, the more likely it is that potential trial participants will be dispersed.[164]

The other hard reality of drug trials is that, at any given time, few people qualify for a trial or choose to enroll. Trial criteria require enrollees to be at a particular disease stage, to have some level of dissatisfaction with their current treatment, to live near or be able to travel to a trial site, and to be willing to undertake any other trial requirements. People may be excluded if they have comorbid conditions or take medications that might confound results.

Most new drugs are approved for conditions that affect less than five million Americans and many target patient populations numbering in the tens or hundreds of thousands. Only a small fraction of potential recipients actually qualify and enroll in the trial.[165] Today, fewer than 10% of Americans say they have participated in any kind of clinical trial, and an even smaller percent say they have taken part of a trial testing a new drug.[166] This is why the CFF's efforts were such a game changer for Vertex's willingness to develop a CF drug.

A number of startups are trying to change clinical trial economics, either by increasing the number of clinicians who qualify to run sites or using AI and other sophisticated digital marketing to recruit participants more efficiently. Both approaches will help, but the gains are unlikely to transform trial risks in a fundamental way. This is because all recruitment starts too late, only *after* a trial is designed. Life for Health creates the possibility of flipping the process, estimating and aggregating demand ahead of a trial's approval, potentially even helping shape the trial's design. Participants can be prequalified on a continual basis using health narrative data, identifying conditions, treatments, or real-world outcomes studies for which they might enroll.

As with the discussion of time machines, this may sound far-fetched, but consider the illustrative case of Frank, who qualified for multiple trials based on various medical factors. Yes, I created that persona and purposefully peppered it with attractive disease targets to highlight Life for Health's potential. But, while some of Frank's issues were more extreme or immediate, they are the same ones that most of us will fact at some point, including a major chronic condition, cancer, and some aspect of neurodegenerative disease. The sooner we qualify ourselves for future research, using actual data or predictive risk models, the faster we will be able to harness demand and make trial participation a more natural part of chronic disease treatment, as it now is for advanced cancer.

Equally valuable will be the ability to accelerate design and completion of post-FDA trials to confirm real-world outcomes. Highly touted by FDA leaders (including current commissioner, Dr. Marty Makary), conducting these trials has proven to be complicated in practice. Here, too, Life for Health is a gamechanger, providing both a clinical infrastructure and data tracking to pre-qualify participants. Drugmakers, too, should be enthused since Life for Health participants are more likely to be receiving concurrent services that increase the odds of treatment adherence.

Outcomes-Based Annuitized Pricing: A New Deal for Breakthrough Drugs

With that as backdrop, let's look closer at how outcomes-based annuitized pricing (OBAP) works. OBAP begins with the insight that a drug's price is actually a bundle of three distinct components, which together compensate drugmakers for (a) the cost to manufacture the drug, (b) sunk R&D costs, and (c) the value of the drug's clinical benefit. Under Hatch-Waxman, drugmakers' "excess margins" during patent exclusivity periods provides for the second and third components. Once the drug goes generic, the patent owner's revenue shrinks dramatically.[167]

It's understandable that compensation for past R&D costs should go to zero, but why also does their share of clinical value go away? And, if a drug's future efficacy is potentially great, but uncertain, why is the drugmaker compensated for that before the value is known? A much better approach is to maximize recovery for the first two elements during patent exclusivity periods, with drugmakers' share in clinical value spread out over time along with that of recipients and insurers. This at least ensures that drugmakers remain interested in the quality of clinical care that drug recipients receive after starting to take their products.

OBAP unbundles the three price components, providing a fixed payment during the first three years that a person takes a drug. This allows drugmakers to recover production and R&D costs. However, prices would be much lower than current levels to increase access. Also, prices would be uniformly set and published as a net price, avoiding PBM machinations that reward artificially high list prices and equally large rebates. Thereafter, drugmakers continue to receive a fixed, annual payment reflecting the clinical value of their product, conditioned on recipients' continuing to have good outcomes. This ties the value of highly effective or one-time therapies to results over time, aligning drugmakers, clinicians, insurers, and participants (as drug recipients). Everyone is better off if the treatment is working, and everyone is aligned to ensure that the clinician and participant are having ongoing and effective discussions about treatment and outcomes.

Here's how this works in practice. For the first two to three years that a person is taking a drug, a branded treatment that costs $6,000 a year might instead cost something like $2,000 a year. Thereafter, drugmakers would receive a preset annual payment per person prescribed the drug, for example $200 to $500 a year, with the amount set at the time of approval based on the disease target and efficacy, and could increase with the recipient's age or inflation. Threshold outcomes for payment would be set by drugmakers based on metrics used in the drug's approval. In addition, drugmakers might earn a one-time bonus for recipients who achieve long-term health outcomes such as being disease-free for a decade, or entering Medicare without the condition that they had when they started therapy.

OBAP is most valuable for drugs that have transformative effects across multiple organs or systems or induce long-term remission of chronic, age-related, or life-threatening disease.[168] This includes GLP-1 therapies (which are discussed at greater length later in this chapter), biologic drugs to treat autoimmune conditions, cell therapies like CAR-T treatments for cancer or autoimmune conditions, and one-time gene therapies.

Would drugmakers agree to lower prices during patent exclusivity periods in exchange for lower clinical trial costs and a right to earn more over time? Yes, especially for breakthrough drugs, those that are administered less frequently (or even just once), and those which are expected to show greater value over time. This is because OBAP solves a number of drugmakers' problems.

First it gets therapies to market faster, and more cheaply. Second, it increases access (and therefore revenue) in the years following initial approval. Most drugs take a number of years to ramp up sales while drugmakers haggle with insurers over formulary placement. This is tremendously inefficient and delays access to breakthrough medications in private insurance and Medicaid. Third, drugmakers earn little or nothing on their innovation once the drug loses patent protection. Annuity payments allow them to continue sharing in the drug's clinical value. Fourth, it ensures drugmakers have an ongoing stake in how well their therapies are being prescribed by clinicians and access to services that increase recipients' chances of a good outcome. Fifth, it shortens the timeframe to understand how well a treatment is working among different recipient populations, why, and how the drug might be improved or combined with other therapies to improve outcomes. Finally, it gives drugmakers a strong incentive to produce their own authorized generic or underwrite reputable generic companies' manufacturing capacity, improving the odds that high-value drugs will be adequately supplied after going generic.

Case Study: Hep-C and Failure of Hatch-Waxman Pricing

The benefits of OBAP and the failure of Hatch-Waxman is illustrated by looking at what happened in the 2010s relating to a breakthrough drug class called direct action antivirals (DAAs), developed to counteract Hepatitis-C, a chronic and ultimately fatal liver disease. For decades, scientists had known about Hepatitis A and B, but a vexingly large number of people treated for both strains still developed liver disease. In the early 1990s, researchers isolated a third hepatitis strain which they named Hep-C.[169] The new version was more insidious than the A or B variants. It could go undetected much longer, without causing external symptoms, but it was also irreversible using conventional treatments. Those infected would inevitably develop cirrhosis or liver cancer, at which point the only option is a liver transplant, which is costly and risky and depends on a suitable donor organ being available.

By 2000, public health experts realized they had an enormous Hep-C liability on their hands. Hundreds of thousands of blood transfusion recipients from the mid-1960s to late-1980s had been infected, especially wounded Vietnam War soldiers. Although contaminated blood had been eliminated by 1990, the virus had gained a second avenue of transmission through intravenous drug abusers sharing needles. By 2010, an estimated 2.5 million Americans had Hep-C. Treatments to slow disease progression required expensive annual treatments, and eventually stopped working. As of 2015, the future cost to treat end-stage Hep-C patients was estimated to be somewhere between $100 and $200 billion—an amount that, at the time, exceeded Medicare's total annual spending on all prescription drugs. Most of the eventual cost would fall on public insurance programs for veterans, older Americans (Medicare), or the poor (Medicaid).

Faced with this massive disease, approval of the first DAAs in 2012 was like manna from heaven. They were the closest thing to a functional cure, inducing long-term remission after a single, four-month course of treatment. The best drug was marketed by Gilead, the leading HIV drugmaker, which made an incredibly savvy and timely purchase of a smaller rival in 2011 on the strength of its soon-to-be-approved Hep-C drug.[170] Gilead moved quickly to maximize revenue, setting an initial list price at $84,000 per treatment. Insurers were gobsmacked, even as Gilead argued that the price was justified given the hundreds of thousands of dollars of future advanced liver disease treatments that its drug would prevent.

Gilead was right, but only if Hep-C infected people could access the drug, and if viral remission over many years proved to be true. However, State Medicaid programs, subject to annual appropriation cycles, could not rationalize the massive spike in outlays required to make the drugs widely available. Gilead was willing to negotiate discounts but was unwilling to spread payments out over time. Gilead also argued that the drugs would provide long-term protection against Hep-C based on strong, but relatively short-term, clinical trial data. Actually realizing this value, they argued, was the responsibility of clinicians and insurers.

Seeking to avoid a messy fight over veterans, Gilead agreed to a reduced price with the Veterans Health Administration. Medicaid programs ended up paying in the $50,000–$60,000 range per person treated, based on data from some states and Gilead earnings reports. Yet, even at reduced prices, treating the estimated 2.5 million Americans with Hep-C would cost about $125 billion. Medicaid program directors in Louisiana and Washington tried a different approach, settling on a subscription price model, dubbed "Netflix pricing" in which they agreed to pay a fixed dollar amount for an unlimited supply of doses. This capped how much the states would have to pay out but shifted responsibility onto state agencies to reduce the per person cost by getting as many people treated as possible.

If the goal was to stop Hep-C, Hatch-Waxman pricing clearly failed.[171] By 2020, just a third of Americans thought to have Hep-C had received *some* treatment, with many not even receiving a full course of injections.[172] Since then, treatment volumes have flat-lined at about 100,000 people a year, essentially treading water given the estimated rate of new infections.[173]

Treatment access delays while insurers haggled with Gilead worsened outcomes. Individuals who progressed to advanced liver disease while awaiting treatment had much worse outcomes than those treated with earlier-stage disease.[174] Insurers prioritized access to older Americans and those who already had severe liver disease—another case of the Prevention Paradox at work—even though the best long-term results could be realized among younger recipients.[175] As a result, there are still about 1.5 million Americans with Hep-C, with future liver disease liability in the neighborhood of $100 billion.

Gilead's commercial success was applauded by investors and others in the industry, generating over $40 billion in the five years from 2014 to 2018 when their drug was the market leader. However, it's worth asking if Gilead's results, and those of other drug companies, would have been even better under OBAP? What if Gilead had heeded George Merck's advice (quoted at the start of the chapter) and pursued a strategy of getting paid based on access and outcomes?

Here's what happened. In 2018, rival drugmaker AbbVie introduced a superior Hep-C drug, and seeking to gain market set their net price at $25,000 per treatment, undercutting Gilead's effective price by about 50%. Gilead had to match AbbVie, and introduced an authorized generic version in 2019 priced at a similar level. Both companies saw the total Hep-C market collapse and today, the two companies each make less than $1 billion a year in US Hep-C drug sales, down about 90% from revenue at its peak.

Now, let's consider what might have happened had Gilead adopted OBAP. Instead of seeking $50,000 up front at the time of treatment, they might have asked for just half of this, slightly more than the comparable stopgap treatment cost. In exchange, Gilead could have asked for up to ten years of $5,000 annual payments for anyone receiving a partial or full course of treatment who did not go on to develop cirrhosis or liver cancer. It might have also agreed to something in-between for people who already had more advanced liver disease, knowing that there was some value in slowing disease progression.

The key factor is how many more people Gilead could have treated early on, including younger people more likely to have remission of a decade or more. At $25,000 a treatment, Gilead drugs could have helped twice as many people during their four-year monopoly, leaving them in roughly the same revenue position. However, they would also be in a position to receive annuity payments totaling between $4 and $8 billion for up to a decade, depending on the number of people treated and their outcomes. All told, Gilead could have earned twice as much, over time, as it did during the five years that it had an effective treatment monopoly.

Would OBAP have dissuaded competitors like AbbVie? No, if anything it should have encouraged them to bring a competitor to market faster. Knowing that their drug was superior to Gilead's, they could have undercut the Gilead price by less than they did, setting the initial treatment cost at, say, $20,000, knowing that under an OBAP regime, they would have the right to receive future annual payments as well. Had OBAP been used in Hep-C, hundreds of thousands, if not millions, would have been treated faster and today both Gilead and AbbView would be making far more than $1 billion a year, even with a much smaller population still to treat. Tens of thousands of advanced liver disease cases would have been avoided, and there would now be a much more robust surveillance infrastructure to track new infections and recipients' outcomes.

OBAP for GLP-1s

In many ways the DAA script has already played out with GLP-1 drugs, limiting access for working class and poorer Americans.[176] Most health policy experts project that prices will decline rapidly once new competitors enter the market, and the earliest GLP-1 used for weight loss, liraglutide, goes generic. So, problem solved, right?

Well, not so fast. For now, GLP-1s must be taken continuously to maintain metabolic benefits, although it may be possible once a person regains their desired weight to spread out or lower doses. Setting aside those who use GLP-1s tactically to achieve short-term weight loss, there is little value in terms of preventing multimorbidity if people with obesity or diabetes cycle on and off the drugs. This scenario may even worsen their metabolic health since the current drugs erode muscle mass and fat in equal measure, increasing the chance that body fat composition will actually worsen after weight regain, or create another as yet unknown metabolic dysfunction. Lower price, alone, does not equal great outcomes. In addition, once earlier GLP-1s go generic, private insurers will have an even greater rationale to limit access to newer, more expensive drugs, limiting access to individuals with higher BMIs. It will be the Prevention Paradox on steroids.

GLP-1s potential value will only be realized if insurers, drugmakers, and clinicians are aligned to benefit *over time* as participants regain and maintain metabolic health. It will also provide better data faster to develop new therapies, or combinations of existing ones, to address unique needs among certain groups, such as older recipients, or those more prone to gastric emptying issues, or versions targeting the brain and not the gut.

So, what might OBAP for GLP-1s include? Pricing could be broken into three components, an "initial period" price, an outcomes-based annuity payment, and a one-time bonus for recipients who start therapy at age 45 or older and enter Medicare without multimorbidity.

The price during the first three years that a person is on therapy would be much lower than current levels, perhaps $100 to $150 per month ($1,200 to $1,800 a year). Thereafter, drugmakers would receive an annual amount for each participant who meets or exceeds metabolic health thresholds, assessed remotely or at in-person visits. The annuity could be simple to calculate, perhaps as a function of age like the Health Outcomes Payment. For example, the annuity might equal participant's age multiplied by $10, yielding $400 for a 40-year-old who meets metabolic thresholds, $580 for a 58-year-old, and so on. Drugmakers would continue to receive the annuity even after their treatment loses patent protection, separate and apart from any payment to the generic manufacturer. The payments would cease if a participant starts taking a different drug.

Finally, drugmakers could qualify for a one-time bonus paid after a recipient enters Medicare with the bonus amount tied to improvement in their metabolic function from the time they started treatment until they enter Medicare. That bonus might be worth thousands or tens of thousands of dollars per recipient entering Medicare without multimorbidity.

OBAP for GLP-1s would avoid the situation that played out with Hep-C drugs. Metabolic syndrome is a much larger potential market, but the same basic issue exists. How do we broaden access as quickly as possible, especially to poorer Americans, ensure people continue to benefit from therapy, and provide data and signals for new and better drugs? OBAP approaches will also accelerate clinicians' understanding of the interplay between medical and non-medical interventions. Once again, in Life for Health, synchronizing science and finance ensures better health and financial outcomes for all.

ENDNOTES

161 The width of the range reflects how opaque drug pricing is within the RPS Vortex. High end estimates include the cost of subsidies and rebates that are traded among insurers, drug companies, and pharmacies; the lower end estimate reflects the net price paid by insurers.

162 Two others treat late-stage autoimmune conditions and one is for a group of blood cancers that tend to correlate with age.

163 Eastern Research Group, "Drug Development," Final Report to Office of the Assistant Secretary of Planning and Evaluation, HHS, September 26, 2024, 31-34.

164 Cancer is one exception to this rule because novel therapies tend to be tested first in people with recurrent or relapsed disease. These individuals are more often treated at large cancer centers all of which are qualified to be trial sites.

165 For example, consider a condition that affects 1% of the US population, or about 3 million people. Perhaps 50,000 to 100,000 people are newly diagnosed each year, about 150 - 300 people per day, at any of perhaps a thousand offices or hospitals. That equates to 0.15 - 0.3 people who potentially qualify per location, per day. Even if everyone is eligible for the trial, only 5-10% may be willing to enroll or live within a reasonable distance of a trial site to complete in-person exams.

166 Even in cancer, when people are much more likely to agree to participate in a trial, just one in five people with cancer enroll in any clinical research, with about half that number (13%) contributing tissues to a biorepository. See Joseph M. Unger et al., National Estimates of the Participation of Patients With Cancer in Clinical Research Studies Based on Commission on Cancer Accreditation Data. JCO 42, 2139-2148(2024). Enrollment in treatment-related trials was four times higher at NCI comprehensive cancer centers compared to other academic or hospital-based settings—22% of NCI center patients enrolled in a trial versus 4% - 5.7% at other locations.

167 The ability to receive some value continues for longer with biologic drugs, which are derived from living organisms and involve more complex protein synthesis. However, as generic drugmakers have gotten better at formulating biosimilar versions of branded biologics, the price advantage for the original product has begun to erode much faster after patent expiration.

168 In 2018, a team of drug pricing experts, led by Dana Goldman and Karen Van Nuys at the University of Southern California, proposed to divide pricing into three period. Pricing in the first, "Evaluation period" would be set as low as possible to encourage access and use -- as is true under outcomes-based annuitized pricing. Data from the initial period would inform pricing during a second period. Drugs that work well would have higher prices; drugs that fizzle in the real world would see prices go down. Then, after an undefined period, prices would drop -- akin to what now happens under generic competition. See: Goldman, Dana P., et al. "A new model for pricing drugs of uncertain efficacy." NEJM Catalyst 4.6 (2018).

169 For discovering Hep-C and describing its mechanism of action, scientists Harvey Alter, Michael Houghton, and Charles Rice shared the 2020 Nobel Prize in Medicine.

170. Gilead brought two main Hep-C drugs to market, sold under the brand names Solvadi and Harvoni. Both drugs were acquired in purchasing a smaller biotech, Pharmasset, in early 2012.
171. Success in treating veterans has been the one potential bright spot. Before DAAs entered the market, the VHA deployed a program to identify Hep-C positive veterans. By 2020, it had treated about 85% of the 150,000 veterans who had Hep-C in 2010. Teshale, Eyasu H, Henry Roberts, Neil Gupta, and Ruth Jiles. 2022. "Characteristics of Persons Treated for Hepatitis C Using National Pharmacy Claims Data, United States, 2014–2020." Clinical Infectious Diseases 75 (6): 1078–80. https://doi.org/10.1093/cid/ciac139.
172. Wester C, Osinubi A, Kaufman HW, et al. Hepatitis C Virus Clearance Cascade — United States, 2013–2022. MMWR Morb Mortal Wkly Rep 2023;72:716–720.
173. Ibid.
174. See, e.g. Kramer JR, Cao Y, Li L, et. al. 2002. "Longitudinal Associations of Risk Factors and Hepatocellular Carcinoma in Patients With Cured Hepatitis C Virus Infection." Am J Gastroenterol. 2022 Nov 1;117(11):1834-1844.
175. DAAs' greatest long-term value is among younger recipients and those with fewer years of Hep-C infection. Yet the under 40 demographic group has the lowest treatment rates by age, especially in Medicaid. See Wester, 2023
176. As of Fall 2024, Medicaid coverage of GLP-1s was available in just 13 states. See: Williams, E., Rudowitz, R., Bell, C., Medicaid Coverage of and Spending on GLP-1s, Kaiser Family Foundation, November 4, 2024.

30. ENSURING MEDICARE'S SOLVENCY

> The projections in this year's report continue to demonstrate the need for timely and effective action to address Medicare's remaining financial challenges—including the projected depletion of the [Hospital Insurance] trust fund, this fund's long-range financial imbalance, and the rapid growth in Medicare expenditures. Furthermore, if the growth in Medicare costs is comparable to growth under the illustrative alternative projections, then policy reforms will have to address much larger financial challenges than those assumed under current law.
>
> –2024 Medicare Trustees' Report to Congress

To read reports about Medicare's solvency such as the Trustee's report above, is to see how thoroughly government officials accept the soothing narcotic that ballooning costs can be solved by financial means alone. Nowhere in the 2024 Trustees' Reports are words like "diabetes," "obesity," "cancer recurrence" or "dementia." It is bizarre, as if the medical substrate that feeds health costs is a kind of dark matter about which the less said the better.

As a result, there is no politically viable path to restore Medicare solvency. Even as official Washington clings to financialism, none of the options to curtail benefits are politically viable. Raising the eligibility age or changing the ramp-in of Social Security benefits (which retirees increasingly use to cover out-of-pocket health costs) disproportionately affects middle and low-income Americans, already facing higher multimorbidity rates and shorter healthspans. Both Medicare for All (liberal

Democrats' preferred reform) or Medicare Advantage for All (Republicans' preferred reform) outsource care to private insurers, which ironically—in the current paradigm—will only increase everyone's reliance on government rulemaking to control multimorbidity-related costs.

What's a financialist to do? Perhaps pray that GLP-1 prices are forced down and can be dispensed like vitamins. Inevitably both political parties will ratchet up pressure on their least-favored part of the RPS Vortex with Democrats going after drugmakers and large health conglomerates while Republicans focus on Medicaid, fraud, and administrative waste. This is the insular game on which the RPS Vortex thrives, as weaker players are forced to be acquired or to exit, increasing incumbents' ability to resist statutory or regulatory changes. No magic elixir of physician payment reforms or financial engineering will undo the relentless scientific march of chronic disease.

Campaigns to improve Americans' health including the Trump-inspired "Make America Healthy Again" movement are helping to shift the focus onto chronic disease, as is increased scrutiny of mega-conglomerate UnitedHealth. However, these positive forces are offset by countervailing sentiment against public funding of research and the emergence of pharmaceutical and vaccine skeptics. RPS Vortex entities will happily exploit signs of division over priorities or methods to try to splinter coalitions. The worst case as insurers see it is that they might be forced into utility-like regulation, limiting profitability while protecting their primacy within the system.

In this respect, Life for Health offers something every politician values, an escape from a political no-win. It has something for everyone, a focus on chronic disease and metabolic issues for MAHA supporters, a longer-term framework around which health startups and new insurance models can thrive (to please clinicians and investors), and a way to reduce costs without having to cut benefits. Health Outcomes Payments and the possibility that a participant might face premium increases if they fail to realize health improvements appeal to conservatives seeking to inject a measure of personal accountability into health care, while shrinking health insurers' influence and lowering drug prices will appeal to liberals. Health insurers are the main economic losers in a Life for Health world, but they need not be wiped out, just cut down to size and refocused on Routine and Emergency/Elective Medicine.

The big conceptual leap for elected officials will be to accept the logic of separating acute and chronic care. It runs counter to decades of practice and will require potential winners from a change including life insurers, large employers, and clinicians fed up with the status quo to advocate in Washington DC and state capitals for a separate system to vanquish chronic disease.

As we saw in Chapter 16, it is possible to get total health spending back to current levels within two decades of starting Life for Health. This is within the time window to secure Medicare's long-term solvency without cutting benefits or changing eligibility rules. Ultimately, there is no alternative to reversing and preventing multimorbidity. Anything else will be insufficient to keep Medicare's promise to older Americans.

31. ENGINEERING FOOD FOR HEALTH

"We're up against powerful biochemical mechanisms created by food addiction. Willpower becomes useless when industrial junk food and sugar are in charge of your brain chemistry. Fake foods have hijacked our brains, our hormones, and our metabolism. These Frankenfoods have literally created a vicious cycle of hunger and cravings. There is no such thing as junk food. There's just junk, and there's food."

–Dr. Mark Hyman

The tragedy of metabolic syndrome is that America spends hundreds of billions of dollars on medications and hospital stays to counteract damage caused by consuming hundreds of billions of dollars of unhealthy food. As we saw in Chapter 9, decisive shifts in agricultural policy in 1973 led to wider use of sweeteners and ultra-processed ingredients at the same moment that the schism between science and finance elevated short-term thinking, shifting health insurers from solving disease to managing symptoms.

Food production in the age of obesity is starting to change, but progress is slow. Efforts to produce food without pesticides or growth additives took almost a quarter century to reach mainstream appeal, but from 2000 onwards, grew rapidly as grocery chains like Whole Foods and Sprouts popularized access to locally produced and organic products. In 2023, natural and organic food and supplement sales topped $100 billion, accounting for almost 10% of total supermarket sales, an encouraging growth in market share. However, market penetration has been uneven, with just a third of organic goods being sold in mass-market supermarket chains, and most packaged food still containing many ultra-processed ingredients.

Some healthy food activists would kickstart efforts by resurrecting public opinion and litigation tactics used to confront Big Tobacco. This would be a delicious irony since Big Tobacco originally borrowed tactics used by sugar growers to counteract charges about the harms of smoking and nicotine. Lawfare against food producers would bring it full circle.

Still, as lucrative as product liability lawsuits can be, they take years to wind through the courts and are risky. It's hard to prove that certain ingredients were decisive in causing metabolic disease or that food producers intended to cause overeating. One jury or judge may find a food maker liable while another does not. Another challenge is that food production and sales are a much bigger part of the economy than tobacco, accounting for 6% of US GDP and 13% of household consumer spending. Agribusinesses in the Midwest, West, and South along with big box retailers, supermarkets, and restaurants nationwide are large employers with effective lobbying arms.

One alternative deployed in other parts of the world and in some US cities is to impose excise taxes like soda taxes, targeting sweeteners. These can be blunt instruments with most of the financial burden falling on consumers. The net effect is to suppress demand rather than forcing food producers to reformulate their products broadly. Soda and sugar taxes are doubly problematic in states with higher obesity and diabetes prevalence, which have lower median incomes and already rely to a greater degree on sales taxes to generate revenue.

A better approach is to quantify the costs of treating metabolic health issues, reframing it as an industry wide externality, akin to the way air pollution is managed in the auto industry and power generation. There, carmakers and power plant owners face caps on certain air emissions, monitored at the tailpipe or smokestack. Annual, industry-wide limits decline at a measured rate, giving industry participants time to adapt, either to deploy new technology, or compensate the public by buying emissions credits or paying fines. Today, carmakers that sell low or zero-emissions vehicles earn credits to sell companies that make higher polluting models. Emissions markets have generated billions of profit for Tesla, for example, which amasses credits on its all-electric fleet, selling them to Ford, GM, and others. A similar "cap and trade" approach has been used for decades in power generation to get plant owners to invest in pollution control equipment or build cleaner-burning gas plants or renewables. Market-oriented approaches like these garner support from affected industries, which tend to prefer them to prescriptive technology mandates.

Life for Health would provide valuable data and a framework to stand up a market for health-related externalities. Participant outcomes will provide strong real-world evidence about how reversal of metabolic syndrome alters the type and volume of food intake, even within the same socioeconomic strata and geographies. This data will be buttressed by longitudinal data associating metabolic function, biomarkers of metabolic health, and longitudinal nutritional and behavioral data. Life for Health data can also help validate nutritional scoring approaches, confirming which labeling approaches most effectively correlate with purchasers' metabolic health.

Structuring markets for metabolic pollution would require experimentation and refinement. Markets might be designed based on geography, socioeconomic factors, or prevalence of metabolic disease, thereby ensuring that efforts to improve nutritional quality has greater value and impact in areas with higher multimorbidity prevalence and risk. Food companies' initial allowances might be based on existing sales over recent periods, decreasing over the following decade. Companies exceeding allowance limits would pay a penalty, based on the market clearing price for a credit, with proceeds going into a fund to defray metabolic health treatments for working age adults and retirees. These measures could be paired with clearer front of packaging nutritional labeling, which studies in Europe and Asia have shown to impact purchasing behavior in general, as well as among individuals with chronic disease.[177]

This is just one among many possible approaches to break the synergy between industrial food producers and the RPS Vortex. Life for Health will act directly on the latter to end sick care, but elected officials will need to pressure food makers to rethink how food is made, distributed, and marketed. The best outcome will be for producers to realize that it is better for their brands, reputation, and finances to make food less harmful, and ideally even, demonstrably healthy.

Just as trying to compress the full value of a breakthrough drug into the amount paid when it is taken is suboptimal, so too, the price of food is far more than amount paid at purchase. The benefits or harms accrue over time, and food makers should profit or pay in some measure, accordingly.

ENDNOTES

177 See e.g., Egnell, Manon, Isabelle Boutron, et. al. 2022. "Impact of the Nutri-Score Front-of-pack Nutrition Label on Purchasing Intentions of Individuals With Chronic Diseases: Results of a Randomised Trial." BMJ Open 12 (8): e058139. https://doi.org/10.1136/bmjopen-2021-058139; and Yu, Tao, Shu Zhang, Ryota Wakayama, Tomohito Horimoto, et. al. 2024. "The Relationship Between the Dietary Index Based Meiji Nutritional Profiling System for Adults and Lifestyle-related Diseases: A Predictive Validity Study From the National Institute for Longevity Sciences—Longitudinal Study of Aging." Frontiers in Nutrition 11 (July). https://doi.org/10.3389/fnut.2024.1413980.

32. CONCLUSION: LOOK LONG, AND BEGIN

"So we argue and we wrestle and we claim conviction
But we might as well be flipping coins
More would be revealed if we'd adjust the focus
Of the shortest distance between two points."

"Look Long", Indigo Girls

Over and over in the media, at medical conferences, and on podcasts, we hear health experts and clinicians lament "if only." If only the system valued long-term improvements. If only the system rewarded prevention instead of treatment. If only people had a stronger reason to take ownership in their health situations. If only clinicians could spend more time with people to understand their situations, instead of spending so much time on paperwork and fighting insurers. If only the system reduced societal inequities and helped change the environmental factors that worsen health.

Life for Health is the answer to "if only."

It confronts the overwhelming reason that healthspan is shrinking as costs go up—rising chronic disease prevalence and the current system's inability to reverse and prevent it.

It is economically viable, repurposing funds misspent within health insurance on sick care in a new system centered around healthspan. It provides a financial structure to reward investments to reverse disease and maintain healthier trajectories for decades thereafter.

It focuses on the most urgent threat, metabolic syndrome, with the goal of minimizing multimorbidity, an approach that can be extended to other chronic issues.

It focuses on outcomes as the key metric of success, applying that lens to help participants and clinicians continually assess progress and adjust measures as participants' circumstances change.

It uses the long-term nature of life insurance to align insurers, clinicians, participants, and drugmakers to share the value of reversing and preventing disease. It recognizes that reversing existing disease is a prerequisite to end multimorbidity, but that the bulk of value accrues over many years. An effective system to roll back chronic disease must do both, working at both ends of the chronic disease cascade simultaneously, to reduce existing and future prevalence.

It provides an alternative for clinicians who lament the current system's short-termism and fragmentation.

It transforms the clinician's role, rescuing their decision-making from insurer second-guessing but requiring transparency and tracking over time about patient outcomes. It attacks fragmentation by granting authority while creating accountability. It re-establishes clinical practice as a profession that requires a mix of knowledge, skill, relationship-building, and judgment, all now aided by richer data and context. It expands the remit of clinicians treating chronic disease, whether they are credentialed as primary care, pediatricians, obesity medicine experts, endocrinologists, or cardiologists. All who aspire to solve disease holistically will have to become both experts and coaches informing and motivating participants to persevere towards better health and longer healthspans.

It provides employers—especially self-insured companies and public sector entities—a means to regain control over worker health costs, ensuring that chronic disease risk and prevalence actually declines. It will not be tolerable for employers just to off-load financial responsibility for chronic disease coverage onto workers and hope for the best.

It provides governments and publicly financed health plans new capabilities to intercept and prevent disease earlier, get enrollees onto better health trajectories, and restore Medicare's long-term solvency.

It gives life insurers interested in underwriting healthy longevity a vast opportunity to grow their customer bases, directing premiums to far more productive ends. It is a way to rebalance longevity risk among the relatively wealthy and healthy that constitute an overwhelming proportion of their current customer base.

It resets participants' role, giving individuals agency in setting health outcome goals, treatment plans, and visibility into how daily choices build up over time to improve healthspan.

Above all, *Life for Health* realizes the greatest systemic "if only" of all, providing a way to value preventive medicine, making forestalling of illness coequal with treatment.

It creates a new ethos around the value of health data and biosamples, accelerating work to understand complex drivers of disease risk and resilience, identify predictive biomarkers, and a longitudinal discipline to refine detection, prevention, and treatment continuously. In particular it enables us to reapply insights gained in solving metabolic multimorbidity to advance work to understand, predict, and prevent cancer and ADRD.

Life for Health's long-term, outcomes-focused approach provides a new framework to price breakthrough drugs, increasing access and reducing upfront prices, while allowing innovators to realize even greater returns over time.

All of this is possible because *Life for Health*—as a system and as an enterprise—synergizes science and finance, reestablishing trust, reconnecting medicine with long-term gains, and creating a rewards structure that shares risk and value.

So many of the limitations in health care that we are acculturated to treat as "givens" are really cornices disguising flawed assumptions and outdated paradigms. Letting go of these shibboleths will be scary for some, but liberating for most.

So how do we start?

There is no statutory or regulatory barrier to launching Life for Health, only institutional will, a willingness to step around the established barricades. This is the flip side of having a real answer to "if only" lamentations. Who is willing to begin?

Do leaders of self-insured companies really want to improve workers' health and lower medical costs? Do clinicians and startups advocating for new clinical models and participant relationships really want to invest themselves to build a system apart from the RPS Vortex? Do life insurers, reinsurers, or other investors want to create a new category of health improvement and savings vehicles? For elected and appointed officials overseeing Medicaid programs: do they really want to improve beneficiaries' situations, now and in the future, inside and outside the system?

Life for Health does not pretend to have all, or even most, of the answers. This book is at best a rough first draft. Real progress will come in the doing, in working with participants and clinicians to learn and improve. Life for Health can begin in a few cities or states, bringing together insurers and reinsurers, investors, large public and private employers, clinicians, and if possible, elected and civic leaders.

Some who have discussed *Life for Health* with me admire the concept but question how much energy and will is required to overcome the status quo. I do not underestimate how hard change will be, but in the RPS Vortex, I also see a system that knows it is spent, that knows it is inadequate to the scientific challenge of chronic disease but is (justifiably) petrified of owning up to it. There is a hunger for new ideas and better ways, even within the system, and the enthusiasm with which a new idea may gain momentum will provide a momentum of its own.

Every time a health care outrage bubbles up, health insurer overlords counsel patience. "We're working to fix it." Sorry, you've had your time. We will be patients, and patient no longer.

ACKNOWLEDGMENTS

Life for Health would not have been possible without the support and encouragement of family, friends, and colleagues over many years. To John Gardner, Jim Pinkerton, Hanns Kuttner—colleagues of many decades—my thanks and appreciation for your time to read drafts and provide helpful suggestions and edits. To Chris Schroeder for decades of sponsorship and counsel.

My thanks to all the expert patients at HealthCentral from 2005 through 2011 who inspired many ideas in this book, and to Susannah Fox, who provided valuable insight about writing and publishing a book even as she was putting the finishing touches on her own. I am grateful time and insights from clinicians Victoria Croog, Michael Johns, Azra Raza, and Beverly Tchang and economists Liran Einav, Ralph Koijen, and Stijn Van Nieuwerburgh.

I appreciate the Milliman team of Deana Bell, Riley Heckel, Al Klein, and Bryce Platt for their feedback on key parts of Life for Health's design. To the wonderful team at The Asset Path who produced this book, many thanks for your care and dedication. And finally, to the great librarians and employees at the public libraries of Manhattan Beach, California; Chapel Hill and Durham, North Carolina; and Bethesda, Maryland where much of this book was written.

ABOUT JEREMY SHANE

I was introduced to the health care world in 1991 when I became a policy aide in the US Justice Department. Those years, leading up to Bill and Hillary Clinton's health care reform in 1993, were a period of intense policy ferment. Congress and Medicare reset how physicians were paid. The Justice Department ramped up efforts to prosecute increasingly sophisticated health frauds empowered by a new law limiting physician self-dealing. The Bush Administration and some states pushed to limit medical malpractice awards, while health insurers intensified efforts to limit coverage for Americans with pre-existing conditions. Even then, the health care system was rife with complexity and controversy.

After leaving government, I spent a decade plus in the wholesale power business, where I learned how to structure multi-decade risks, a "given" in an industry that requires very large capital commitments in the face of much economic and regulatory uncertainty. Returning to health care in 2006, while facing my own medical challenges and others within my family, brought home the practical issues of dealing with chronic disease. Later, I learned about the barriers to medical education (while creating degree programs for nurse practitioners and physical therapists), and while running medical publisher Medscape, the extraordinary administrative and informational burdens on all physicians. Collectively, these experiences gave me a close-up view of health care as it is, but free from the bias that comes from being part of a clinical, hospital, or insurer entity.

After the Great Financial Crisis, academics began to speak of health care, along with education and poverty, as "wicked problems," ones that are practically insoluble. However true this was, or is, it also engendered a sense of futility about the possibility of lasting change. This seemed to me to be too much of a capitulation in advance. Studying diplomatic history in college along with Enlightenment thinking, it was clear that seemingly impregnable empires or enterprises could be overthrown. It required a new conceptualization of the problem, technological breakthroughs, and the hardest of all, serendipitous events, but even complex and entrenched systems could be upended. Why not in health care as well?

In a landmark paper reexamining a thorny issue in quantum physics, Nobelist Richard Feynman wrote, "The only reason that we cannot do this problem of superconductivity is that we haven't got enough imagination." Feynman's novel solution began by visualizing how atomic particles might behave in particular situations. Instead of trying to extend established theories, he reasoned from ground truths towards an explanation to fit the facts.

So, too, with the shortcomings of our health care system. The immutable facts of chronic and age-related disease are long time dimensions, they play out over decades, and variability in causes, progression, and treatment response. It is inescapable that solutions must meet these challenges on their terms, creating decades-long arrangements that prevent and delay disease and reduce treatment uncertainty. If the existing system cannot do this, and it is manifestly clear it cannot, it is incumbent on us to imagine and fashion one that can. It's that simple.

INDEX

A

ACT-UP 209, 210
Affordable Care Act (ACA) 118
Agency for Healthcare Quality Research (AHRQ) 27, 28, 42, 124
Alzheimer's Disease (ADRD) xxi, 47, 172, 205, 220, 221, 222, 226, 243, 249, 255, 260, 261, 262, 263, 264, 265, 270, 295
  amyloid hypothesis 261, 262, 263, 264
  predicting/preventing 221, 264
American Medical Association (AMA) 66, 99, 108
Arrow, Kenneth 91, 92, 100
Artificial Intelligence 9, 67, 105, 108, 184, 200, 222, 229, 234, 235, 236, 238, 275
Atherosclerosis Risk in Communities (ARIC) study 220, 221, 225, 226
Attia, Peter 9, 63
Autoimmune conditions 15, 55, 59, 90, 98, 99, 133, 198, 215, 224, 271, 277, 284

B

Biomarkers 59, 139, 226, 255, 291, 295
Biosamples xviii, 17, 63, 128, 200, 216, 220, 225, 228, 261, 295
Body Mass Index (BMI) 24, 42, 45, 97, 100, 141, 149, 198, 282

Boyer, Stanley 98, 99
BRCA gene mutation 252, 255, 259
Bush, Vannevar 64, 68, 69, 91, 218
Butz, Earl 94, 95

C

Cancer xiii, 10, 13, 47, 48, 49, 74, 98, 147, 207, 208, 251, 252, 259, 267, 284,
  Early detection, MCED tests, screening, and 107, 204, 253, 251, 252, 253, 254, 255
  Increased risk from chronic disease, and xii, 12, 33, 37, 55, 59, 61, 72,
  life insurers, and 7, 179, 180, 183
  Life for Health, and xvii, xviii, xix, 42, 133, 140, 145, 146, 153, 160, 161, 172, 190, 204, 205, 249, 251, 260, 264, 295
  Longitudinal data, and 243, 275, 276
  Metabolic surgery, and 45, 50, 116, 118
  Targeted therapies for 270, 271, 277
  Treatment at National Cancer Instittute Comprehensive Cancer Centers (NCI-CCCs), and xviii, 7, 10, 256, 257, 258
  Value-Based Care, and 111, 112

Womens' Health Initiative (WHI) and, 223, 224
Cardiovascular Disease (see Heart Disease) xv, 5, 15, 54,
   ARIC study, longitudinal data, and 220, 221
   Barriers/failures in solving 74, 80, 81, 82, 83
   Example of how to solve chronic disease 12, 73, 74, 75, 76, 77, 78
   Framingham Study, and 78, 79, 82, 220, 225
   Life for Health, and 135, 138, 139
   Pharmaceutical investment in 270, 271
   Relationship between heart health & healthspan 21, 45, 49,
   Women's Health Initiative (WHI), and 221, 223, 224
Center for Medicare and Medicaid Innovation (CMMI) 110, 111, 112
Centers for Disease Control (CDC) xiv, 24, 42, 75, 101
Cholesterol xvi, 35, 37, 49, 58, 78, 81, 90, 98, 107, 115, 141, 151, 152, 197, 270, 273
   LDL receptors, discovery of 98, 115
Christensen, Clayton 102, 127
Chronic Disease (see also Multimorbidity) xii, 9, 11
   barriers to solving xiv, xv, 55, 105, 106, 107, 148, 288, 294
   cost of 34, 35, 36, 37, 38, 39
   health insurance, and 8, 14, 15, 53, 175
   heterogeneity/variability of xv, 8, 11, 12, 17, 32, 46, 49, 55, 242, 299
   how to solve xiii, xvii, 8, 9, 16, 17, 19, 99, 112, 128, 155, 224
   ICHRAs, and 121, 122
   Life for Health, and xvi, xvii, xviii, 9, 154, 158, 159, 176
   Life insurers, and 6, 183, 184, 180, 185
   longitudinal data, and 17, 218, 222, 242, 243
   MAHA movement, and xvi, 287, 296
   preventing xi, 18, 59, 198
   science of xii, xiii, xiv, xxi, 11, 54, 60
   spending on xiv, 158, 159, 161
   Value Based Care (VBC), and 110, 111, 112, 117, 121
   value in reducing prevalence / solving, xix, xx, 39, 40, 41, 42, 44, 45, 47, 48, 49
Chronic disease cascade 10, 12, 18, 19, 24, 27, 28, 35, 36, 37, 38, 39, 40, 49, 59, 97, 105, 112, 154, 159, 199, 240, 241, 294
Clinical trials 70, 72, 202, 226, 235, 237, 238, 257, 268
   Complexities and costs, of 212, 213, 214, 217, 270, 274, 275, 277
   Life for Health, and 139, 143, 152, 168, 204, 206, 269, 275, 276
Clinician in Charge 134, 139, 142, 144, 146, 148, 149, 190, 204, 205
Cohen, Edward 98
Cohen, Herbert 98
Collins, Francis 13
Courcoulas, Anita 50, 116, 118
COVID 13, 72, 90, 91, 202
   Long COVID 215, 216
Cuban, Mark 165, 197, 201, 202
Cystic Fibrosis 200, 212
Cystic Fibrosis Foundation (CFF) 212, 213, 214, 215, 217
   Beall, Robert, and 212, 213, 238
   Vertex Pharmaceuticals, and 213, 214, 215, 217, 275

D

Diabetes (Type 2) xxii, 4, 8, 11, 19, 45, 47, 58, 74, 81, 106, 147, 184, 189, 198, 206, 271, 286
- ADRD, and 261
- Cardiovascular / metabolic syndrome, and xii, xv, 15, 41, 49, 60, 79, 133, 155, 225, 237
- GLP-1s, and 272, 282
- Prevalence of 24, 25, 26, 29, 35, 42
- Life for Health and 141, 151, 154, 167, 237, 250
- Metabolic surgery, and 5, 45, 46, 50, 115, 116, 118, 154, 207

Dialysis/Hemodialysis 86, 87, 88, 89

Drug development, marketing, use, and pricing 270, 271, 272, 273,
- Branded, and 267, 268, 269, 272, 284
- Generic, and 112, 249, 267, 268, 269, 270, 271, 273, 276, 278, 282, 283, 284
- Hatch-Waxman, and 269, 270, 273, 276, 280
- Outcomes Based Annuitized Pricing (OBAP) 268, 269, 276, 277, 278, 280, 281, 282, 283
- Pharmaceutical company role in RPS Vortex 105, 270
- Risk and expense of developing drugs 274, 275, 276

E

Emergency/Elective Medicine xx, xxi, 36, 41, 58, 60, 62, 63, 138, 139
- Insurance coverage of 156, 166, 173, 175, 190, 288

Employers
- Frustration with rising insurance costs 120, 121, 122, 123, 124, 177, 178, 288
- History of employer coverage 64, 65, 70, 71, 93
- Life for Health, role in 132, 133, 135, 136, 138, 141, 145, 146, , 152, 158, 172, 174, 175
- Self-insured employers and Life for Health 114, 135, 136, 146, 158, 163, 164, 165, 166, 167, 168, 169, 170, 171, 177, 178, 296

End Stage Renal Disease (ESRD) Program 87, 88, 89, 100, 111
- Dialysis versus transplants, in 86, 87, 88, 89, 100

F

Fauci, Anthony 210

Financialism and financialists xiv, xv, 12, 30, 90, 91, 93, 99, 286, 287

Food, role in chronic disease xvi, 9, 11, 46, 55, 161, 199, 289, 290
- Changes in ingredient production, 1973 90, 91, 94, 95, 96, 100
- Dietary guidelines 58
- Life for Health, and xxi, 16, 129, 160, 250, 291, 292
- Ultraprocessed foods, and 199, 239

Food and Drug Administration (FDA) 81, 90, 99, 104, 202, 209, 210, 214, 262, 269, 270, 274, 276

Fragmentation (clinical) 8, 15, 74, 81, 131, 148, 294

Framingham Study 78, 79, 82, 220, 225

G

Gilead Sciences 279, 280, 281, 282, 285

Glazer, Shep 85, 86, 87, 89

GLP-1s 6, 24, 59, 113, 160, 264
- Use against metabolic diseases 8, 129, 159, 182, 189, 198
- Outcomes of 46, 115, 154

Index 303

Participant access in Life for Health 142, 153
Pricing of xxi, 267, 268, 271, 277, 282, 283, 285
Women's health, and 224, 225
Goldman, Dana 47, 48, 50, 254, 259, 284
Group life insurance
    Life for Health, and 135, 136, 145, 146, 169, 170, 175, 178, 189, 190, 192

H

Hall, Kevin 199
Hatch-Waxman Act 269, 270, 273, 276
Health insurance / insurers xx, 17, 33, 118, 177, 289
    Affordable Care Act (ACA), and 137, 174, 178
    Behavior in RPS Vortex 106, 107, 108, 109, 110, 254
    Designed for acute, not chronic xiii, xiv, xvi,
    Dissatisfaction with 8, 123, 124, 296
    Drug pricing, and 267, 287
    Health Maintenance Organizations (HMOs), and 90, 91, 92, 93, 123
    History of and emergence of employer-paid coverage 65, 69, 70, 71, 85, 87
    Life for Health, and xxi, 63, 128, 129, 132, 135, 136, 137, 138, 139, 141, 145, 146, 153, 156, 158, 159, 163, 164, 165, 166, 168, 171, 173, 183, 244, 288
    Life insurers, and 113, 114, 115, 179, 180
    Medicare Advantage, and 14, 107, 108, 117, 164, 177, 186, 287
    Multi-year health insurance 175, 176, 178
    Opposition to metabolic surgery 5, 6, 113, 114, 115, 117, 118, 119
Health Maintenance Organizations (HMOs) 90, 91, 92, 93, 123
Health narratives 128, 200, 205, 206, 227, 228, 229, 230, 234, 240, 261, 263, 275
Health Outcome Payments 142, 143, 145, 190, 241, 242, 245
Healthspan xi, xiii, xv, xx, 9, 17, 18, 38, 89, 106, 122, 161, 180, 206, 240, 251, 286
    Extending healthspan, magnitude and value of xix, 21, 22, 23, 41, 42, 44, 45, 46, 47, 48, 198
    Life for Health, and xvi, 31, 133, 138, 150, 153, 155, 156, 183, 184, 264, 293, 294, 295.
    Medicare, and 178, 250
    Measuring progress/metrics of, 19, 20, 23, 24
Heart disease (See Cardiovascular Disease)
Hepatitis-C (Hep-C) 213, 278, 279, 280, 281, 283, 284, 285
    Veterans Health Administration, and 33, 280
Herrup, Dr. Karl 263
HIV/AIDS 3, 13, 90, 200, 209, 210
    ACT-UP and 209, 210
    Elite controllers, and 211, 215
    Fauci, Anthony, and 210
    White, Ryan and 209
Hospitals xx, 17, 27, 86, 226, 286
    Historical role in US system, and xiii, 13, 54, 55, 57, 58, 61, 64, 65, 69, , 70, 71, 72, 90, 91, 92, 99
    Life for Health, and 149, 164, 165, 167

Impact of chronic disease/multi-
morbidity on 15, 30, 31, 33, 34,
37, 42, 82, 251
Role in the RPS Vortex, and 43,
53, 102, 103, 105, 106, 107, 108,
110, 111, 112, 116, 117, 119, 139
Hyman, Mark 9, 289

I

Individual Coverage Health Reim-
bursement Arrangement
(ICHRAs) 121, 122
Life for Health, and 149, 173

J

Jobs, Steve 208, 216, 256
Johnson, Lyndon Baines 84, 85
Joint replacement surgeries 59, 117

K

Kaiser Permanente 71, 110
Kaiser, Henry 71, 92, 122
Kidney disease 71, 72, 110, 124

L

Lacks, Henrietta 201
Lauterbur, Paul 98
Life for Health
As a concept/system xi, xvi, xviii,
xx, xxi, 16, 17, 18, 293, 294, 295,
296
As a business xvii, xviii, xix, 9, 15,
16, 131, 132, 133, 134, 135, 136
Benefits of, for life insurers 9, 128,
158, 164, 172, 184, 185, 186
Benefits of, for participants
(See, Health Outcome Pay-
ments) 142, 143, 145, 190, 241,
242, 245

Cancer, and xvii, xviii, xix, 42, 133,
140, 145, 146, 153, 160, 161, 172,
190, 204, 205, 249, 251, 260,
264, 295
Cardiovascular disease, and 135,
138, 139
Chronic disease, and xvi, xvii, xviii,
9, 154, 158, 159, 176
Clinical trials, and 139, 143, 152,
168, 204, 206, 269, 275, 276
Coverage portability 174, 175
Diabetes, and 141, 151, 154, 167, 237,
250
Drug pricing, and (including
Outcomes Based Annuitized
Pricing) 268, 269, 276, 277,
278, 280, 281, 282, 283
Employers, role in 132, 133, 135, 136,
138, 141, 145, 146, , 152, 158, 172,
174, 175
Food issues, and xxi, 16, 129, 160,
250, 291, 292
Healthspan, and xvi, 31, 133, 138,
150, 153, 155, 156, 183, 184, 264,
293, 294, 295.
Health insurers, and xxi, 63, 128,
129, 132, 135, 136, 137, 138, 139,
141, 145, 146, 153, 156, 158, 159,
163, 164, 165, 166, 168, 171, 173,
183, 244, 288
Hospitals 149, 164, 165, 167
Life for Health entity, role of xvii,
166, 167, 169, 170, 171, 172, 173,
190, 191, 192
Metabolic Surgery, in
Multimorbidity, and 172, 241, 243,
294
Life insurance policies in 135, 136,
145, 146, 169, 170, 173, 175, 178,
189, 190, 192

Life insurers' role in 16, 132, 135, 136, 137, 138, 140, 143, 153, 169
Longitudinal data in xxi, 130, 142, 145, 162, 200, 249
Medicaid, and xxi, 16, 31, 188, 189, 190, 191, 192, 193, 244
Medicare, and 152, 159, 164, 172, 176, 188, 249, 250
Metabolic Surgery, and 142, 163, 166, 205, 206, 207
Multimorbidity, and 172, 241, 243, 294
Participants in xvii, xviii, 16, 128, 129, 130, 132, 133, 134, 135, 136, 137, 138, 142, 143, 144, 145, 146, 148, 149, 151, 152, 153, 154, 159, 171, 172, 176, 182, 183, 240, 294, 295
Predictive/Preventive Medicine in 41, 134, 138, 156, 160, 164, 173, 197, 204, 205, 206, 240, 244, 245
Life insurance / life insurers xvii, 3, 4, 5, 6, 7, 179, 180, 288, 295
Risks and risk management in Life for Health 181, 182, 183, 244, 245
Benefits to, from Life for Health 9, 128, 158, 164, 172, 184, 185, 186
Life insurance policies in Life for Health 135, 136, 145, 146, 169, 170, 173, 175, 178, 189, 190, 192
Life for Health, role in 16, 132, 135, 136, 137, 138, 140, 143, 153, 169
Lilly, Inc. 46, 267, 271
Liver disease 45, 115, 162, 278, 279, 280, 281, 282
Data, longitudinal 17, 225, 226
Blockchain, and 235, 236, 237, 238
Health narratives, and 128, 200, 205, 206, 227, 228, 229, 230, 234, 240, 261, 263, 275
Compensating contributors 200, 231, 235
Life for Health approach to xxi, 130, 142, 145, 162, 200, 249
Predictive/Preventive Medicine, and 225, 226, 231, 233, 242, 243
Privacy and control 231, 232, 233, 235, 237, 238
Use and value in solving disease 115, 159, 160, 215, 216, 291

M

Magnetic Resonance Imaging (MRI) 90, 98, 253, 254
Make America Healthy Again (MAHA) xvi, 287, 296
Medicaid xix, 33, 84, 92, 159, 164, 165, 177
Incorporating Life for Health into xxi, 16, 31, 188, 189, 190, 191, 192, 193, 244
Coverage of metabolic disease treatments 114, 115, 118, 278
Hep-C treatment, and 279, 280, 285
Medical Loss Ratio (MLR) 137, 273
Medicare 13, 43, 84, 85, 92
End Stage Renal Disease (ESRD), and 87, 88, 100
Experiments with Value Based Care (VBC) 107, 108, 110, 111, 112
Life for Health, and 152, 159, 164, 172, 176, 188, 249, 250
Multimorbidity, and 14, 27, 33, 37, 38, 39, 117, 177, 178
Maintaining solvency, and politics of doing so, xii, xxi, 34, 250, 286, 287, 288, 295
Outcomes Based Annuitized Pricing (OBAP), and 274, 277, 279, 283

Medicare Advantage 14, 107, 108, 117, 164, 177, 186, 287
Medicine, Four Types of xvii, 57, 58, 59, 60, 61, 62, 63, 123
Mendosa, David 4
Metabolic surgery 4, 5, 6, 7, 8, 10, 46, 129, 139
    Long-term outcomes of 45, 46, 50, 116, 118, 154, 198
    Health insurers' opposition to 5, 113, 114, 115, 117, 118, 119
    Life for Health, and 142, 163, 166, 205, 206, 207
Metabolic Syndrome xvi, xxii, 11, 19, 23, 30, 42, 45, 49, 87, 114, 261, 294
    Obesity, and 97, 250
    Food issues, and 96, 289, 291
    Clinical approaches to 80, 81
    Drug pricing, and 274, 283
    How to solve 129, 199
    Life for Health, and 16, 133, 138, 149, 151, 152, 153, 154, 205
    Life insurers, and 181, 182
    in Medicaid 188, 189, 192
Monoclonal Antibodies (MAbs) 90, 97, 98, 271
Multimorbidity (see also Chronic Disease entries) xii, xx,
    Barriers to solving 80, 105, 106, 107, 117, 267, 273, 282
    Definition of xi, xxii
    Median age of onset 19, 20, 23, 24
    Metrics of progress 18, 19
    Chronic disease cascade, and 12, 27, 28, 35, 36, 37, 38, 39, 162
    Cost of xiv, 165
    How to solve 47, 48, 78, 79, 82, 175, 177
    impact on healthspan 21, 22, 23, 44

    Life for Health, and 172, 241, 243, 294
    Life insurers, and 180, 183, 244
    Medicaid, and 31
    Medicare, and 14, 15, 37, 38, 39, 250, 283, 288
    Metabolic issues, and 24
    Poverty, and 28, 29, 30, 31, 43, 291
    Prevalence in the US, of xii, 24, 25, 26, 27, 28
    Prevalence outside the US, of 20, 31, 32,
    Value in reducing prevalence xix, 40, 41, 42, 153, 154, 160, 178
Multiple Cancer Early Detection (MCED) tests 107, 204, 253, 251, 252, 253, 254, 255

N

Narratives, health 128, 200, 205, 206, 227, 228, 229, 230, 234, 240, 261, 263, 275
National Cancer Institute Comprehensive Cancer Centers (NCI-CCCs) xviii, 7, 10, 256, 257, 258
National Institutes of Health (NIH) 13, 20, 69, 88, 100, 105, 199, 202, 209, 210, 216, 223
Neurodegenerative disease (cross ref with ADRD) xxi, 47, 172, 205, 220, 221, 222, 226, 243, 249, 255, 260, 261, 262, 263, 264, 265, 270, 295
Nixon, Richard Milhous 53, 85, 90, 92, 94, 95, 270
Novo-Nordisk 46, 267

O

Obesity xii, xv, 35, 41, 45, 82, 96, 97, 101, 133, 135, 138, 139, 146, 149, 151, 154, 161, 189, 193, 226

Diabetes, and 11, 15, 24, 25, 26, 29, 42, 225
Food issues, and 90, 96, 100, 250, 289, 290, 291
GLP-1s, and 24, 46, 224, 272, 282
Health insurers, and 114, 115
Metabolic surgery, and 4, 5, 8, 50, 118, 198
Obesity medicine specialist 80, 81, 142, 294
Primary Care Physicians, and 58, 113, 116, 117, 119

O'Connor, Sandra Day 260
Olshansky, Jay 47, 251
Outcomes Based Annuitized Pricing (OBAP) 268, 269, 276, 277, 278, 280, 281, 282, 283

P

Participant(s) xvii, 17, 18, 46, 127, 291
Data contributions and controls over use, by 228, 229, 230, 232, 233, 234, 235, 237, 238, 243
Health Outcome Payments, and 142, 143, 145, 190, 241, 242, 245
Involvement in clinical research/trials 199, 200, 201, 202, 203, 204, 205, 206, 216, 219, 222, 225, 226, 228, 250, 255, 256, 257, 264, 269, 274, 275, 276
In Life for Health xvii, xviii, 16, 128, 129, 130, 132, 133, 134, 135, 136, 137, 138, 142, 143, 144, 145, 146, 148, 149, 151, 152, 153, 154, 159, 171, 172, 176, 182, 183, 240, 294, 295
in Medicaid 190, 191, 193

Life for Health coverage portability 174, 175
Reallocation of insurance premiums 163, 166, 167, 168, 169, 170
Pharmacy Benefit Managers (PBMs) 103, 120, 272, 273, 274, 277
Pinkerton, Jim 12
Predictive/Preventive Medicine xvii, xx, xxi, 13, 58, 59, 60, 63, 175, 176, 190, 201, 211, 225, 233
Cardiovascular disease, and 73, 74, 77, 79
In Life for Health 41, 134, 138, 156, 160, 164, 173, 197, 204, 205, 206, 240, 244, 245
Longitudinal data, and 225, 226, 231, 233, 242, 243
Prevention Paradox 24, 198, 199, 240, 241, 280, 282
Primary Care Physicians 55, 57, 69, 79, 92, 99, 104, 113, 116, 119, 294
Proteomics 221, 226, 255

R

RAND Institute 35, 37, 39, 43, 111, 112, 117
Raza, Azra 251, 252
Rock Paper Scissors (RPS) Vortex 103, 120, 123, 163, 176, 177, 296
Entities within 104, 105
Operating principles of 106, 107, 108, 109, 287
Metabolic surgery, and 113, 114, 115, 116
Resistance to preventive medicine 198, 203, 218, 230, 239, 250, 292
Rockefeller, John D, Jr. 66, 208
Roosevelt, Franklin Delano 67, 68, 69, 70, 71, 91

Routine Medicine / routine care xiii, xx, 18, 31, 32, 36, 54, 58, 60, 61, 63, 70, 79, 122, 132, 138, 157, 166, 173, 175, 190, 288

S

Scarcitarianism 12, 91
Schwaber, Jerrold 98
Scott, Andrew 9, 48, 50
Serious Medicine xvii, xxi, 58, 59, 62, 63, 73, 75, 77, 128, 197, 204, 205, 206, 211
Sinclair, David 48, 50
Statin drugs 76, 77, 90, 98, 107, 197, 226, 270, 273

T

Topol, Eric 216
Transplants 61, 76, 278
    Kidney transplants 86, 87, 88, 89, 100
Truman, Harry S 57, 84, 85
Tuskeegee Experiments 201

U

UK Biobank 219, 220, 225, 226, 255, 259
UnitedHealth Corp. 120, 272, 287
United Kingdom 76, 226

V

Value-Based Care (VBC) 110, 111, 112, 117, 121
Value-Based Insurance Design (VBID) 111
Van Tulleken, Chris 9

W

White, Paul Dudley 21, 77, 82
Women's Health Initiative 223, 224
Wyss-Coray, Tony 222

Y

Yurkiewicz, Ilana 131, 147, 149

www.ingramcontent.com/pod-product-compliance
Lightning Source LLC
Chambersburg PA
CBHW070802040426
42333CB00061B/1801